Psychonarratology

Foundations for the Empirical Study of Literary Response

Psychonarratology is an approach to the empirical study of literary response and the processing of narrative. It draws on the empirical methodology of cognitive psychology and discourse processing as well as the theoretical insights and conceptual analysis of literary studies, particularly narratology. *Psychonarratology: Foundations for the Empirical Study of Literary Response* provides a conceptual and empirical basis for this interdisciplinary approach that is accessible to researchers from either disciplinary background. An integrative review of the classic problems in narratology – the status of the narrator, events and plot, characters and characterization, speech and thought, and focalization – is presented. For each area, Bortolussi and Dixon critique the state of the art in narratology and literary studies, discuss relevant work in cognitive psychology, and provide a new analytical framework based on the insight that readers treat the narrator as a conversational participant. Empirical evidence is presented on each problem, much of it previously unpublished.

Marisa Bortolussi is Professor at the University of Alberta and holds a joint appointment in the Departments of Modern Languages and Cultural Studies and of Comparative Literature, Religion, and Film/Media Studies. She is the author of two books on children's literature and has published articles on contemporary Hispanic literature.

Peter Dixon is Professor of Psychology at the University of Alberta and has published on a wide range of topics in cognitive psychology. A Fellow of the American Psychological Society, he is currently the editor of the *Canadian Journal of Experimental Psychology*.

Psychonarratology

*Foundations for the Empirical Study
of Literary Response*

MARISA BORTOLUSSI

University of Alberta

PETER DIXON

University of Alberta

PUBLISHED BY THE PRESS SYNDICATE OF THE UNIVERSITY OF CAMBRIDGE
The Pitt Building, Trumpington Street, Cambridge, United Kingdom

CAMBRIDGE UNIVERSITY PRESS
The Edinburgh Building, Cambridge CB2 2RU, UK
40 West 20th Street, New York, NY 10011-4211, USA
477 Williamstown Road, Port Melbourne, VIC 3207, Australia
Ruiz de Alarcón 13, 28014 Madrid, Spain
Dock House, The Waterfront, Cape Town 8001, South Africa

http://www.cambridge.org

© Cambridge University Press 2003

First published 2003

Printed in the United Kingdom at the University Press, Cambridge

Typeface Palatino 10/13.5 pt.   *System* LaTeX 2_ε [TB]

A catalog record for this book is available from the British Library.

Library of Congress Cataloging in Publication Data
Bortolussi, Marisa.
Psychonarratology : foundations for the empirical study of literary response / Marisa
Bortolussi, Peter Dixon.
p.   cm.
Includes bibliographical references and index.
ISBN 0-521-80411-6 – ISBN 0-521-00913-8 (pbk.)
1. Narration (Rhetoric)   2. Literature – Psychology.   I. Dixon, Peter, 1952–   II. Title.
PN212 .B67   2002
808'.001'9–dc21   2002017394

ISBN 0 521 80411 6 hardback
ISBN 0 521 00913 8 paperback

To our children, Robert Adelchi and Alina Katharine Bortolussi Dixon, without whose understanding and indulgence this book would not have been possible.

Contents

List of Figures and Tables

Figures

Tables

Acknowledgments

We are very grateful to the Social Sciences and Humanities Research Council of Canada for their support of our psychonarratology project.

A special thanks is due to our research assistants and others who have contributed to this research over the years. These include Patricia Hughes-Fuller, Benjamin Berger, Maria Kotovych, Joseph Iyekekpolor, Carmela Bruni-Bossio, Colleen Irwin, Valerie Henitiuk, Kimberly Tannas, Leslie Twilley, and Chuck Anderson.

1

Introduction

"fear is a failure of the imagination"
          T. Findlay, *Not Wanted on the Voyage*

The Study of Narrative

Narratives in one form or another permeate virtually all aspects of our society and social experience. Narrative forms are found not only in the context of literature but also in the recollection of life events, in historical documents and textbooks, in scientific explanations of data, in political speeches, and in day-to-day conversation (Nash, 1994: xi). In fact, narrative discourse seems to be intrinsic to our ability to use language to explain and interpret the world around us, and there is an abundance of evidence suggesting that the manner in which we process narrative affects our cognitive and linguistic behavior in general. Therefore, understanding the dynamics of narrative can be instrumental in gaining knowledge about how the mind works (Chafe, 1990); how individuals behave in social and personal relationships (Tannen, 1982, 1984); how they acquire and organize knowledge and analyze themselves, the world, and others around them (Potter & Wetherell, 1987; Lamarque, 1990); how they shape their experience of reality (White, 1981; Ricoeur, 1983); and how they are affected by cultural codes and norms.

Because of narrative's ubiquitous nature and its perceived importance in all aspects of social life, it is not surprising that narrative "is no longer the private province of specialists in literature (as if it ever should have been)" (Nash, 1994:xi), and that it is now studied across a wide range of disciplines, such as literary studies, cultural studies, linguistics, discourse processing, cognitive psychology, social psychology, psycholinguistics, cognitive linguistics, artificial intelligence, and, as Nash points out, ethno-methodology and critical legal studies (Wieder, 1974). Now generally subsumed under the broader cross-disciplinary category of "discourse," narrative is studied from a variety of theoretical perspectives that focus on its pragmatic functions and effects on individuals. It is not surprising that so many disciplines are engaged in the study of narrative comprehension, for, as Emmott explains, "reading a story is an astonishing feat of information processing requiring the reader to perform complex operations at a number of levels" (Emmott, 1997:v). In all these disciplines, this emphasis on the recipient of narratives can be seen as the result of a paradigm shift that exposed and transcended the limitations of purely formalist models. In literary theory, it is marked by the transition to reader-reception and -response theory. In linguistics, it is witnessed by the transition from the focus on *langue*, or language as a system, to *parole*, or individual speech utterances. In discourse processing, it is illustrated by the passage from research on story grammar to the investigation of the reader's "search after meaning" (Bartlett, 1932; Graesser, Singer & Trabasso, 1994). What all these developments clearly indicate is that the forms of narrative discourse are only meaningful when understood in the context of their reception.

Although there has been extensive research on narrative in a wide range of fields, the flow of research findings across disciplinary boundaries is still minimal. Important advances in different scholarly traditions do not always inform each other, and research findings often remain isolated and largely unintegrated. For the most part, cross-fertilization is still limited to fields that have been traditionally perceived as complementary. For literary scholars, "interdisciplinary" is still generally understood as comprising the same "human science" fields with which literary scholars are more familiar: philosophy, history, sociology, film studies, anthropology, and ethnography. By the same token, scientific interdisciplinarity is typically limited to fields within the sciences. This bias has given rise to some curious situations. For example, although linguistics and literary studies are considered complementary, as are linguistics and cognitive psychology, the association between literary studies and cognitive psychology has not been developed until recently (see Duchan, Bruder & Hewitt, 1995; Gross, 1997; Spolsky, 1993; Turner, 1991). As late as 1990, John Knapp called for the association between literary studies and cognitive psychology, but shyly concluded that "no one would ever assume an unproblematic affair, much less a marriage, between literary critics and mainstream psychology" (Knapp, 1990:359). An unfortunate consequence of this lingering closed-door policy is the loss of fundamental insights. As Catherine Emmott pointed out, psychologists are generally uninformed about "the significance of discourse structure in their text-processing models" (1997:x) developed in literary studies, particularly narratology, and literary scholars are unaware of important research on text memory, coherence, and inference. However, given the common interest in and research on reading and narrative, it stands to reason that a sustained dialogue among the disciplines of literary theory, narratology, cognitive psychology, discourse processing, and linguistics is a prerequisite for a more rigorous inquiry into how narrative functions.

Objectives

One of our goals in this book was precisely to bridge the gap between at least some of the disciplines in which the most promising and outstanding advances have been made and to put the methods of cognitive psychology at the service of understanding what we argue is the least understood dimension of narrative: its cognitive processing. To date, there exists no exhaustive exploration of the ways in which research in cognitive psychology can serve to advance our understanding of the reading of literature. On one hand, a review of literary scholarship reveals that none of its theories (phenomenological, hermeneutic, structuralist, semiotic, reader-reception or reader-response, narratological, or cultural-studies-based approaches) are well informed by research on reading in discourse processing and cognitive psychology. Although narratology in particular has contributed a very sophisticated body of knowledge on the forms and features of literary narrative, this scholarship has been developed independently of detailed theories of the reader. More broadly, critical interpretations of literary works frequently become the resource pool from which scholars draw to make general inferences about the cognitive processes involved during the act of reading. We believe that this is an inadequate heuristic approach to the study of cognitive processing. On the other hand, research on narrative in discourse processing has often proceeded independently of the knowledge and insights garnered in literary theory. Even though cognitive psychology has made outstanding contributions to our understanding of the cognitive processes involved in reading, its understanding of narrative per se is limited relative to the advances made in literary studies. Drawing from the range of our joint expertise, we set out to establish vital links between literary studies (in particular, reader-response theory and narratology), cognitive psychology (in particular, discourse processing), and branches of linguistics.

This book is the result of a nine-year collaboration during which we developed an interdisciplinary framework for the empirical study of the reception of narrative. We refer to this approach as *psychonarratology*. Psychonarratology combines the experimental methods of cognitive psychology with the analysis and insights available from a range of literary studies. The fruits of this collaboration provide not only evidence on a variety of specific mechanisms of narrative processing but also a demonstration of the promise of the general approach. In this book, we elucidate that framework and describe a variety of new evidence and concepts relevant to the processing of narrative. We believe that this work provides a substantial contribution to a variety of fields. By putting the methods of cognitive psychology at the service of literary processing, we hope to advance our understanding of the cognitive processes involved in the reading of narratives. And by bringing to cognitive psychology the rich comprehension of narrative achieved by literary scholars, we hope that researchers of that discipline will be inspired to extend their experimental approach to more complex narrative issues.

As background for this anticipated multidisciplinary contribution, we provide in the following section a brief sketch of the research related to narrative processing that has been done within several fields. We point out the epistemological and methodological limitations of these approaches and preview some of the ways in which they can be transcended. We first discuss reader-oriented literary studies, including reception theory; second, the formal study of narratology; third, discourse processing in cognitive psychology and psycholinguistics; fourth, some related work in the field of linguistics; and finally, some previous empirical approaches to literature. Following this review, we present the elements of our new approach, psychonarratology.

Reader-Oriented Literary Studies

Recognition of the reader's productive role in the construction of meaning has led to the emergence of one of the most interesting and fundamental challenges to literary scholarship. Indeed, as Rabinowitz explained, "the turn toward the reader may well be the single most profound shift in critical perspective of the post-war years" (Rabinowitz, 1995:403). Antecedents of reception theory can be found early in this century in the work of the Russian Formalists and the Czech Structuralists. The principal impetus for this focus on the reader began in the sixties with the work of the Constance School scholars Jauss and Iser, followed by a veritable boom in reader-oriented criticism that ensued during the seventies and eighties. So much has been written on the general topic of reader response that it has become almost impossible to count the number of published titles. However, as Rabinowitz pointed out, this vast but scattered body of scholarship "is neither united by a common methodology nor directed toward a common goal" (quoted in Selden, 1995:375), which led Rabinowitz to conclude that it had not achieved an "advance in knowledge according to traditional paradigms" (401).

Without discounting the insights and contributions of research on reader response, we agree that for several reasons it has not led to a significant advance in our understanding of readers and the reading process. Perhaps the most obvious reason is the exclusive reliance of these models on purely intuitive speculation formulated in the absence of an objective method of validation. Scholars turning to this body of work in the hopes of gaining knowledge about readers and their reading encounter a vast body of contradictory, divergent theories that have never been tested. Moreover, the approaches are often mired in a vicious circularity: "Readers" are constructed in accordance with the logic of a given theoretical framework, be it sociological, formalist, psychoanalytical, or hermeneutic, so that the characteristics of the theory provide evidence for various narrative competencies, while the existence of a particular competence provides the evidence for a particular characteristic of a theory. Another difficulty with this area of study has been the propensity to adopt vague, almost idiosyncratic, terminology that is not ratified by any form of consensus. Still another problem is the failure to resolve the relationship between individual and collective reading experience, leading to an exclusive reliance on a single, unitary conception of the reader. This indulgence in circular logic, speculative hypothesis, capricious use of terminology, and monolithic views of reading experience runs throughout all the reader-oriented approaches in literary studies, from the earliest to the most recent trends.

Early Conceptions of the Reader

As early as 1917, the Russian Formalists stressed the role of the reader's perception in the definition of literariness (reprinted in Shklovsky, 1965). Later, the Czech Structuralists emphasized the role of a public's changing norms and tastes on our perception of aesthetic and literary value. However, neither the Russian Formalists nor the Czech Structuralists (Mukarovsky, 1970) succeeded in describing specific interactions between particular populations of readers and particular texts. "Readers" in these approaches are understood as universal, aggregate, hypothetical entities responding in unison.

The Aesthetics of Reception

The same is true of Jauss's concept of the "horizon of expectations." This concept was central to a new branch of literary studies known as the aesthetics of reception (Jauss, 1970). In the hopes of revitalizing the sense of history that was missing from Formalism and Marxism, Jauss argued that literary studies should include in literary history the process of production and reception (quoted in Holub, 1989:57). He believed that the connection between past and present could be achieved by reconstructing the "horizon of expectation" of a work's readers. Holub is but one of many scholars who has aptly critiqued the vagueness of this term; it appears to refer to "an intersubjective system or structure of expectations, a 'system of references' or a mind-set that a hypothetical individual might bring to any text" (Holub, 1989:59). Laudable as the appeal to consider history may be, Jauss's lack of a workable methodology and his reliance on a purely intuitive and hypothetical notion rendered his ambition of a history of aesthetic experience more of an unattainable dream than a realistic goal.

Reception Theory

Less concerned with the history of aesthetic response, Wolfgang Iser's reception theory focused on the interaction between the text and the reader. Drawing from phenomenological sources, he attempted to describe the reading process in terms of the reader's "concretization" of textual features, in particular, gap-filling activities activated by the text's indeterminacies, or "schematized aspects." In describing these concretization activities and responses, Iser coined the term "the implied reader" (1974). The extensive discussion that ensued as to what precisely Iser might have intended by this term has generated the consensus that it refers to a text-based concept of the reader, implying that the reading process entails the generation of the meanings already inscribed in the text. The circularity of his theory is evident: From his theory of the text he extrapolates a concept of the reader, and the reader's presumed activities confirm his hypothesis regarding the text. Although Iser's intuitive descriptions of the reading process provide some interesting insights, they remain purely speculative because his text-based approach offers no method of validating the hypotheses. Consequently, his theory sheds little light on what actually transpires in the mind of readers during the reading process. In his defense, it must be pointed out that Iser did acknowledge the limits of purely speculative approaches and argued that empirical modes of inquiry were needed. In his preface to *The Act of Reading*, he explained that his concern was "to devise a framework for mapping out and guiding empirical studies of reader reaction" (Iser, 1978:x). His point that empirical research needs to be guided by a framework of issues and questions is well taken, but such a framework conceived independently of the research itself is unlikely to be helpful.

Reader-Response Theory

Prominent among the American reader-response theories are the works of Stanley Fish (1980) and Norman Holland (1975). Both critics have attempted to validate their hypothesis by means of empirical observation of real readers, but in both cases the methods used are flawed, rendering the conclusions drawn from them unconvincing. For example, to prove that meaning is less in the text than in the reader, Fish merely observed students in one of his own literature classes, and Holland informally assessed the reactions of five of his students. In neither case was there any attempt to compare the behavior of the students to that which might be obtained under other circumstances, making it difficult to say for certain what might have caused the responses that these authors reported. For example, it is quite possible that in both cases the subjects were led (or misled) to produce precisely the results expected by the researchers, and it is unclear whether comparable findings would obtain under more representative reading conditions.

Reader-response theory is often framed in terms of the hypothetical response of ideal or universal readers. This has led to a plethora of elusive terms, each with its idiosyncratic orientation and bias. Some of these terms include, for example, the "ideal reader" (Culler, 1975b), the "implied reader" (Booth, 1961; Iser, 1974), the "informed reader" (Fish, 1970; Wolff, 1971), the "super reader" (Riffaterre, 1966), "communities of readers" (Fish, 1980), and gendered or sexed readers, such as the "resisting reader" (Fetterley, 1977). Some form of generalization is important if one wishes to do more than catalogue the behavior and responses of particular individuals. However, a missing methodological component of the generalized readers often discussed in reader-response theory is the relationship between the theoretical concept of the reader and the actual readers of real texts. We have more to say about how this problem may be solved in Chapter 2.

Hermeneutics

Within the field of hermeneutics, a myriad of contradictory theories and insights has been developed to account for the reader's interpretive activity. Some claim that texts encode determinate meaning that can be decoded by using reliable methods (Hirsch, 1976). Some argue that only the readings of qualified critics are reliable and enlightening (Krieger, 1981). Others defend the view that all interpretations are to be considered on equal footing (Bauer, 1972). Others still proclaim that all interpretations are either subjective and idiosyncratic (Bleich, 1978; Holland, 1975; Slatoff, 1970) or erroneous (de Man, 1983). And still others remain uncommitted by simply asserting ambiguously that some interpretations are more appealing than others (Iser, 1980). In short, this body of research has left us with much confusion and no consensus as to the nature of the text, the reader, or the reading experience.

Sociological, Historical, and Cultural Approaches

The belief that reading is "essentially a collective phenomenon" and that therefore "the individual reader" should be regarded "as part of a reading public" (Suleiman & Crosman, 1980:32) has led many scholars to attempt in different ways to define the cultural codes and conventions that intervene in the reception of literature. Sociological, historical, and cultural approaches to readers' responses to narrative are so numerous and diverse that it is impossible, and indeed un-necessary, to review them all here. Nevertheless, to the extent that it is possible to generalize the characteristics of these divergent trends, the general object of inquiry, as Susan Suleiman and Inge Crosman have concluded, is "the relationship between specific reading publics (varying with time, place, and circumstances), and either specific works or genres, or else whole bodies of works that make up the literary and artistic tradition of a given society" (32).

A central limitation of this branch of reader-oriented approaches is their propensity to reduce the reader to a predetermined set of over-generalized laws and models. This in turn springs from the failure to recognize the element of difference, divergence, and contradiction due to individual variation. For example, it is often presupposed that individuals belong to a single homogenous and autonomous group or social class at any given point in time. As has been only too well rec-ognized, this view oversimplifies a highly complex reality because, in fact, no one member belongs to just one social group at any given time, but rather to several, and not all members of the same class belong to all the same subgroups. Further, individual readers do not react solely as members of a given reading public. Even if a collectivity could be identified on the basis of obvious, common characteristics, it would never be the case that all members comprising it would share exactly the same values, aspirations, ideas, opinions, or, in short, the same life experience. After we reject monolithic notions of reading publics, we can no longer justifiably believe that the reading experience of all members of any given group will be identical and reducible to intuitive hypotheses about collective responses.

The ethnographic studies within feminist, post-colonial, and cultural studies propagate the flaws of earlier sociological and historical reader reception approaches. Beach (1993) pointed out that one of the major limitations of cultural studies approaches to reading publics is that "the theorists make questionable claims about the ways in which *groups* of readers or viewers are socialized to accept the ideological reading formations of texts.... Such sweeping generalizations are often insensitive to the variation of individual responses" (Beach, 1993:150). Other critical analyses of some of these approaches include Ebert (1988), Hartley (1987), and McRobbie (1990). However, missing from these and other similar critiques are concrete suggestions for improving the methodology and incorporating compelling empirical evidence. The importance of the ethnographic approach to reading and reception makes it clear that this is necessary and overdue.

Our conceptual approach to this tension between individual and collective response is outlined in Chapter 2. In any event, we believe, like Fludernik, that "paradoxically, we still know much too little about narrative to indulge in any easy generalizations about its commitments to, and ensnarements by, its political, societal and ideological embedding" (1996:2). Thus, an understanding of narrative processing is a prerequisite to further research on the effects of cultural factors on narrative reception.

Narratology

Narratology is fundamentally concerned with the identification and theoretical description of formal characteristics of narrative texts. Its "classical" period, influenced by the work of the Russian Formalists and Saussurean linguistics, spanned the sixties through the eighties.

One of the most influential concepts reinforced during this period was the Aristotelian distinction between story (mimesis) and discourse (diegesis), that is, between the told and its narration, or telling. Much of the scholarship of this period concentrated on the definition and description of plot (Barthes, 1966; Bremond, 1966, translated 1980; Greimas, 1971). Genette set the narratological agenda for posterity in 1973 with the publication of his book *Figures III*, which detailed topics such as the representation of temporality (e.g., narrative time and story time), narration (who speaks and the relationship between the speaking voice and elements of the story world), and focalization (who sees) (see also Genette, 1980, 1983). Although different narratologists organize the object of study into different classification frameworks, they all incorporate these main categories. A summary of the research on each of these categories would exceed the scope of this introductory chapter but will be provided in subsequent chapters, each one of which is devoted exclusively to one of these problems. More recently, this narratological project has been extended by drawing on the findings of other fields, such as deconstruction, feminism (Lanser, 1995), psychoanalysis, cognitive psychology, and philosophy. Traditional concepts such as the story–discourse distinction have been challenged, and the object of inquiry has been extended beyond the literary to include all narrative discourse. This fostered the move toward the study of narrative pragmatics and speech act theory.

Many narratologists have recognized that a more solid understanding of narrative requires an analysis of how it functions for readers. For example, Booth (1961) suggested that readers construct an image of the implied author in the course of understanding a literary work. According to Gerald Prince's own definition, narratology also considers the "functioning of narrative," which implies a reader, and attempts to both "characterize narrative competence" and "account for the ability to produce and understand" narrative (Prince, 1987:65). More recently, Prince (1990:3) noted that modern narratology "can account for certain responses to texts," thus expanding the field of inquiry of narratology to include narrative pragmatics. Lanser (1981) has claimed that narratives need to be considered in terms of speech act theory, in which readers construct some representation of authors and their intentions. Rimmon-Kenan (1983) argued that the story of narratives must be constructed by readers. O'Neil's (1994) entire book illustrated the importance of the reader's role in the construction of narrative features. Margolin reminded us that characters are constructed by readers who draw inferences about them based on textual cues (1989), and that the determination of textual properties, which can vary across individuals and contexts, "belongs probably to pragmatics" (1992:54). Monica Fludernik attempted to "redefine narrativity in terms of cognitive ('natural') parameters, moving beyond formal narratology into the realm of pragmatics, reception theory and constructivism" (Fludernik, 1996:xi). Espousing the belief that "spontaneous conversational storytelling" (13) sheds light on the production, forms, and reception of "the study of all types of narrative" (15), her goal was to provide an account for "organic frames of reading" (xi). Even a cursory review of narratological articles appearing in a variety of scholarly journals reveals a plethora of attempts to characterize the reader's cognitive activities. However, as Jahn remarked, "despite the fact that recourse to readers, readers' intuitions, and reading plays an important role in narratological argument, the contribution of mainstream narratology to a dedicated cognitive approach is meager and often counterproductive" (1997:465).

Fludernik's (1996) attempt to ground the study of narrative in a sophisticated description of cognitive experience constitutes a step in the right direction. Nevertheless, her descriptions of readers and the reading process remain entrenched in vague generalities, as demonstrated by her following claim:

When readers are confronted with potentially unreadable narratives, texts that are radically inconsistent, they cast about for ways and means of recuperating these texts as narratives – motivated by the generic markers that go with the book. They therefore attempt to recognize what they find in the text in terms of the natural telling or experiencing or viewing parameters, or they try to recuperate the inconsistencies in terms of actions and event structures at the most minimal level. This process of narrativization, of making something a narrative by the sheer act of imposing narrativity on it, needs to be located in the dynamic reading process where such interpretative recuperations hold sway. (34)

It may well be that by default readers "actively construct meanings and impose frames on their interpretations of texts just as people have to interpret real-life experience in terms of available schemata" (12). But intuitive as the insight may be, it remains only a plausible hypothesis. Fludernik's correlation between storytelling and natural modes of human experience may be a powerful way of explaining the production and forms of narrative, but it is too vague and general to explain narrative processing and reception. How readers process narrative is essentially an empirical question that can only be answered by systematic observation of actual readers reading actual texts; it cannot be answered solely on the basis of intuition, anecdotal evidence, or even sophisticated models of human experience. Moreover, the answer to this question inevitably will be complex: Readers' mental processes will vary with the characteristics of the individual reader, the nature of the text, and the context in which the reading takes place. This means that what is required is a large body of empirical evidence on how these variables operate, how they interact, and how they combine to determine readers' processing.

That is not to say that empirical research should not be driven by theoretical intuitions about how narrative works. In fact, the remaining chapters in this book provide empirical validation for an intuition about narrative processing that intersects Fludernik's theory in several ways. Our view is that approaches such as ours and Fludernik's need to be twofold. First, a theoretical treatment of the reading process must be developed with sufficient precision and rigor that unambiguous and testable predictions are made. Second, those predictions must be evaluated empirically by observing the response of actual readers. This is the line of attack that we have taken here.

Discourse Processing

Historically, the main focus of research on discourse processing has been the nature of the processes used to construct mental representations of the text, and it has generated a substantial body of evidence and theorizing on the mental processes readers use. For example, an abundance of evidence on the nature of inferences drawn during reading suggests that inferences are drawn in the service of what is termed a "search for meaning" (Graesser et al., 1994); there is a body of compelling and insightful evidence on how people construct mental representations of the spatial and configural relationships in the story world (e.g., Morrow, Greenspan & Bower, 1987); a considerable amount of work exists on the role of causal and relational connections in inference and textual memory (e.g., Trabasso & van den Broek, 1985); and there are crucial findings concerning the interpretation of perspective cues in narrative (e.g., Tversky, 1996). A recent concern has been relating the information in the text to perceptual and motor representations in the mind of the reader (e.g., Lakoff & Johnson, 1999; Glenberg, 1997). However, discourse-processing research has been only minimally informed by the conceptual advances and distinctions that have been developed in narratology, and much of the field has been concerned with narratives that have an exceptionally simple form, often created by the researchers themselves. Thus, the theoretical developments in discourse processing, although well grounded in empirical evidence, tend to have a limited scope when compared to the breadth of issues and variety of texts investigated in narratology.

The "Text-as-Communication" Framework

Perhaps the most obvious incompatibilities between discourse processing and literary studies have to do with the presumed function of narrative. In much of the discourse-processing field, written discourse is thought of as a communication between the author and the reader. Thus, the goal of the reader is to decode the message intended by the author and to represent it internally (e.g., Clark & Chase, 1972; van Dijk & Kintsch, 1983). Typically, it is assumed that the mental representation of the text consists of an organized list of propositions (Kintsch, 1974), and that an index of the effectiveness of the discourse and its comprehension can be obtained, at least in principle, by comparing the derived propositions to those propositions intended by the author. Research based on this "text-as-communication" view has helped to identify a wide range of processes and representations used in discourse processing. These include lexical processes (e.g., Seidenberg & McClelland, 1989), the representation of syntactic structures (e.g., Frazier & Rayner, 1982), the processing of anaphoric reference (e.g., Chang, 1980), inferences generated for textual cohesion (e.g., Singer & Ferreira, 1983), the processing of figurative language (e.g., Gibbs, 1990), the productive use of language (Glenberg & Robertson, 1999, 2000; Kaschak & Glenberg, 2000), and structures for representing larger segments of text (e.g., Mandler, 1984).

One of the ways in which the text-as-communication model has been applied is to assume that the author's intended message is unambiguously coded in the text and that the reader's task is to decode this message. This assumption leads to an interpretation that successful comprehension is determinantly related to the text itself. Thus, often research in discourse processing has an implicit assumption that readers' responses to a text are generally homogeneous, and that any variation is due either to comprehension "errors" (in which the intended message is not correctly decoded) or unusual, idiosyncratic, or task-specific goals or reading strategies. Examples of this type of supposition can be found in Fletcher and Bloom (1988), McKoon and Ratcliff (1992), Trabasso and Sperry (1985), and a wide range of other work. This presumption is not that much different from the notions of homogeneity made by some reading-response theorists. Our view is that the text is a stimulus to which readers respond, and that this response is potentially subject to any number of influences in the reader's mental makeup or the reading context. Such influences need to be taken into account in a systematic and fundamental manner.

Further, we argue that the text-as-communication model is inadequate to explain the complexities of literary processing. For example, there is no simple sense in which literature can be construed as a communication from the author to the reader because the apparent speaker of the words of a literary text is the narrator, not the actual author. Further, there are important aspects of what readers do with literary texts that are unlikely to have been intended by the author and hence difficult to describe as an aspect of communication (Dixon & Bortolussi, 2001). More sophisticated views of the interaction between the author and the reader have been built within the communication framework that ameliorate some of these concerns (e.g., Bruce, 1981; Clark, 1996; Gerrig, 1993). Although each of these approaches is helpful, we argue that they have limitations as approaches to the empirical study of literary narrative. In general, even though the research on discourse processing provides a rich set of constructs and representations that undoubtedly play a role in the processing of literature, we believe that the view of narrative as communication between the author and the reader requires important modifications in order to make further progress concerning literary processing (Dixon & Bortolussi, 2001).

Theoretical Concepts

In much of the work to be presented here, we build on some important theoretical ideas that have been developed and applied in discourse processing. We describe a few of these here.

A central advance in discourse processing has been the careful delineation of various forms of inferences. Graesser et al. (1994) identified four broad classes of inference: local coherence inferences, explanatory inferences, global coherence inferences, and communicative inferences. As described in Chapter 3, we take issue with some aspects of this analysis. In particular, Graesser et al. suggested that communicative inferences are generated on the basis of the pragmatics of communication between the author and the reader. We believe, however, that it is not useful to conceptualize narrative as communication between the author and the reader, and that hence it is more appropriate to think of these communicative inferences as pertaining to the narrator. Further, we argue that many aspects of such narratorial inferences should be considered in term of conversational processes. Readers treat their representation of the narrator much as they would a representation of a conversational participant. The instances of "communicative" inferences considered by Graesser et al. become more coherent and productive when described in such terms. Nevertheless, the distinctions among inference types represented by Graesser et al. are critical to the development of a theoretical understanding of how readers process narrative.

A common assumption in discourse processing is that readers represent not just the text itself but also that to which the text refers. In narrative, this is in effect the reader's representation of the story world. Various authors have termed this type of representation a referential representation (Just & Carpenter, 1987), a situation model (van Dijk & Kintsch, 1983), or a mental model (Johnson-Laird, 1983). One of the crucial insights of this line of research has been that the nature and qualities of the referential representation depend on the reader's prior knowledge and expectations. For example, the referential representation may change depending on the reader's goals (e.g., Anderson & Pichert, 1978), background knowledge (Spilich et al., 1979), or expectations concerning genre (McDaniel et al., 1994). Recently, it has been noted that referential representations of meaning cannot simply be abstract and symbolic but must also include perceptual information about how objects look, sound, or feel and motoric information about how actions might be performed. Such information falls under the general heading of "embodied" representations of meaning (Lakoff & Johnson, 1999; Glenberg, 1997). Regardless of the precise nature of such representations, the notion of a referential representation must be central to theories of literary processing because many of the interesting aspects of literary texts concern the content of that referential representation rather than aspects of the text itself.

Another problem of central importance is the role of memory in comprehension. Although the research described in this volume is not specifically concerned with memory for text, many of the processes and structures that have been explored in this literature are relevant to the issues we address. In particular, we view three types of memory as central to the processes we discuss. The first is most commonly subsumed under the term "working memory" (cf. Baddeley, 1986). Although there are many different views of working memory and its role in comprehension, a critical ingredient to many of these views is the idea that working memory maintains the current context, goals, and themes as one reads the text. In this sense, working memory subsumes the discourse pointer (Just & Carpenter, 1987), focus (e.g., Sanford & Garrod, 1981), or given information (Haviland & Clark, 1974). A second memory representation is related to the notion of long-term working memory discussed by Ericsson and Kintsch (1995). In our usage, this representation is based on those processes that allow one to organize and structure the large bulk of the information garnered and inferred from the text so that it may be easily and reliably retrieved when necessary. Ericsson and Kintsch suggested that a situation model provides the necessary organizational mnemonic. However, as will be developed more fully in Chapter 3, we argue that the reader's representation of the narrator and his or her knowledge is more likely to be relevant for memory retrieval in the processing of narrative. Finally, another process that is likely to be important is memory resonance (Myers & O'Brien, 1998). Memory resonance processes include those mechanisms that allow readers to retrieve relevant information automatically from memory based on their similarity or close relationship to the textual information currently being processed. As developed by O'Brien and colleagues, memory resonance processes allow the reader to retrieve information that had been encountered earlier in the text. However, we hypothesize that resonance-like processes may also be crucial in allowing readers access to their own personal experience and idiosyncratic world-knowledge during comprehension.

As we indicated earlier, a central limitation of a large portion of the work in discourse processing has been an implicit endorsement of some form of the text-as-communication view. Most commonly, text is conceived of as a communicative transaction between the author and reader (in which it is the reader's task to divine the author's intention) or as an unambiguous code for meaning (that the reader must translate). Such an approach makes it difficult to discuss literary narrative with any depth, and one of our main goals is to recast the suppositions of this research in terms that are more congenial to our purposes; the basic elements of this approach are discussed later in this chapter. We believe that such an enterprise does little damage to the substantive contributions that have been made to the study of discourse processing but allows a more productive analysis of narrative and literature in particular. Crucial to our research, though, are the methodological advances common in the empirical study of discourse processing. As we discuss in Chapter 2, the methodologies we propose to use build on this research and include the careful and objective measurement of the dependent variables, precise control over stimulus materials, and rigorous standards for drawing conclusions from the evidence. The traditions of scientific rigor developed in experimental psychology and discourse processing are carried over to the research presented here.

Linguistics

Linguists interested in narrative discourse have developed a large number of important distinctions that are central to the study of narrative. These include the analysis of language forms related to space and spatial descriptions (e.g., Levelt, 1996), the modes of conveying represented speech and thought in discourse (e.g., Banfield, 1981), and the means by which point of view is determined in a text (Erlich, 1990). For our purposes, one of the limitations of much of the work in formal linguistics is that it is often based on introspective distinctions made by the researchers themselves. For example, a variety of scholars have developed a painstakingly meticulous tracking of perceptual and discursive shifts in the now famous sentence from Colette's *La Chatte* ("Elle le regarda boire et se troubla brusquement à cause de la bouche qui pressait les bords du verre") based solely on the formal treatment of the text with little regard for readers' processing (Bal, 1983; Bronzwaer, 1981; Nelles, 1990; Vitoux, 1984). Although we would not dispute the validity of such distinctions per se, it is an open, empirical question as to how important such linguistic variations are for most readers of most narratives. In some cases, such fine-grained analysis may have no impact on processing at all. One of our tasks in the succeeding chapters is to extract what we feel are the most central and compelling aspects of the linguistic analysis and carefully measure their effects on the reading of actual narratives.

While many linguists have focused on the local relationships among words and sentences, a few have tackled the broader problem of narrative structure in general. One example is the work of Emmott (1997). She proposed an approach that consists of formulating "hypotheses about text comprehension by looking at the text rather than the reader" (94), on the explicit understanding that these hypothesis must be subjected to empirical testing, without which "we can only say that it seems likely that a particular mental representation is formed" (95). Although her approach is laudable for its treatment of real and full-length narratives, the insights gained seem to be largely reformulations of common intuitions. For example, to make connections between different portions of text, she argued that readers must retain in memory information gathered from previous passages, and, in her words, making the connections "involves looking at places in the text where an inference must be made if textual coherence is to be established, such as the inferencing necessary to assign referents to pronouns" (95). Our analysis is that the thrust of this approach is dedicated to describing the minimal conditions of competent reading. Furthermore, Emmott's analysis is comparable to literary critics' hypothetical presuppositions about the reader in that she relies mainly on her own intuitions about what reading stories entails.

Conversational Processes

Although we argue that the communication model in general is inadequate to explain the complexities of literary processing, elements of conversational dynamics are crucial to the theoretical treatment we propose. First, an essential insight is that in conversation, a language user maintains a mental representation of the other participant, and that this representation must include information about the other's intentions in the conversation, the knowledge that he or she has of the conversation and its relevant background, and the perceptual information he or she has available (e.g., Clark & Schaefer, 1989). Under many circumstances, it becomes crucial to note that the mental representation of conversational participants is potentially recursive, so that, for example, a speaker's representation of the hearer includes information about the hearer's model of the speaker. This kind of representation is critical in making sense of how conversational participants negotiate a common understanding of the conversational topic and how misunderstandings are detected and corrected (e.g., Schegloff, Jefferson & Sacks, 1977).

Second, conversational participants come to a conversation armed with a collection of assumptions about how participants should behave; these are the so-called conversational postulates of Grice (1975). The first postulate is the maxim of quantity: Speakers should make their contribution informative and provide only necessary and sufficient information. The second is the maxim of quality: Speakers should only say that for which they have evidence and that they believe to be true. The third is the maxim of relation: Speakers should only make relevant contributions. Finally, the fourth is the maxim of manner: Speakers should be brief and should avoid ambiguity and obscurity. These assumptions allow language users to make a variety of different kinds of inferences during a conversation on the assumption that speakers are generally cooperative, that is, they attempt to follow the conversational postulates.

Third, related to the notion of conversational postulates, is the concept of conversational implicature. For our purposes, an implicature can be understood as an inference that is licensed by the assumption that speakers are being cooperative. For example, if the speaker seems to violate a conversational postulate and one assumes that the speaker is cooperative, then an inference can be generated about what the speaker knows or believes that would make the seeming violation appropriate. Often such implicatures may be related to the speakers' model of the audience. For example, suppose a speaker commands the audience simply to "bring me the big one," but there are several big items one might bring. If one believes the speaker is cooperative and intends to supply sufficient information, one could infer that the speaker believes that the audience knows or can infer which item he or she is interested in. As we develop further in Chapter 3, the notion of implicatures is central to our view of how readers represent and process the narrator. In particular, we argue that readers assume that the narrator is cooperative and, based on that assumption, draw narratorial implicatures concerning the narrator's mental state and intended message.

Empirical Research on Literature

Empirical Science of Literature

One of the first to actually attempt and promote the study of real readers in the study of literature was Siegfried Schmidt (1980). His pioneering work provided inspiration and impetus to researchers involved in the current empirical research on literary processing. As early as the 1970s, Schmidt and his collaborators in the Bielefeld University research team developed the concept of ESL, the empirical science of literature. In so doing, he began constructing a bridge between the humanities and the sciences (Schmidt, 1980, 1981, 1983).

Schmidt distinguished between "empiricized conceptions of literary studies" that rely on sociological or psychological methods, and ESL, which attempts to "construct a science of literature as a homogeneously founded and oriented net of empirical theory-elements" (Schmidt, 1983:19). The import of this phrasing is not altogether clear, but it is partially elucidated by his statement: "in contrast to concepts of empirization, ESL, I think, attempts to provide an autonomous paradigm for the study of literature" (19). Schmidt's objection to "empirization" seems to be the fear that the dependency on scientific methodologies leads to an obliteration of the concern for the special qualities of literature. This is by no means a trivial or unfounded concern. Often, when literature becomes the object of sociological or psychological inquiry, it can become subordinated to the concerns of those fields and may not be studied with a view to furthering the understanding of literature itself. A classic example is Bartlett's (1932) investigation of the comprehension and memory of folktales. This highly cited research is a cornerstone of so-called "schema" theories in cognitive science, and it is often used as an important demonstration of the effects of prior knowledge and expectation on comprehension. However, the fact that readers in his experiments were processing literary texts has become largely irrelevant to the volume of research following in Bartlett's tradition. Deep-seated distrust of the use of literature by the scientific community explains Schmidt's emphasis on the need to establish the conditions of applicability under which empiricism can contribute productively to literary studies. His insistence that empiricism be theory-dependent can be understood as a plea to devise safeguards against unrestrained and inapplicable empiricism. The theory he himself develops is intended to explain processes comprising the LITERATURE-system, that is, the activities of "producing, mediating, receiving, and processing" (Schmidt, 1981:322). Inspired by Schmidt, a variety of European scholars have pursued this theoretical vein quite extensively (e.g., Hauptmeier, Meutsch & Viehoff, 1989; Larsen & Viehoff, 1995; Rusch, 1995; Schmidt, 1995). However, the actual empirical evidence produced in this research program is rather scant. Although there is no denying the importance of reflecting on one's scholarly activities, theoretical disquisitions on the proper uses of empiricism cannot replace sound empirical investigation, and the benefits of reflection are quickly exhausted if not accompanied by practice. The empiricism practiced by Schmidt and his collaborators is admirable for its pioneering spirit. Relative to the mass of evidence collected by researchers in discourse processing and cognitive psychology, however, their empirical contribution is limited.

One of the main objectives of this book it to demonstrate that it is possible to put some of the sound and rigorous empirical methods of the sciences at the service of literary studies, that is, to reconcile Schmidt's ideal for autonomous literary–empirical studies with sound empirical methods. In Chapter 2, we will elaborate an inter-disciplinary methodological framework that meets Schmidt's theory-dependency and applicability criteria, and that focuses on one of the activities of the literary system, the cognitive processing of literary texts.

A common concern among numerous literary critics was the fear that the empirical study of real readers would degenerate into sheer interpretive randomness. But this "interpretative anarchy" has not occurred (Selden, 1995:401); the tendency to reduce reading to purely individual cognitive operations not governed by any form of lawful-ness has not come to constitute a prevalent theoretical position, nor is it a danger of empirical investigation. In fact, from an empirical perspective, idiosyncratic or variable behavior at the level of individual readings does not imply a lack of systematicity and regularity at the level of process and mechanism. For example, Newell and Simon (1972) treated a similar issue in problem solving: Even though the be-havior and approaches to solving a problem were different for each individual and each problem, the form of the information-processing constraints were the same. Newell and Simon were able to provide an insightful and general theoretical account by a careful and objective analysis of an extensive collection of such problem-solving behavior. We do not suggest that a similar analytical approach is necessary or appropriate for the empirical study of literature; our point is merely that variability is not randomness.

Current Trends

Since Schmidt's early advocacy of ESL, a variety of empirical inves-tigations have contributed to our understanding of literature and literary narrative. An important problem has been the role of indi-vidual differences in literary processing. This has been investigated using groups of literary expert and novice readers (e.g., Thury & Friedlander, 1995), the development of scales to measure literary expertise (Miall & Kuiken, 1995), and the assessment of reading history or habits (Dixon et al., 1993). Others have pursued the nature of affective reactions related, for example, to the reader's personal history (Larsen, Lázló & Seilman, 1991), interaction of reading styles and genre (Cupchik, Oatley, & Vorderer, 1998), or identification processes (Tan, 1994). Another class of important problems concerns how readers assess and track essential elements of the story world and characters' knowledge (Graesser, Bowers, Olde & Pomeroy, 1999). Methodologies used in these investigations are varied, but a common technique involves the collection and evaluation of verbal protocols (e.g., Graves & Frederiksen, 1991) or summary evaluations of the narrative (e.g., Dorfman, 1996). The research reported here builds on these efforts. However, we argue that a valuable component of such methodology is the careful manipulation of the text. Incorporating this ingredient allows one to identify covariation between features of the text and corresponding reader constructions and, as we elaborate in Chapter 2, allows much stronger and more precise inferences concerning causes. The net result is much more informative theoretical explanations. Although there are important exceptions (e.g., Andringa et al., 1997), our impression is that this approach to the empirical investigation of literature is relatively uncommon.

Psychonarratology

Psychonarratology is our term for the investigation of mental processes and representations corresponding to the textual features and structures of narrative. The motivation for coining this term is twofold. On one hand, any number of scholars in modern narratology have proposed that a resolution of narratological issues requires some understanding of how actual readers process texts. However, the field of narratology as a whole is ill equipped in some ways to conduct this kind of investigation. Discourse processing and cognitive psychology, on the other hand, have many of the methodological and interpretive tools for investigating reading processes, but for a number of reasons they have been only peripherally concerned with narratorial processing. What we are proposing here is a framework in which the best of narratology and discourse processing may come together to make some progress on these problems. Most of our work follows from two insights: First, to effectively merge the insights and expertise of narratology with carefully collected empirical evidence, it is essential to distinguish features of the text on one hand from the reader's mental constructions on the other. Second, a great deal of progress can be made in understanding how readers process narrative by assuming that the narrator is treated as a conversational participant. Each of these ideas is elaborated later. First, however, we discuss several suppositions that some may view as obstacles to this interdisciplinary enterprise.

Interdisciplinarity: Myths and New Directions

As our review of the literature suggests, the understanding of narrative processing, and of literary narrative in particular, is still limited. In light of this, interdisciplinary cross-fertilization would appear to be a sine qua non for advancing our knowledge of this phenomenon. Promoting this kind of research environment is not without its problems. The greatest are undoubtedly the mutual biases of one field against the other and the stereotypes that still dominate each discipline's perception of the other. These problems explain in part the tardiness of the interaction between literary studies and discourse processing in spite of their common interest in texts and readers. Although there is intuitive agreement among promoters of interdisciplinary studies that it is in the boundaries between disciplines that new and exciting insights can emerge, contact between the humanities and natural sciences is still avoided. In the humanities, this is owing to a deeply ingrained, traditional bias against the "hard-core" sciences as alien and enemy disciplines that have nothing in common with literary studies, and thus have nothing to offer the field. These myths have been subjected to critical scrutiny exposing their basis in popular misconceptions that block our ability to perceive commonalties and imagine fruitful collaboration (Bortolussi & Dixon, 1998; Knapp, 1990; Limon, 1990; Schmidt, 1981). For their part, scientists may reject the insights gained in humanities out of hand as subjective, vague, and imprecise.

The potential for advancing our knowledge of a wide array of problems related to the processing of narrative discourse is great, but so also is the amount of work that must still be done. The first step to meeting the challenges of the future is developing a mutual willingness to share knowledge and adopting an open mind with respect to true interdisciplinary interaction. For literary scholars, this means acknowledging the need for the methods and approaches found in the natural sciences. For natural scientists, this means accepting the expert knowledge of narrative discourse found in literary scholarship. One of our goals in writing this book was to assuage the fear that results from the inability to imagine one's commonality with the alien "other" discipline, and to demonstrate how accessible this kind of interdisciplinary research really is for scholars within these different disciplines. With this in mind, it is worth reviewing some of the myths that have delayed the emergence of psychonarratology and the concerns that lead some to fear it.

One such myth is the objection that the sciences are hopelessly positivistic and concerned only with observable, quantifiable phenomenon to the exclusion of equally valid, intangible aspects of life. In a true Gadamerian spirit, it is argued that these require intuition and interpretation, not scientific method. Consonant with this objection is the argument that the mind cannot be directly observed, and thus the complexities of the mental reading experience are not amenable to empirical observation. It is a subjective experience, and thus outside the domain of science. In the words of one literary scholar, "the field of cognitive studies is insufficiently equipped to deal with the complexity of human thought processes. Practitioners of cognitive science can explain neither the complexity of cognitive aesthetic perception nor the depth and individuality of subjective, affective reactions" (Gross, 1997:294).

However, methodologies for drawing rigorous inferences concerning unobservable phenomena have a long tradition in science; nuclear physics and radio astronomy are obvious examples of disciplines founded on such techniques. Cognitive psychology in particular has developed methods for making inferences concerning how the mind works. Although mental operations such as problem solving, memory retrieval, and language comprehension cannot be observed directly, one can gain knowledge of them indirectly by synthesizing a variety of observable signs such as verbal reports, response latencies, and degrees of accuracy in the performance of specific tasks. Understanding what this network of evidence says about the object of study is guided by a history of logic, theory, and methodological development. The study of the mental processing of literature is, in principle, no different.

A second objection on the part of humanities scholars is the fear that the appropriate scientific techniques are too difficult. Humanities scholars are not trained in the sciences, the argument goes and, therefore, cannot undertake this kind of research. It is true that some technical skills used in various scientific disciplines require years of study and practice. However, there is nothing about a scientific approach, per se, that requires such a background. In fact, most of the lessons to be learned are quite simple, consisting of issues such as how to formulate empirically testable questions, how to distinguish between valid and invalid inferences, and how to determine what counts as objective evidence. In particular, the interdisciplinary research we describe in this book is accessible to all scholars who are interested in the approach, including those in the humanities, and requires no previous scientific training; it requires merely a willingness to think about the problems in a different way. Students of the humanities are sometimes put off by the scientific penchant for reporting statistics and the details of statistical procedures, and some of such details are included in our reports of empirical evidence here. However, we believe a concern about the technical aspects of statistics is misplaced: The required background to carry out statistical procedures such as those we describe is roughly comparable to an entry-level university course and is routinely mastered by a broad spectrum of undergraduates in a handful of weeks. Moreover, our reporting of these results is intended to be accessible to even casual readers. (As a further aid for readers with a minimal background in statistics, a brief overview of the approach used in this book is provided in an appendix.)

For scientists, a corresponding objection might be that much of literary studies is irrelevant. However, we argue that crucial lessons can be learned from many branches of literary studies and narratology in particular. These include narratological components of discourse such as the narrator (a concept largely ignored in discourse processing), the function of narrative communication, and an appreciation of the range and scope of narrative forms. Our sense is that it is shortsighted and naïve to ignore the history of insight and debate that has transpired concerning literature and reading simply because it has not occurred in scientific circles. The approach we have attempted to take here is to conduct rigorous empirical investigations that are inherently informed by the scholarship in literary studies.

Features and Constructions

Many narratologists and other literary scholars share the common supposition that the processing of narratives must be considered in understanding the ways in which narrative functions. However, narratological approaches typically fail to provide an account of the how features of the text interact with the mental processes and representations of actual readers. The first step in elucidating this interaction is to draw a careful distinction between the text and its formal description on one hand, and the reader and the reading process on the other. We use the term *textual feature* to refer to anything in the text that can be objectively identified. Textual features include many of the distinctions made in classical studies of narratology, such as narration styles (first- or third-person narration, heterodiegetic versus homodiegetic narration), speech styles (direct, indirect, free-indirect speech), techniques for marking discourse and story time, and aspects of characterization. We believe that these and other features in principle could be identified objectively by an explicit algorithm. Thus, one could envision designing a (relatively sophisticated) computer program to find and measure such features. In practice, we use trained observers to find textual features; if such observers are provided with sufficiently detailed and specific definitions of the features, they should be able to find the features reliably and consistently.

In contrast, *reader constructions* are events and representations in the minds of readers. Reader constructions include mental representations of various sorts, changes in readers' attitudes or beliefs, and affective reactions. Crucially, reader constructions are subjective, in the sense that they can vary across readers, and contextual, in the sense that they vary with the reading situation and readers' goals and expectations. Although logical analysis and theorizing might be useful in identifying textual features, it does not suffice for the investigation of reader constructions. Instead, empirical evidence is necessary to determine what representations were constructed or what processes transpired. However, in many cases the procedure for collecting such data is relatively straightforward; for example, in many of the experiments we report in this book, we have simply asked readers specific questions about their reactions and attitudes concerning the narrator and the narrative and collected responses using numerical scales. The critical ingredient is the simple recognition of the fact that readers need not, in principle, process or interpret a text in a predetermined way; in order to make claims concerning reader constructions, actual reading behavior needs to be assessed in the context of a particular narrative and reading task. An important point for our approach is that even though reader constructions are variable, they are knowable in an aggregate sense. That is, one can attach a certain amount of statistical certainty to generalizations as long as they are sufficiently delimited with respect to reading context and to reader population.

To repeat an earlier argument, this means that what is required is a large body of empirical evidence on how these variables operate, how they interact, and how they combine to determine readers' processing. Psychonarratology is an empirical approach that targets one dimension of the general problem of narrative processing: It is designed to measure systematically how particular groups of readers process specific features of narrative. Narratology and linguistics guide us in our description of these features, while cognitive psychology and discourse processing inspire our measurement of reader constructions.

The Conversational Narrator

A common assumption shared by several disciplines is the idea that narrative reception and processing are best understood in the context of real-life models. Within literary studies, there has been a distinct move away from the elitist notion of "literariness," or the intrinsically literary nature of certain fictional texts. The field of discourse analysis is grounded in the assumption that literary language is not distinct from, but rather an instance of, ordinary language, and that consequently it is processed as such by readers (Tolliver, 1990). This focus on what readers naturally do with narrative texts constitutes the basis of Fludernik's "natural narratology," which in turn was inspired by the trend in cognitive linguistics to focus on "naturalist" linguistic models (Dressler, 1990). Linguistics has produced an abundance of research on the general topic of how people use narratives in everyday life, as in, for example, the work of Deborah Tannen. Within cognitive psychology, specialists like Ray Gibbs have argued that literary studies and studies of discourse in general need to account for the cognitive factors that intervene in people's experience of meaning;

he believed that these factors are analogous to "the cognitive processes that operate when we understand human action of any sort"
(Gibbs, 1999:4–5).

In keeping with this theme, a central component in much of the theoretical development presented here is the view that readers treat the
narrator of a narrative much as they would a conversational participant. The details of this idea are developed more fully in Chapter 3.
It is useful to note at this point, though, that this view is distinct from
the more common supposition that the reader communicates with the
author via the text. In particular, we explicitly avoid any suggestion
that the relationship between the narrator can be described as communication in any real way. Indeed, because the narrator is not a real
person, he or she cannot be said to have intentions or messages to
communicate to the reader. Instead, our thesis is that readers process
the narrator *as if* they were communicating with such an individual in
conversation. As we develop in succeeding chapters, the implications
of this view of reader processing of narrative are many and profound.
It dictates the possible effects of having narrators be absent or present
in the story world; it determines how readers interpret elements of
plot and story structure; it provides a mechanism for understanding
perspective and focalization; and it unifies how readers interpret and
analyze speech and thought presented in the narrative. However, it
is important to note that this is essentially an empirical hypothesis
concerning the nature of reader constructions related to the narrator.
The evidence presented in succeeding chapters provides some support for this view, but it will undoubtedly require, at a minimum,
further elaboration and refinement beyond what we present here.

The Promise of Research in Psychonarratology

The succeeding chapters of this volume describe our program of research in psychonarratology. Chapter 2 begins by outlining some
methodological issues involved in our approach. These involve criteria and techniques for identifying textual features, the tension
between the description of individual reader responses to text and
the description of readers in aggregate, how to deal with variability
in empirical evidence, and the role of textual manipulations in generating causal explanations. Following these preliminaries, we discuss

the reader's mental representation of five categories of textual features, to which we devote one chapter each. The central issue of the representation of the narrator is discussed in Chapter 3. Because all aspects of the narrative are mediated by a narrating agent, and on the assumption that the interpretation of the text hinges upon this mediation, we discuss how the representation of the narrator is determined by the reader's knowledge, goals, and reading context. Chapter 4 examines the cognitive processes that condition the reader's experience of discourse elements as events and plot. In Chapter 5, we draw from research in social psychology on person perception and attribution theory to highlight the similarities between interpreting literary characters and real people, and in the light of this, we develop a framework for character analysis that accounts for how real-life experience mediates the process of character construction. Chapter 6 provides a framework for understanding textual features pertaining to perceptual information and discusses some hypotheses for related reader constructions. In Chapter 7, we consider the readers' constructions related to represented speech and thought in narrative and consider how the voice of the narrator is distinguished from those of the story-world characters. Although these categories pertain to the major theoretical issues in narratology, they do not, by any means, exhaust the problems that might be addressed, and a few other issues are mentioned in Chapter 8.

We begin each chapter with a critical scrutiny of the narratological theories relevant to each of these areas, demonstrating that the seemingly irreconcilable variety of frameworks and ongoing debates are often due to the failure to make a clear distinction between the text and its formal description on one hand, and the reader and the reading process on the other. Relevant research in discourse processing and related fields is also briefly reviewed. Following this background, we present a synthesis of these ideas that provides a workable framework for textual features related to each of these narratological problems and some hypotheses concerning the associated reader constructions. Each chapter provides empirical evidence pertaining to these hypotheses.

By bringing together the fields of discourse processing and narratology, we hope not only to lay the foundation for a science of psychonarratology but also to make contributions to both of the component disciplines. Narratologists are increasingly aware of the need to consider reader constructions and the reception of narratives to understand the ways in which narratives function; our work should enable them to incorporate into their field the empirical investigation of how narratives are actually processed. Psychonarratology thus provides the means for narratology "to account for what should be one of its prime considerations, the cognitive mechanics of reading" (Jahn, 1997:464). We expect to contribute to discourse processing by providing it with the analytical tools for studying complex narrative texts and by introducing the critical concept of narratorial representations. We also anticipate that the results from the research will have broad implications for understanding the function of narratives wherever they are encountered in our society. For example, when narrative is used as a vehicle for conveying information in instruction manuals, political speeches, legal arguments, and any of a wide range of other contexts, we expect that the interpretation of the message will be colored by the comprehender's representation of the narrator and the narrator's intent. Our research should provide evidence and conceptual insight relevant to such mechanisms.

Summary

In this chapter, we have outlined the background and elements of a new, interdisciplinary enterprise, psychonarratology. This approach is motivated by the emphasis placed on the reader in a variety of reader-oriented approaches to literary studies. In particular, we draw on the formal analyses of narrative found in classical narratology, and the problems we address in this work are, to a great extent, the central issues that have been framed in that field. However, our view is that both formal and reader-oriented approaches are not deeply informed by compelling empirical evidence concerning the behavior of real readers interacting with actual texts. For that, we turn to the methodologies and inference techniques found broadly in the fields of discourse processing and cognitive psychology. In our approach, we make use of many of the processes and representations that have been developed in theories of discourse comprehension; these include inference forms, referential representations, and memory processes. We argue, though, that the immediate application of much of the work in discourse processing to literary narrative has been hampered by the implicit assumption that text should be thought of as communication between the author and the reader and by a relatively unsophisticated analysis of narrative forms. Thus, in psychonarratology we attempt to draw together the insights and analytical tools of narratology and related branches of literary studies together with empirical techniques used to investigate cognitive processes found in discourse processing.

We introduce two central theses that represent the underpinnings of our approach. First, it is critical to distinguish carefully textual features from reader constructions. Textual features are derived by a suitable, objective analysis of texts; reader constructions, on the other hand, can only be verified by empirical evidence concerning the cognitive processes of readers and are potentially variable, subjective, and contextual. The second thesis is a framework for a broad collection of hypotheses concerning such reader constructions: We propose that readers often process narrative in much the same way that they would process conversation. Borrowing the linguistic concepts of conversational cooperation and conversational implicature allows us to generate a rich set of hypotheses concerning how readers process narrative. The succeeding chapters of this volume develop some of these and present a collection of empirical evidence in their support.

2

Preliminaries

In the present chapter, we present a framework and methodology for the empirical study of psychonarratology and discuss some of the epistemological issues that form the background for this kind of research. Following a discussion of the domain of psychonarratology, we elaborate on four aspects of the methodology that are central to its study. First, we discuss the distinction between features and constructions introduced in Chapter 1 and describe criteria for developing useful textual features. Second, the term "statistical reader" is introduced; this term describes an approach in which aggregate measures of groups of individuals are used to provide insights into the general characteristics of populations of readers. Third, we sketch some of the epistemological assumptions involved in conducting empirical research in psychonarratology and outline the theoretical goals. Fourth, we argue that the strongest inferences about reading processes can only be obtained by conducting "textual experiments" in which the text is manipulated and concomitant changes in readers' responses are observed. Together, these notions provide a foundation for the empirical investigation of the problems of psychonarratology.

This chapter was designed in part to address the needs, interests, and concerns of literary scholars who may be intrigued by the empirical study of literary response but lack the confidence to pursue it on their own. In particular, we have endeavored to outline the fundamentals of empirical research without recourse to specialized knowledge or vocabulary. As we discuss in Chapter 1, the very word "statistics" may have unpleasant connotations for literary scholars. We hope that the following sections will demonstrate not only that these connotations are ill-deserved but, more importantly, that statistical concepts are relevant to literary studies. The actual mechanics of using statistical formulas are generally not important to understanding the theories and evidence we present in this book. However, the elements of these calculations are described in the Appendix, and this material could serve as a resource for those individuals who wish to proceed and try their hand at this kind of research. To those individuals, we would also reiterate our belief that the epistemological and conceptual underpinnings provide the greatest barrier to conducting empirical research and that the process of manipulating the numbers is relatively simple.

The Domain of Psychonarratology

The goal of psychonarratology is to understand the psychological processing of narrative form. As described in Chapter 1, one of the major advances in recent work on narratology is an agreement that what readers do with the text is crucial for an understanding of narratives and how they function. In our view, there is a common supposition that the process of reading must be considered to understand the way in which narratives function. However, there is much less consensus on how to proceed from that starting point. Our view is that narratologists have been unable to pursue that agenda effectively to date because the important issues are essentially empirical questions that can only be answered by systematically observing readers as they read. Inevitably, the answer to the question "What do readers do with the text?" will be complex: What readers do will vary with the characteristics of the individual reader, the nature of the text, and the context in which the reading takes place. This means that what is required is a large body of empirical evidence on how these variables operate, how they interact, and how they combine to determine readers' processing. Although this is a daunting project, it is essentially tractable and can be addressed with established methodologies and experimental paradigms.

In fact, in psychology and psycholinguistics, there is already a great deal of evidence and theorizing on how readers process text. This work provides a solid foundation for discussing a range of problems, including the mechanics of reading (i.e., how the eye is moved over a text and how words are recognized), the identification of sentence structure and local textual coherence, the role of working memory in on-line processing, and the variables involved in remembering and learning from text. Although important, this work does not bear on the processing of narrative form directly and literary processing generally. There are also substantial areas of discourse processing, some of which are briefly reviewed in Chapter 1, that are more directly relevant to narrative. Problems such as the structure and use of referential representations, the generation of inferences, and the role of causal structure all form a background for the present work. However, since the pioneering work of Rumelhart (1975) and others on story grammars, relatively little of this work has been concerned with narrative form per se, and the history of scholarship in narratology and literary studies has had a minimal impact. In a sense, psychonarratology can be viewed as an extension of discourse processing that is concerned precisely with narrative and that builds on the knowledge and insight gained in decades of work in narratology and allied fields of study. As such, it depends on epistemological underpinnings that are common in psychological research but that are rarely discussed explicitly. In this chapter, we attempt to make some of these foundational notions clear.

The field of narrative processing is very broad and includes such things as how readers process whole texts, different genres, works from different periods, as well as how any of these is affected by culture, class, gender, and so on. In the present work, we focus primarily on how a relatively circumscribed collection of readers process a limited set of textual features. Consequently, the work and theoretical analyses we present here comprise only a starting point. This seems appropriate given the limited empirical evidence we have in this domain: It is necessary to start at a basic level before tackling deeper and wider problems. For example, the present work may be a building block for other inquiries in cultural studies or other allied disciplines.

Features and Constructions

Applying Features and Constructions

A distinction between text features and reader constructions eliminates some critical obstacles to the scientific study of narrative. For example, as we elaborate in Chapters 3 and 5, narratologists have devoted effort to defining the nature and locus of the narrator and characters in narrative. Is the narrator "in" the text, a property of the communicative transmission of information from author to reader, or some generalization of reader response? In our view, questions such as these have been difficult or controversial to answer because of a failure to carefully distinguish between textual features (i.e., objective and identifiable characteristics of the text) and reader constructions (i.e., subjective and variable mental processes). In fact, we would argue that the narrator is simultaneously both "in" the text and "in" the reader: There are identifiable narratorial features in the text (such as speech styles, proper nouns, deictics, and propositions attributing thought and action to agents) that provide cues and information to the reader; readers in turn commonly use such cues to construct a representation of the individual who might be producing that narrative, that is, the narrator (cf. Dixon & Bortolussi, 2001b). Some hypotheses concerning the content of this representation are taken up in Chapter 3.

We believe that a distinction between features and constructions is essential to bring the right tools to bear on different aspects of the problem of understanding narrative processing. A reasonable model of how this can work can be found in the field of psycholinguistics. Psycholinguistics involves the use of empirical methods from cognitive psychology to investigate how features of language are processed by language comprehenders. In many cases, formal linguistics provides the conceptual distinctions and interesting variables for this investigation, while cognitive psychology contributes the empirical methods and interpretive tools. As a small example, consider that formal linguistic analyses indicate that the structure of sentences with reduced sentential complements are momentarily ambiguous as they are being read. Following this kind of analysis, psycholinguists have used experimental techniques such as the measurement of the duration of eye fixations to understand how readers process that ambiguity (e.g., Frazier & Rayner, 1982). By analogy, we use the term "psychonarratology" to refer to the interdisciplinary investigation of narratorial processing. In our view, psychonarratology should consist of the empirical investigation of how the distinctions and variables identified by narratologists are processed and how they affect readers.

The Nature of Textual Features

At the heart of the successful development of psychonarratology is the identification of textual features. Here we present some criteria for what a valuable textual feature should be. We suggest that features should be objective, precise, stable, relevant, and tractable. A discussion of each of these criteria follows.

First, a textual feature must be *objective*. Objective means that the definition of the feature is public, clear, and understandable. It is not useful, for example, to describe a text as having "a sense of intimacy" because it is unlikely to be clear to many what that means exactly, and there would probably be little agreement as to which of a collection of texts have a sense of intimacy and which do not. In contrast, the presence of a first-person narrator is a much more objective feature; it is likely that most researchers would be able to agree on which of a set of texts were written in the first-person mode. Objectivity may be thought of as a continuum, and the definitions of features may evolve and become more objective. For example, one may start with a subjective insight that a text is "intimate"; subsequently, one may define an intimate text in terms of other properties of the text, such as first-person narration, the presence of substantial amounts of self-reflection, and personal judgments of other characters. As each of the elements of this definition is made more and more explicit and detailed, the definition of what it means to be an "intimate" text becomes more objective. One way of thinking about objectivity is to conceive of a test procedure that can be carried out in a more-or-less mechanical manner that would distinguish the presence of the feature from its absence. If there is such a procedure, and if it can be communicated to other knowledgeable individuals, then the feature is objective. Difficulty in conceiving of such a test suggests that the feature may not be sufficiently objective or explicit. As a proposed feature becomes more objective, the nature and content of the corresponding test becomes more clear and detailed.

Related to the notion of objectivity is that of *precision*. With a perfectly precise definition of a textual feature, it would always be clear when a text has a feature and when it does not. Imprecise features admit of a substantial number of ambiguous cases in which it is unclear whether the feature is present. Although related, precision can be distinguished from objectivity. For example, the feature of having a substantial amount of quoted speech is perfectly objective: The testing procedure might consist of simply counting the percentage of words that appear in quotes. However, the definition, as it stands, is imprecise because it is not clear how large a percentage is needed to count as "substantial." It might serve, for example, to distinguish a text in which 80 percent of the words are quoted from one in which there is no direct speech at all, but what about a text that has 60 percent quoted speech? Or 30 percent? A lack of precision is usually not a serious problem as long as the definition can, in principle, be extended or elaborated to handle those cases that lie in the gray area. One might, for example, say that greater than 75 percent quoted speech is "predominant," greater than 40 percent is "substantial," greater than 20 percent is "significant," and less than that is "minor." In this way, the definition of the feature becomes more articulated and precise as the need for such precision arises.

A third criterion for a textual feature is that it be *stable*. By stability we mean that it is an enduring property of the text and does not vary with the reader or the reading situation. For example, "evokes a feeling of sadness" is not a stable feature because it might easily be the case that some readers do not experience this emotion while other do. It would be better instead to describe the text as having a depressing topic, or describing sorrowful moods in characters, or one in which the narrator is depicted as depressed, as the case may be. Indeed, "evokes a feeling of sadness" is a description of a construction on the part of the reader, and, as we argued previously, it is crucial to distinguish reader constructions from textual features. However, as a stepping stone to more objective and stable definitions of features, we believe that it would not be remiss to include a certain amount of potentially ill-defined interpretation as part of the definition of a feature. For example, one might begin by describing the narrator's voice as having a dejected tone, even though one has only limited insight into the textual details that conspire to produce that tone. Eventually, one would hope that such a description would develop sufficiently so that such global interpretation would not be necessary in the definition. It may be defensible in the interim, though, as long as informed readers can generally agree on that interpretation. In this sense, the definition could be relatively stable over different readers, even though it may not be completely objective.

A fourth criterion for a useful textual feature is that it be *relevant*. There are a plethora of possible features that one might define for texts that are perfectly objective, precise, and stable. One could count the number of words that have *e*'s in them, or measure the average number of words between occurrences of compound sentences, for example. However, features such as these would not be useful in developing a theory of psychonarratology because they are unlikely to have any impact on readers' processes. It is, of course, ultimately an empirical question as to whether a particular feature is relevant. For example, whether or not a text has a substantial amount of quoted speech might affect how readers process a text, but it might not. In general, one cannot know whether a feature is relevant until suitable evidence has been gathered. Our goal in stating relevance as a criterion is to indicate that, in describing texts, one should begin by seeking features that are important for readers, and our sense is that a little introspection and common sense can go a long in way in delimiting the initial search for relevant features. In contrast, logical coherence, elegance, or parsimony are of little value in a system of features if those features have little impact on most readers.

Finally, a textual feature should be tractable. Our goal is to investigate how textual features are related to reader constructions, and that inevitably involves the conduct of research in which features are measured or manipulated. Tractability of the features means that research can be carried out in a manner that is efficient and cost-effective. For example, one might categorize a novel's plot as typical or atypical by surveying a large sample of popular fiction, rating the similarity between the novel and each of the popular works, weighting that rating by the number of copies sold, and then calculating the average. Although such a measure might easily have an impact on the reader (mediated, we expect, by reader expectations), it would be expensive in terms of time and money to construct, and we would regard it as not very tractable. Although it is occasionally important in science to go to great lengths to measure aspects of the world that are otherwise unknown, our view is that such circumstances are unlikely to arise in the immediate development of psychonarratology. In this instance, plots might be classified as typical or atypical purely on the basis of the intuition of the researcher. Although such a measure is not completely objective, suffers from a certain degree of imprecision, and may not be entirely stable, it is simple and inexpensive, and probably a good place to start. More precise and stable measures can be developed as needed.

In many cases, definitions of textual features may be imperfect and may contain a variety of deficiencies with respect to these criteria. This is not, in itself, a fatal flaw. The essential aspect of this enterprise is simply that investigators agree on the criteria. Then, as deficiencies become clear, new and better definitions can be developed as the need arises. One need not have a perfect, pristine set of carpentry tools to build a house; one simply starts to work with the tools at hand and then obtains new ones if the old tools prove inadequate.

Measuring Reader Constructions

A second component of our methodological framework is the measurement of reader constructions. There is a wide range of techniques for measuring such constructions; the approaches we have used in our research represent only a tiny fragment. It is sometimes suggested that the empirical investigation of literary processing requires the development of new, sophisticated measurement methodologies that are specially suited to the domain (Schmidt, 1981). Sophisticated tracking of eye movements during reading or the detailed analysis of verbal protocols might be suggested, for example. Although the intelligent use of such methods can be very insightful, they can also be extraordinarily expensive and time-consuming. Further, we disagree that such methods are always necessary. Instead, we believe that the most mundane methods imaginable (such as simply asking readers direct questions concerning the text) are often sufficient when they are combined with a careful delineation of features and constructions and when the investigation is conducted with due regard for the need to make strong inferences concerning their relationship. Nevertheless, there are likely to be many circumstances in which one may wish to consider other ways of assessing reader constructions, and here we mention what we believe are some important criteria for such measurements. In particular, we argue that the measurement of reader constructions should be direct, replicable, and concise.

A measurement is direct when what is actually recorded corresponds closely to the construction of interest. Any empirical investigation of mental processes involves a significant degree of what can be termed "operationalization." For example, one may wish to measure the extent to which a reader sees the narrator as similar to him or herself. One cannot see inside the reader's mind to make this measurement, and the researcher must instead be satisfied with a somewhat more indirect approach, such as asking readers to rate their similarity to the narrator. In this instance, readers' rating response is an operationalization of the construction of interest, readers' perceived similarity; one would say that perceived similarity has been operationalized as a rating response. With a little care, the two measurements are likely to be closely related so that the operationalized measure provides a good index of the reader construction. However, even in this simple example, they need not be precisely the same; some readers may be motivated for some reason to lie in their questionnaire response, or they may misinterpret the questions in some way. Having a measurement with minimal operationalization means that the link between the reader constructions and what is actually measured is relatively short and direct and that the likelihood of such extraneous effects is small. In the vocabulary of measurement theory, a minimal operationalization has "face validity."

Replicability refers to the ability of other researchers to conduct a similar investigation and measure the same reader construction. For example, if readers fill out a questionnaire under controlled circumstances, those measurements are usually quite replicable because another researcher need only know the precise wording of the questions to conduct virtually the same investigation. In contrast, if a researcher simply reports that readers failed to appreciate the import of a given work, such a measurement is likely to be difficult to replicate, even if the report is correct. The problem in this case is that it is difficult to ascertain what precisely might be meant by "failed to appreciate" and that the import of a work is potentially open to interpretation; as a consequence, other researchers might easily not find that reported result. In general, replicability is greater when the measurement instrument is described objectively and when all the relevant details of the measurement procedure are explicit.

Conciseness in a measurement instrument means that the results of the measurement can be communicated in an efficient manner. Unabridged verbal protocols, for example, might easily reflect reader constructions in a manner that is direct and replicable. However, they do not provide, by themselves, a particularly useful measurement instrument because they cannot be easily communicated. To be useful, protocols typically need to be summarized and scored in some manner. Only then would they be appropriately concise and useful as an index of reader constructions. However, the method of scoring and summarization must properly be thought of as part of the measurement. As such, they must be suitably direct (i.e., the summarization itself should reflect reader constructions) and replicable (i.e., other researchers should be able to summarize the same protocols and get similar summaries). In contrast, numerical measurements almost always provide concise measurements because the methods for summarizing and describing a body of numerical measurements are well established, and under most circumstances one may reasonably assume that standard descriptive statistics provide a direct and replicable description of the original data set.

The Statistical Reader

One of the greatest challenges for empirical approaches to literary reception is the need to reconcile two seemingly contradictory assumptions concerning the nature of the reader. On one hand, there is the recognition that the response to and interpretation of a literary work is not homogeneous within any group of readers, and that, instead, there is a range of responses and reactions that must be explained. On the other hand, there is the assumption that literary processing is not entirely idiosyncratic, and that the processes used by readers are amenable to scientific investigation and description. We have developed an explicit formulation of this problem in our notion of the "statistical reader" (Dixon et al., 1993). This development derives largely from some basic tenets of probability and statistics; hence the term "statistical." It may be apparent that the view we are proposing here is not new, but rather a restatement of many of the implicit assumptions involved in standard data analysis procedures. However, there are crucial advantages in making these notions explicit for the development of the present methodological framework.

Central to this issue is the question of how variability in reader constructions is interpreted. We do not believe that such variability should be interpreted as random noise or error; each reader's constructions must be viewed as valid and appropriate given that reader's knowledge, background, goals, and personality. At the same time, we do not believe that the study of reading processes should be limited to simply describing specific and idiosyncratic interpretations of a text, as some radical reader-response critics have done (e.g., Holland, 1975, 1980). Instead, we view the task of a science of psychonarratology as the description of the properties of the processing that are common to groups of readers in aggregate. Moreover, we posit that scientific claims about literary processing and interpretation cannot be made in the abstract, but only with respect to some explicitly defined population of readers. However, reader populations are unlikely to be uniform and monolithic with respect to interesting aspects of narrative processing. Instead, we view any given reader population as consisting of a complex collection of overlapping and nested groups, each with potentially distinct reading processes. In this respect, we believe that the concept of the statistical reader is an advance over the vague, informal, a-historical, and essentialist notions of the reader that have often prevailed in literary studies.

The notion of the statistical reader is thus based on two powerful concepts: population and measurement distributions. We first present a relatively formal description of these concepts in their simplest form. We then describe how these notions form the basis for a description of variables and relationships.

Population

A population is a collection of individuals about which interesting claims might be made. For example, a population might be all undergraduate students in the United States and Canada; another might be skilled readers of English; still another might be literary critics who have published papers on Borges. We propose that any scientific claim about reading, processing, and interpretation must be prefaced with a description of the population to which the claim applies. In other words, scientific claims cannot be justified in the abstract, but only with respect to a particular domain of reference. However, there is no restriction on size, scope, or criteria for defining a population, and there may be any number of populations about which interesting claims might be made. In particular, literary processing in one population might proceed in one way, and in an interestingly different way in another. Moreover, the multitude of interesting populations may be related in complex ways: They may be nested, so that one population is a subset of another; they may be disjoint, so that no individuals in one population are in another; or they may overlap, so that some individuals in one population are also contained in another. Sorting out the facts that apply to these various populations is a difficult but empirically tractable problem. However, its solution requires that the populations be specified at the outset.

Measurement Distributions

A measurement is anything that one can assess or evaluate about an individual, his or her behavior, or his or her situation. Measurements are objective in the sense that it is possible to explicitly describe the procedure by which the measurement was collected; this procedure is the measurement instrument. Although measurements are often quantitative, they need not be. Measurements might be disjoint categories (e.g., good reader or bad reader), lists (e.g., the books read this year), or even open-ended verbalizations. The set of measurements that might, in principle, be collected from an entire population is referred to as a measurement distribution. The notion of a measurement distribution is crucial because it admits the possibility that populations are heterogeneous with respect to any given measurement. In particular, we assume that measurements inevitably vary and are generally different for different individuals or on different occasions. However, despite this variability, a measurement distribution can be described. Two classes of descriptions are common: Descriptions of *central tendency* (e.g., the mean or average) indicate what measurements are likely to be found in the population; descriptions of *variability* (e.g., the standard deviation) index the range of possible measurements. Although measurements are generally collected from some small sample of individuals, those measurements may provide a substantial amount of information about the measurement distribution for the population. In fact, well-established procedures are available for generating precise mathematical descriptions of the distribution from relatively small samples selected from that distribution. For example, if measurements are randomly selected from the measurement distribution, the mean of the sample provides an estimate of the mean of the distribution, and the precision of that estimate increases in a lawful manner with the size of the sample. Similarly, the variability of the distribution (described, for example, by the standard deviation) can be estimated by the standard deviation of the sample. That is, one may infer, with some degree of confidence, properties of the measurement distribution from a restricted sample of measurements. Thus, an empirical approach, in which measurements are assumed to be sampled from a measurement distribution, provides a mechanism for describing not only how individuals and their reactions tend to be the same but also how they differ. Both are required for a clear understanding of readers' constructions.

Measurements are also made of texts. For example, one might identify whether a text has a particular feature or how much of a feature a text has. However, because texts are not (usually) sampled from some population, there are typically no corresponding notions of central tendency or variability. (It is worth noting, however, that this view is not universally held. For example, following Clark (1973), it is common in psychology to treat words, sentences, and other verbal materials statistically as if they were randomly sampled from a population of comparable materials. See Wike and Church (1976) and Clark et al. (1976) (for some of the debate on this practice). Texts do vary, though, from one to another, and this is a critical ingredient in the identification of relationships between textual features and reader constructions.

Variables and Relationships

Describing distributions and their characteristics is the first step in identifying variables and relationships. For our purposes, we define a variable as a set of measurements that can be indexed in a systematic manner. For example, suppose we are interested in whether readers believe the narrator of a story is male or female. The measurement instrument in this case might be a rating response in which readers select a number on a scale with, for example, 1 corresponding to "certain to be male" and 7 corresponding to "certain to be female." The population might be University of Alberta undergraduates. The measurement distribution would correspond to all the ratings that might be produced by the individuals in that population. In this situation, a variable would be generated by collecting several sets of related measurements. For example, ratings might be collected by having readers report their perception of the narrator in several different works; the index in this case would be those works. For each value of the index (i.e., for each different work), there would be a corresponding measurement distribution.

Variables can be classified in terms of the nature of the measurements. In the previous example, the measurements are of reader constructions; consequently, the generated variable can be referred to as a *construction* variable. When the measurements are of texts or textual features, we may refer to a *text* variable. For instance, one might classify different works on the basis of whether the main character is male or female. As mentioned earlier, text measurements typically do not involve sampling from a distribution. Nevertheless, such measurements can be indexed and can be used to generate variables. Thus, having a male or female main character can be a variable, indexed by different works. An important third class of variables pertains to different types of reader populations and can be referred to as *reader* variables. For example, one population of readers might be undergraduates at the University of Alberta; another might be graduate students in literary studies at the University of Alberta; still another might be literature instructors at the University of Alberta. The measurement distributions in this case are indexed by the type of reader (corresponding roughly to level of expertise). Although reader variables are, in principle, central to the study of psychonarratology, we will have relatively little to say about them in the present work.

Inferences in empirical investigations are possible only when variables are related to one another. A relationship in this sense means that there is concomitant variation between two variables that are indexed in the same way; in other words, the variables covary. For example, it might be the case that works that have a female protagonist are more likely to be viewed as having a female narrator than those that have a male protagonist. In this instance, having a female or male protagonist is a text variable indexed over works; viewing the narrator as female or male is a construction variable also indexed over works. The variables are related because, as one goes from one work to another, the measurements tend to change together: male protagonist and the perception of a male narrator in one case, female protagonist and the perception of a female narrator in the next, and so on. In the research that is presented here, most of the relationships will be of exactly this type: Textual variables, indexed over different texts, will be related to construction variables, also indexed over texts. However, other relationships are important as well, such as those between construction variables and reader variables.

It is important to distinguish *meaningful* relationships from trivial ones. A meaningful relationship is one that bears on interesting theoretical considerations. Typically, this means that the covariation is of a magnitude that is sufficient to distinguish one theoretical view from another. One could identify a great many possible relationships in the processing of narrative that, although real, are of little importance in developing a theory of psychonarratology. For example, it could be the case that novels that begin with a question lead to somewhat more active processing on average than those that begin with a declarative sentence; perhaps further, this small difference in processing has a miniscule persisting effect over the course of the book, so that readers end up with a very slightly more elaborate representation of the story world by the novel's end. If this chain of reasoning is correct, it implies that there should be some (very small) covariation between the form of the initial sentence and number of details in readers' representation of the story world. Such covariation would be exceedingly difficult to detect with an empirical study. Moreover, even if it were detectable, the magnitude of the effect is likely to be so miniscule that there would little point in developing one's theoretical analysis of narrative processing in order to incorporate such influences. In other words, the potential relationship is trivial. Although this example is clear, the magnitude of the covariation required to make the relationship meaningful in most situations is a matter of debate. However, our point is that the mere existence of some degree of covariation is not necessarily interesting or relevant to the development of a theory; a relationship must be meaningful as well. To be meaningful, covariation must always achieve some minimal magnitude, and anything smaller than that is simply not of concern.

Theory and Explanation

As described in Chapter 1, our goal here is to develop a framework for the theoretical and empirical investigation of the psychological processing of narrative. Although we do not have a complete theory of this domain as yet, we have some sense of what such a theory would entail. In particular, we believe that a theory consists in large part of a set of causal explanations. A causal explanation indicates that variables are related because one causes another. For example, one might observe that a narrator tends to be interpreted as sympathetic to a character when that character's thoughts are commonly presented in the narrative. A causal explanation of this observation is that the textual characteristics cause that reaction in readers. It is critical in developing such theories to distinguish the *observation* (i.e., that readers' reactions tend to co-occur with particular aspects of the narrative technique) from its *explanation* (i.e., that readers' interpretations are caused by the use of that technique). An observation is subject to validation and replication but cannot be refuted by argument or opinion; an explanation, on the other hand, must always be considered a hypothesis subject to further support or testing and can never be proved beyond doubt.

Clearly, causal explanations in psychonarratology would not allow a simple, unequivocal determination of what a reader's reaction is likely to be. Instead, they must be understood as describing tendencies or proclivities that operate in conjunction with a network of other influences. For example, although presenting a character's thoughts in the narrative might lead the reader to see the narrator as more sympathetic to the character, it is not the only variable that might produce that reaction, and these other influences might produce the reaction even in the absence of the character's thoughts in the narrative. Similarly, there may be other factors that lead the reader to perceive the narrator as relatively unsympathetic, and these other influences may prevail even when the character's thoughts are present. An appropriate way to view this situation is to conceive of two otherwise identical situations, one in which the textual feature is present and one in which the feature is absent; if the causal explanation is correct, readers should see the narrator as relatively more sympathetic in the former. In other words, the hypothesized causal explanation is that, all other things being equal, putting the character's thoughts in the narrative should lead to a stronger perception of a sympathetic narrator.

Any given observation typically admits of a variety of causal explanations. For example, it may not be the presence of the character's thoughts per se that leads the narrator to be seen as sympathetic, but rather the fact that the character's thoughts provide a sensible and coherent explanation of the character's behavior. Alternatively, it may be the case that whenever the author intends to present a sympathetic narrator, a variety of techniques are used, including the presentation of the character's thoughts, but only a few of these are causally related to the reader's interpretation. More complex causal explanations must also be considered. For example, the relationship between the narrative technique and the reader's reaction may only obtain if readers are predisposed to reflect on the attitude of the narrator or if other aspects of the narrative make the attitude of the narrator salient. Identifying and distinguishing at least a few of these possibilities is the substance of the theory we present in this book.

In our approach, as in any line of empirical investigation, progress at developing causal explanations is of necessity piecemeal. Possible explanations may vary with the situation and characteristics and goals of the reader, and a complete causal explanation of a given reader construction is likely to entail a myriad of interactions among a wide range of textual features. Because of this potential complexity, it is impossible to test or even describe a causal explanation of any depth given our current state of knowledge and evidence. However, we believe that such detailed causal explanations are possible in principle; they merely require a great deal of empirical and theoretical work. Given this perspective, it would be ingenuous of us to suggest that the present approach and set of hypotheses are unassailably accurate. Instead, they merely scratch the surface of the empirical work that is needed on this problem. We believe that progress is made by proposing specific, testable causal explanations and then revising and elaborating those explanations as needed. The crucial ingredient in such progress is compelling empirical evidence.

The Textual Experiment

As described earlier, causal explanations are central to a framework for psychonarratology. We anticipate that the most important causal explanations are likely to be those that explain particular reader constructions as caused by particular features of the text. For example, we might hypothesize that the use of free-indirect speech causes a reader to have a sympathetic attitude toward a character; that the narrative description of multiple hazardous outcomes creates suspense in the reader's mind; and so on. We argue that the best technique for assessing such causation is to conduct *textual experiments*, in which particular features of a text are identified and manipulated by the researcher (Dixon & Bortolussi, 1999c). In a properly designed textual experiment, several versions of a text are created that are identical except for the single, manipulated feature. Experiments of this sort have a special relationship to causal explanations and, as a consequence, should be used whenever possible to evaluate hypotheses concerning the connection between features and constructions.

Covariation and Causation

The logical basis for this claim is illustrated in Figure 2.1. Generally, causes are identified by covariation between two variables, denoted as I and D. Covariation occurs whenever the particular values of one variable tend to co-occur with particular values of the other variable. For example, suppose that I is the presence of a character's thoughts

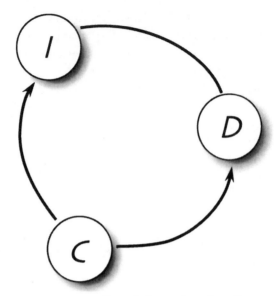

FIGURE 2.1. Covariation and confounding.

in a narrative and D is the reader's view of the narrator's sympathy toward a character. Covariation between I and D would occur if narratorial sympathy occurs more often with texts that include the character's thoughts than with texts that do not. Covariation of this sort is indicated in Figure 2.1 by the arc between the I and D circles.

Whenever two variables covary, there are three possible causal explanations: The first variable can cause the second, the second variable can cause the first, or some other, third, variable may cause both of these. When I refers to features of the text and D refers to a reader construction, we are usually interested in the hypothesis that I causes D. The possibility that D causes I can safely be ruled out on logical grounds: The text precedes the reader's exposure to it and cannot be affected by the reading process and the reader's constructions. However, the possibility that I and D might both be caused by a third variable is very real and compromises any possible interpretation of I as the cause of D. In the vocabulary of experimentation, the third variable is known as a confounding variable. A possible confounding variable C is shown in Figure 2.1, with arrowheads to indicate that it could be the cause of both I and D.

Author Confounds and Other Artifacts

In the course of drawing inferences from observed covariation, an unexpected confound may produce a relationship as an artifact; that is, the relationship may emerge simply because both variables of interest covary with a confounding variable. Although artifactual relationships can occur in any empirical investigation, they are common when variables are indexed over texts. For example, one may find that in a selection of texts, novels with a male protagonist are rated as more literary than novels with a female protagonist, and, because of this relationship, one might consider the explanation that the gender of the protagonist caused the difference in the literariness ratings. However, on further examination, it might turn out that the sample of texts included a large group of popular romance novels (in which the protagonist is typically female) and a large group of eighteenth-century literary works (in which the protagonist is more likely to be male). As a consequence, the relationship between gender and ratings could easily be an artifact of the manner in which the texts were selected. For example, the relationship is confounded with the genre of the work or its period, either of which could have a causal effect on the literariness ratings. Because of these confounds, then, the inference that gender of the protagonist has a causal effect on ratings is suspect.

Figure 2.2 illustrates why confounding is a central problem in the analysis of the effects of literary discourse. Generally, we imagine that texts are constructed by authors who have some intention concerning the aggregate effects of the narrative; such intentions may lead them to construct the text in a particular way with a particular constellation of features and characteristics. This is indicated by the variable A in Figure 2.2. For example, an author may want to portray a narrator who is sympathetic to a character. If the author believes that this might be done by providing the character's thoughts in the narrative, the feature might be included in the narrative. However, the author likely would also provide other features. For example, the character may express actions or thoughts that are likely to generate sympathy on the part of the reader, the narrator might express sympathetic attitudes toward the character explicitly, and so on. These other textual features are indicated by the variable C in Figure 2.2

Preliminaries

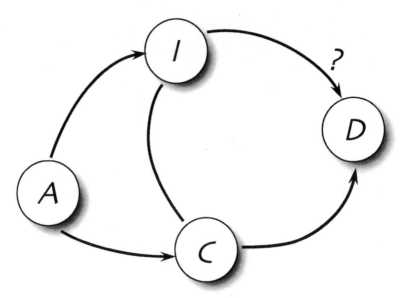

FIGURE 2.2. Author confounds.

and represent a possible confound in the relationship between the feature of character thoughts (I) and the reader's interpretation of the narrator (D). In naturally occurring narrative, the aggregate of techniques that follow from the author's intention may be the ultimate cause of both variables. Because the reader's constructions might be caused purely by these other textual features rather the feature under consideration, the covariation between I and D does not necessarily imply causation. We refer to this situation as the problem of "author confounds."

The solution to this inferential dilemma is to manipulate the text experimentally, that is, to conduct a textual experiment. For example, we, as the researchers, might construct a modified version of the author's text in which all the character's thoughts have been removed. If the reader's construction is determined purely by variables other than the character's thoughts, such a manipulation should have no effect; on the other hand, if the character's thoughts in the narrative has a causal role, one should observe some change in the reader's reactions. This situation is illustrated in Figure 2.3. In this case, only the presence or absence of character thoughts (I) varies across the texts used in the study; all other characteristics of the text

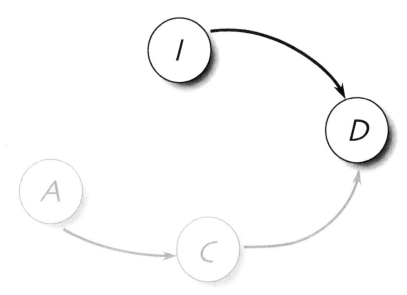

FIGURE 2.3. Unambiguous causal inference in a textual experiment.

(as well as the author's original intentions) remain the same. In textual experiments, *I* is referred to as the independent variable in the experiment and *D* is referred to as the dependent variable. In our example, any covariation between the features of the narrative and the reader's constructions can be attributed unambiguously to a causal connection between that manipulated feature and the corresponding reader construction. Such an unambiguous causal inference is an overwhelming advantage in constructing theoretical accounts of readers' processing, and it accrues uniquely to textual experiments.

Designing Textual Experiments

The logical power of textual manipulations is clear in principle. However, the technique requires that one be able to manipulate one variable without inadvertently changing other, potentially confounding variables. In turn, this requires a sophisticated theory of the text and its features and structure. Thus, the success of empirical research in psychonarratology builds on the availability of detailed and elaborate theoretical analyses such as those found in narratology. Analyses of this sort allow one to manipulate particular features of the text confidently without introducing confounds.

Even with a sophisticated theoretical description of textual features, however, confounds might be introduced inadvertently. For example, suppose one were conducting an experiment on the effects of mental access, that is, the provision of information about a character's internal thoughts and reactions. The following text fragment would provide mental access:

The child thought his parents couldn't hear him crying.   (1)

In a textual experiment, this fragment might be changed so that it does not provide mental access, and the following replacement might be used:

The child's parents couldn't hear him crying.   (2)

This particular manipulation is potentially confounded: Although both text fragments describe the same situation, the first seems to suggest the possibility that the parents could in fact hear the child, despite his impression, while the second does not. In other words, the manipulation of mental access is potentially confounded with the information conveyed about the situation. Typically, such artifacts arise because of an incomplete analysis that fails to consider important variables. (Indeed, based on our analysis of represented speech and thought described in Chapter 7, we would argue that, in this particular example, the manipulation is confounded with conversational properties of the narrative.) Although undesirable, this potential confound is not a fatal flaw in the method of textual experiments, and two aspects of the methodology allow one to recover from such problems.

First, under many circumstances, an incomplete analysis that fails to identify a confound may simply lead to a weak manipulation that produces few changes in reader constructions. For example, suppose one were interested in evaluating whether mental access alters the reader's interpretation of the narrator's attitude toward the character; in particular, the hypothesis might be that eliminating mental access would lead the reader to see the narrator as less sympathetic to the character. According to this hypothesis, the narrator should be seen as less sympathetic with fragment (2) than with (1). The slightly different information provided in these two excerpts may not compromise this hypothesis because, if anything, the situational information conveyed by (2) makes the narrator seem arguably more sympathetic to the character, not less. Thus, if results of the study confirm the hypothesis, it would be difficult to attribute those results to the confounding variable. Another way of saying this is that, although the manipulation is confounded, the expected effect of the confound is contrary to the hypothesis of interest and, as a consequence, cannot be used as an alternative explanation. If the analysis of the confound is correct (i.e., the information conveyed by (2) leads the narrator to be seen as more sympathetic), the causal inference based on the expected result remains sound.

Second, the presence of confounding variables can be readily evaluated by further experimentation. For example, if one were concerned about the possibility that the difference in the information conveyed by (1) and (2) has an effect on the dependent variable, one could simply test whether that information, by itself, has an effect. In this case, one might compare the results obtained with (1) to those obtained with the following fragment in which the new information is conveyed explicitly:

The child thought his parents couldn't hear him crying, and he was right. (3)

The data obtained from this further textual experiment would either confirm or disconfirm the causal effect of the new manipulation and would indicate clearly whether the data from the original experiment was confounded or not. A series of control experiments of this general sort can eventually lend great confidence to a particular causal inference. In general, the possibility of potential confounds is not an inherent defect in the method of textual experiments; rather, potential confounds are empirical questions that need to be addressed by (further) careful experimental investigations.

Identifying Meaningful Relationships

After the data from an empirical investigation have been collected, one needs to decide whether a meaningful relationship exists. For example, in a textual experiment, one would need to decide whether there was a relationship between the manipulation of the text (the independent variable) and readers' constructions (the dependent variable). In this case, it is common to say that each different version of the text defines a treatment condition, and the task of identifying relationships amounts to asking whether a dependent variable varies with condition. There is a long history of debate in statistics on the appropriate way in which to solve this problem. The approach that is commonly used in psychology and many other disciplines is sometimes referred to as "null hypothesis significance testing" and derives in part from ideas proposed by Fisher (1925) and Neyman and Pearson (1928). Although this approach is widely used and taught, it suffers from a variety of well-known flaws and logical inconsistencies, not the least of which is that it fails to distinguish between meaningful relationships and trivial ones. Without going into any details, we find the arguments against null hypothesis significance testing compelling and will not report such tests here. Instead, we use an alternative method described by Dixon and O'Reilly (1999) and modeled on the approach suggested by Edwards (1992), Fisher (1955), and Goodman and Royall (1988).

The approach to identifying meaningful relationships adopted here involves reporting the evidence for different competing interpretations of the results. Typically, one wishes to compare the interpretation that the independent variable (the textual manipulation) is related to the dependent variable (the reader measurement) to an alternative interpretation that the variables are unrelated. Each of the two interpretations may match the obtained results more or less well. For example, given the interpretation that there is no relationship, any obtained difference between the conditions would be error and would count against the interpretation that the conditions are actually the same. Alternatively, given the interpretation that there is a meaningful relationship of a specified size, an obtained difference that is smaller would count against that interpretation. The evidence for one interpretation relative to the other can be succinctly captured by calculating a likelihood ratio. The likelihood ratio indicates how likely the data are given one interpretation divided by how likely the data are given the other. Large values provide support for the first interpretation, while small values less than 1 provide support for the second. As a rule of thumb, a likelihood ratio of 10 or greater (or 0.1 or smaller) constitutes clear evidence for one interpretation over the other. (For readers familiar with null hypothesis significance testing, "clear evidence" generally implies rejecting the null hypothesis with $p < .05$; Dixon, 1998). Likelihood ratios of this sort are readily calculated by recombining the elements of more traditional statistical calculations; a summary of some of these methods is presented in the Appendix. Because likelihood ratios provide a convenient and intuitive summary of the strength of the evidence for a relationship obtained in an experiment, they are used here to document the effects we discuss.

Summary

In the present chapter, we provided some foundational concepts and methods for an empirical investigation of psychonarratology. We began with the distinction between textual features and reader constructions: Features are objectively described properties of texts, while constructions are variable mental representations generated by individual readers. The statistical reader provides a basis for assessing reader constructions empirically. Populations of readers must be explicitly identified and sampled, and the characteristics of the measurement distribution must be calculated on the basis of the sample. We argue that sound causal inferences concerning the relationship between features and constructions can only be obtained by making use of the textual experiment in which features of the text are systematically manipulated and concomitant variations in reader constructions are measured; to do otherwise admits author confounds and other artifacts. Finally, we discussed some data analytic procedures: We avoid here the common procedure of null hypothesis testing and replace it with likelihood ratio calculations.

3

The Narrator

In literary studies, it is commonly assumed that the presence of a narrator is one of the features distinguishing fiction from nonfiction (Makaryk, 1993). In natural narratives and nonfictional discourse, the argument goes, the speaker of the utterance speaks directly in his or her own voice, whereas in fictional narratives the utterance is delivered by the mediating voice of a narrator, an entity distinct from the historical author. Although the nature of this distinction and the relationship between author and narrator are matters of debate, virtually all agree on the distinction's importance. Indeed, it is conceivable that even in natural narratives and nonfictional discourse, storytellers or conversational participants may "project" themselves into a speaking function distinct from themselves. But certainly in the case of fictional narratives, the story and all the details pertaining to the story world – characters, events, situations, setting, and so on – are mediated by the voice of a narrator. Inevitably, this mediation affects the reader's responses to the fictional world. The most immediate implication of this fact of narrative is that readers must create a representation of the narrator, that is, a representation of the person who seems to utter the words of the text. Further, in our approach, the reader may represent the narrator as if the reader and the narrator were participating in a communicative situation. The presence, in the mind of the reader, of this communicative situation colors virtually all aspects of the text and its interpretation.

Readers' representations of the narrator are likely to vary with the perceived relationships among authors, their narrators, and the fictional world. In some texts, the distinction between the author and the narrator, at least on a superficial level, is more obvious than in others. For example, the narrator of Kamau's *Flickering Shadows* is a ghost; one of the narrators of William Goyen's *The House of Breath* is a river; and the narrator of Ana Castillo's *So Far From God* is a town. Clearly, the reader must distinguish such narrators from the historical author. Yet, even though the distinction at the level of personal attributes is obvious, the overlap in points of view is more ambiguous. In other narratives, such as Milan Kundera's *The Book of Laughter and Forgetting,* in which one of the narrators is Milan Kundera, the similarities in personal attributes are closer, but the degree of distinction at other levels is more ambiguous. Personal familiarity with the author and knowledge of the author's life and works may provide some insight; nevertheless, there is no clear method for determining the precise relationship between the author and narrator, and readers are left to draw whatever inferences they can. In certain reading situations, readers may well associate the two, while in others they may be led to ponder why a given author might create a particular kind of narrator. We will return to this point later in the chapter. However, regardless of the degree of possible overlap between author and narrator, it is the direct voice of a narrator that the reader confronts.

In the next section, we first review some of the analytical schemes for categorizing the narrator, his or her relationship to the story world, and the textual signs for the narrator's presence. Then we turn to an analysis of the levels of communication that have been identified in narrative and the narrator's role in this analysis. In a third section, we outline in detail our conception of a representation of a conversational narrator and then describe some hypotheses concerning the processing of such a narrator. Finally, we discuss the concept of identifying with the narrator and present some relevant empirical evidence.

Previous Analytical Concepts of the Narrator

In this section, we sketch a brief overview of a few of the main issues that have been and remain central to narratological theory pertaining to the narrator. Three main issues emerge from this research: the nature of the narrator, the classification of different kinds of narrators, and the description of textual signs of the narrator.

The Nature of the Narrator

Narratologists have been concerned with questions such as: "What is a narrator?" and "Do all narratives have narrators?" Answers to the first question include the views that the narrator is merely a voice (Bal, 1985), a narrating agent (Rimmon-Kenan, 1983), a narrative position (Toolan, 1995), an aggregate of textual signs (Doležel, 1989; Margolin, 1990b), or a construction based on readers' inferences (Coste, 1989; Fludernik, 1993; Margolin, 1986, 1998). On the second question there is considerable debate. Some, like Chatman (1978), argued that certain narratives have no narrator, that they were "non-narrated." Others argued from a more radical perspective that the concept of the narrator is not a valid concept, and that what some like to think of as a narrator is really only the author or a character (Walsh, 1997a). Rimmon-Kenan and Toolan categorically disputed any rejection of the narrator, arguing that even in texts presented as pure character dialogue, found manuscripts, epistolary correspondence, or diaries, the presence of the narrator, or higher authority responsible for the organization and presentation of the material, is a necessity. Chatman (1990) eventually came to admit this, having understood that

> every narrative is by definition narrated – that is, narratively presented – and that narration, narrative presentation, entails an agent even when the agent bears no signs of human personality. (115)

However, Chatman's correction is only slightly more intuitive than his previous analysis. Arguing that the earlier position was "a misguided effort to restrict 'agency' to human beings" (116) he went on to specify that his current position requires "a presenter, whether human or not" (116). A nonhuman presenter is plausible because, according to Chatman, "in this age of mechanical and electronic production and reproduction, of 'smart' machines, it would be naïve to reject the notion of non-human narrative agency" (116). Whether or not readers can actually conceive of a story presented by a nonhuman agent is another issue. Chatman was thinking of narratives that appeared to be impersonal, for example, narratives in which inner monologue is presented without the intervention of a narrator's voice. He suggests that the origin of presentation in such narratives is an "implied author." Fludernik (1993) took this argument a step further by arguing that readers tend to conceive of the narrative as told (by someone) unless there is strong indication to the contrary. In our view, it is common sense to analyze the words of the narrative as presented by a narrator, and a departure from this view strikes us as nonintuitive.

Types of Narrators

An important criterion for classifying types of narrators is the relationship of the narrator to the story world. This hinges on the classical distinction between mimesis and diegesis. In Prince's (1987) definitions, diegesis refers to the story itself: the story world, its constituents, and the events that unfold. That is, diegesis is "the fictional world in which the situations and events narrated occur" (20). Mimesis refers to the manner in which the story is presented, that is, the discourse. Narrators can be classified in terms of their relationship to the diegesis. A narrator, for example, might be a part of the story and might be presumed to have knowledge of events and circumstances that are comparable to other characters in the story. Alternatively, a narrator might be external to the story world and relate the story from an omniscient stance. Although frequently criticized for its complex terminology, Genette's (1980) extensive typology is still commonly used as a description of the possible relationships. He distinguished among the following kinds of narrators:

- Extradiegetic – narrators who are external to and not part of the story, such as third-person omniscient narrators (e.g., the narrator of Toni Morrison's *Beloved*);
- Heterodiegetic – narrators who are part of the story world but not participants in the story events (e.g., the narrator of Hoffman's "The Sandman," knows the protagonist but plays no part in the narrated events);
- Homodiegetic – narrators who are also characters in the narrative (e.g., Watson in the Sherlock Holmes stories);

- Autodiegetic – narrators who are the protagonists of their own story (e.g., the narrator of Salmon Rushdie's *Midnight's Children*);
- Intradiegetic – narrators who produce a story as characters within the main narrative. (The commonly cited example is Schezerazade in the *Thousand and One Nights*. Others are the "Night of the Emerald Cloak" as well as the shepherd's story, both in Cervantes' *Don Quijote*, and both Frankenstein and his monster in Mary Shelley's *Frankenstein*).

Typically, extradiegetic narrators are impersonal; that is, there is no identifiable individual to whom one can ascribe the views and beliefs of the narrator, whereas other types of narrators can be thought of as personal.

Chatman (1995) was strenuously committed to the concept of diegetic levels and argued that the story/discourse distinction is crucial in descriptions of the narrator. These and other similar classifications stress that external narrators have unlimited knowledge and access to characters' minds, while narrators within the story are restricted in the source and extent of their information and knowledge. Whether or not readers differentiate between these different categories of narrators, or discern and process all cues regarding the narrator's epistemic capabilities, remains an unexplored empirical question. In other words, how functional these categories are for most readers remains to be determined. Some narratologists have expressed concern for such issues. For example, Shaw argued that convictions such as Chatman's seem "designed to excuse the narratologist from worries about whether his categories are likely to enable interesting readings of individual texts" (1995:313) and was in favor of incorporating the activities of real readers within narratological inquiry.

Textual Features for the Narrator

Some narratologists have analyzed the textual signs that are perceived as constituting a narrating agent (Margolin, 1983, 1990b; Toolan, 1995). Some of the textual conditions or features that constitute the narrator include some of the following textual cues:

- Proper names
- Declarations or statements about the narrator's social identification (e.g., class, race, religion, profession, political affiliation)
- Declarations or statements about the narrator's more personal identity (e.g., age, gender, personality, character, motivations, mental condition, attitude, relations to others)
- Declarations or statements about the narrator's behavior (verbal and physical actions)

(Margolin also includes deictics specifying temporal and spatial position in this list. However, as discussed in Chapter 6, our view is that such features have different properties). These declarations can be made by narrators themselves, or can be offered by other characters or narrators. For example, in Cela's *The Family of Pascual Duarte*, the narrator is a convict writing in the first person for the obvious purpose of justifying his crime. His discourse is framed by a series of letters written by other people who knew him, and these have the effect of making the reader ponder the relationship between different points of view about the narrator. In the classic *Thousand and One Nights*, Schezerade is the narrator of her daily stories, but her discourse is framed by another discourse telling us about her.

The presence of textual signs such as these generally signal a *personal* narrator, either in the story world or external to it. Presumably, characteristics, knowledge, and beliefs of the narrator may be inferred from such information. However, in some cases, the narrator is *impersonal*, that is, he or she does not explicitly profess attitudes, knowledge, or beliefs, and there are no textual signs that explicitly refer to the narrator. In such cases, it is still possible to draw inferences concerning the narrator based on indirect signs. In general, such indirect features derive from the logic that the narrator must select information from the story world and decide to present it in a particular manner. Such decisions relate to aspects of the narrative such as the description of settings, the identification and description of characters, and the inclusion of summaries or commentaries (cf. Rimmon-Kenan, 1983; Toolan, 1995). Such information may indirectly suggest attitudes or judgments of the narrator with respect to the characters and events of the story world and, as a consequence, can be used to make inferences concerning the characteristics or beliefs of the narrator.

Although these analyses provide a reasonable depiction of the kind of information in the text that is relevant to understanding and interpreting the narrator, they say little about the actual processes that readers may engage in. What is missing from these narratological analyses are explanations regarding how textual clues interact with reader's goals, experience, expectations, and so on in constructing representations of the narrator.

Narrative and Communication

Levels of Communication

The function of the narrator is sometimes viewed as one of communication, and the nature of that communication has been the subject of detailed analysis. Some of the most important aspects of this analysis are depicted in Figure 3.1 (cf. Bruce, 1981). The fundamental level of communication is presumed to be between the historical author and the actual reader, and the substance of this transaction typically consists of just the text. However, based on the text itself, one might be able to infer characteristics of the author and his or her state of mind and communicative purpose. This hypothetical individual who seems to be implied by the content of the text is the implied author. As Fludernik explained, the implied author "is generally agreed to be a construct of the text's 'meaning' or of the 'intentions' of the (real) author" (1993:446). Conceptually, the implied author needs to be distinguished from the historical author because the characteristics and intentions that seem to be implied by the text need not actually be true of the historical author. More generally, the function of the implied author can be inferred from the information that is selected for presentation in the text and the choice of the manner in which it is told. Corresponding to the implied author is the intended audience that seems to be implied by the text; this is the implied reader.

What is transmitted from the implied author to the implied reader is the narrative. The speaker of the narrative is the narrator. The narrator in turn needs to be distinguished from the implied author because the intentions and goals that seem to be implied by a work

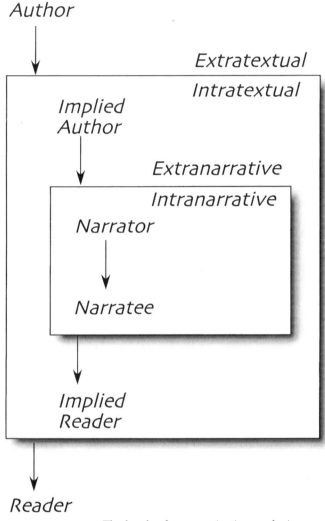

FIGURE 3.1. The levels of communication analysis.

need not be those that are either implicitly or explicitly held by the narrator. The distinction between the implied author and the narrator is particularly salient for first-person fictional narratives. There must also be an explicit or implied audience for the narrator; this is the narratee. Sometimes the narratee is explictly identified in the

narration. Epistolary novels, in which letters are addressed to particular individuals, such as Laclos's *Les Liasons Dangeureuses (Dangerous
Liasons)* or Bram Stoker's *Dracula,* are perhaps the most obvious examples of works with represented narratees. Other examples are
eighteenth-century novels in which narrators directly address their
fictional readers, such as Sterne's *Tristram Shandy.* But more often the
characteristics of the narratee must be gleaned from the language
and depiction of the narrator (Piwowarczyk, 1976). The words of the
narrator form the basis of the communication between the narrator
and the narratee.

Various aspects of this structure have been the subject of debate.
On the assumption that narratives are addressed to someone, and
in an attempt to define this communicative situation, scholars have
developed variations on the structure depicted in Figure 3.1. In some
models, the implied author–implied reader categories are eliminated
(Bal, 1985; Rimmon-Kenan, 1983); others have included all three
categories (O'Neil, 1994:75). Fludernik denied the communicative
purport of the implied author–implied reader level, arguing that
"linguistically speaking, neither communication, telling, utterance
nor any other speech act can be posited for the implied author level"
and that the "so-called 'implied reader' has even less communicative
function" (1993:446). Chatman (1978) regarded the narrator–narratee
relationship as optional, but later argued strongly in favor of an implied author (1990).

While there is considerable discussion about the identity and functions of the author, narrator, implied author, and implied reader, it is
typically the case that the role of the real reader is minimized. For example, Rimmon-Kenan (1983) defended the view that "the empirical
process of communication between author and reader is less relevant
to the poetics of narrative fiction than its counterpart in the text" (89).
Toolan, on the other hand, argued that the author–narrator–real
reader relationship is the only essential one, with the narratee as an
"optional fourth" (Toolan, 1995:77). Nevertheless, his book dedicated
sections to implied authors, narratees, and implied readers, but none
on the real reader. O'Neil limited his discussion of the real reader to
the activity of reconstructing the implied reader. Fludernik's 1993
treatment of the real reader was consistent with other narratologists' views. In concluding that the real reader "needs to suspend

his or her real-life beliefs in order to enter into a co-operative reading experience," (446), she denied the potent effect of the real reader's life experience and the influence of this experience on the reading process. For Fludernik, the real reader must subordinate his or her reality to adopt "a certain stance towards the text, which can be identified with the 'implied reader' construct" (446).

In narratological theory, the issue of the communicative relationship between real reader and narrator is never discussed as such, although scholarship in narratology is strewn with speculative comments about how readers respond to different types of narrators. It is clear that in these comments the reader is never a real or empirically validated reader as much as a hypothesized ideal reader. As mentioned earlier, readers in these narratological studies are always hypothetical constructs extrapolated from the textual features. It is always presupposed that a reader will interpret or respond to a narrator and other instances of the communicative model as a narratologist would, that is, identifying the type of narrator according to the descriptive classification and acknowledging its corresponding logical functions. For example, it is assumed that readers will interpret the discourse of external, omniscient, third-person narrators as the truth, and that they will recognize the authority of other narrators as limited, and thus feel less inclined to take their discourse at face value (O'Neil, 1994). Once again, the actual response of readers to narrators, and the effects of different kinds of narrators on readers, are unexplored, empirical questions. Moreover, as we discuss later, our view is that the conventional description of narrative communication in terms of three distinct levels is not a useful tool for approaching the problem of narrative processing because it disregards the essential communicative transaction between the narrator and the reader. In the following sections, we discuss some of the ensuing difficulties with this "levels" analysis.

The Author–Reader Relation

Consider the claim that extratextual communication is established between real authors and the real audiences or readers they address. Obviously, authors write with the hopes of being read, understood, and appreciated by real readers and have some general sense of their potential readership. However, the relationship between author and reader is very different from the relationship between interlocutors engaged in oral conversation. For this reason, the linguistic communication model is inappropriate for describing the processing of written, fictional narratives. Unlike natural narratives occurring in oral conversations, literary narratives are written in the absence of direct contact between interlocutors. Consequently, the feedback loop and progressive interchange of utterances made possible by the contact of the interlocutors in oral communication are missing. Although one can readily define the interaction between author and reader as a form of communication, much of the theoretical analysis of oral conversation does not apply in any real sense. On balance, stating that real authors communicate with real readers would seem to have little explanatory force.

Gibbs (1999) emphasized the relationship between authors and readers and argued that readers do in fact draw inferences about the historical author's intentions in producing the narrative and are guided by these inferences in their interpretation of the story. We would not dispute the importance of such processes when they occur. However, suggesting that readers can be concerned with the historical author's intention is not the same thing as suggesting that there is a substantive communicative interaction between the author and the reader analogous to what transpires in conversation. Indeed, Gibbs understands that the attempt to "figure out" the author's intentions does not amount to recapturing these intentions in an unambiguous fashion. More generally, in our view, a concern with authorial intention does not entail a communicative relationship like that suggested by Figure 3.1.

The Author–Intended Reader Relation

Clearly, some authors have an image of their intended readers; for example, in some cases they may dedicate a work to a particular individual, such as Lewis Carrol to Alice. However, the author's image of the reader cannot be an exact replica of a reading public. This image is necessarily hypothetical or ideal because all members of a reading public possess their own individual traits, preferences, knowledge, and experience. At most, an author's intended audience may be based on a general understanding of some segment of the real public's social constitution, norms, reading habits, expectations, and so on. So for example, Flaubert wrote for the nineteenth-century middle class of France he knew well; nonetheless, his *Madame Bovary* was rejected by his reading public, and the work was only understood by subsequent audiences. In a sense, Flaubert both did and did not write for the readers of his time. As with Flaubert, an author's imagined reader is more likely to transcend the limitations of his or her time and society, whose norms and values authors frequently set out to defy. Generally, authors may write for intended readers but are read by real readers who may or may not coincide with the author's intended reader, and who may not even reconstruct the implied reader in the same way as the author. In this sense, there cannot be said to be real communication at the extratextual level between an author and a real reader.

The Narrator–Narratee Relation

The idea that narrators address narratees also needs some reexamination. To begin with, the concept of the narratee is often vague and problematic, as some literary scholars have explained (Chatman, 1978). The concept is clear enough when the individual addressed by the narrator is actually a character or reference in the story. For example, in epistolary novels, narrators address specific individuals in their letters; these individuals are fictional recipients existing at the level of the story and on the same ontological level as the narrators. However, when there is no overt narratee and the narrator does not appear to directly address anyone specifically, it may be difficult to discern any difference between the narratee and the implied reader, and it is quite possible that readers would treat the two as the same. According to Prince, the implied reader "is inferable from the entire text," while the narratee "is inscribed in the text" (1987:57). However, identifying this distinction may be problematic even for trained narratologists, as Prince himself recognized. Furthermore, although narrators may address intranarrative narratees, their discourse is read by real readers who may assume the narrative was written for them, thereby confusing themselves as real readers with the narratees and the implied reader. Of course, what real readers actually do is an empirical question and cannot be resolved by theoretical formulation.

Narrator as Reader Construction

In this section, we develop a rather different view of the narrator. Our fundamental departure from the earlier scholarship is to treat the narrator not as logical or abstract characteristic of the text but as a mental representation in the mind of the reader. In other words, the narrator should be viewed as a reader construction. Moreover, we hypothesize that the reader's representation of the narrator is similar in many respects to that which one would construct of a conversational participant. This idea capitalizes on the intuition that communicative processing is central to the processing of narrative without being encumbered by the conceptual difficulties that an assumption of real communication entails. Although the narrator is in the mind of the reader, it is based on identifiable features of the text. We turn first to some of the processes that this proposal implies and then discuss how the approach can be used to reinterpret some of the concepts of the levels-of-communication framework.

Conversational Processes

The assumption that readers represent the narrator as a conversational participant has a number of implications for how narrative is processed. We discuss two of these here. First, readers must attribute to the narrator those properties that are necessary for conversational communication. In particular, the narrator would be assumed to share perceptual ground, language, and culture with the reader. When this is not case, and there is no explicit indication of that in the text, readers will have trouble understanding and remembering material. A clear demonstration of this prediction can be found in a study by Kintsch and Greene (1978). This study was in part a systematic replication of Bartlett's (1932) classic work on remembering. The authors compared two stories – one based on familiar cultural schemas (a Grimm's fairy tale) and one based on unfamiliar cultural schemas (an Alaskan Indian folktale). The recall of the story based on unfamiliar schemas was poor, primarily because of systematic distortions of the material to match the readers' cultural schemas. We believe that the reason readers attempted to apply inappropriate schemas to the Alaskan folktale is that they expected the narrator to share their own cultural schemas.

Second, following Grice's (1975) analysis of conversation, readers must assume that the narrator is cooperating with them and subscribing to conversational conventions. When this does not seem to be the case, readers are invited to make inferences about the narrator's knowledge and beliefs that would render the narrator cooperative. For example, if the text seems to provide extra, unnecessary information, readers may infer that it is in fact necessary and may spend additional time and effort attempting to ascertain how the additional information is relevant or important. On the other hand, if the text provides insufficient information for comprehension, readers will assume that there is a plausible inference that could be made to render the narrative comprehensible, and they are likely to spend time searching for such an inference. In conversation, these kinds of inferences have been termed implicatures by Grice (1975). Analogously, we use the term "narratorial implicatures" to refer to inferences licensed by the assumption that the narrator is cooperative.

In some respects, our proposal is similar to Fludernik's (1993) suggestion that readers assume that a story is being told and construct some representation of the teller who is doing the telling. However, we suggest further that there is a strong analogy between the representations and processes used in conversation and those that are used in understanding narratives. In other words, although there is no real communication in the linguistic, conversational sense, we argue that readers treat narrators *as if* they were conversational participants. This means that readers perceive that the narrator addresses them for some purpose, and they feel naturally motivated to discern this purpose. This position is related to the arguments of Lanser (1981) and others who suggested that narrative texts should be considered as analogous to speech acts and must be interpreted in terms of readers' understanding of the goals and intentions of the author. Although Lanser's view has some merit, it has a number of implications that we are reluctant to embrace. For example, it implies that text should be considered as communication, but, as we have argued earlier, a literary text is demonstrably not communication in the usual sense: The reader and author do not share common perceptual ground, they cannot engage in communicative processes of confirmation and error correction, and the same text can be processed quite differently depending on the context, the knowledge and goals of the reader, and so on. Lanser's solution to these problems was to describe narrative as communication in a special sense that is not really the same as the usage common in communication theory. We prefer to avoid these issues altogether by adopting a crucially different interpretation: Communication and the related assumptions of speech act theory only exist as processing strategies in the mind of the reader. Once again, text is not communication, but it is often treated as if it were by readers. Further, we suspect that this may be a very natural process, and it is possible that people have an almost inevitable tendency to deal with language in this way.

The Narrator and the Author

When the narrator is understood as a representation in the mind of the reader, not as an abstraction related to the text or the hypothetical interaction between the author and the reader, many of the complexities concerning diegetic level, embededness, and the status of the narrator in the text become moot. Indeed, we hypothesize that under many circumstances readers are relatively insensitive to diegetic level and merely respond to the voice of the narrator as if it were directed to them. However, despite the prominence of the narrator in the reader's mind, he or she may also construct a representation of the author. Often, the reader may not clearly distinguish the author from the narrator. Support for this view can be found in the informal observation that students in entry-level university courses on literature typically require substantial instruction to master the concept of the narrator. Under other circumstances, the narrator and the author are logically distinct, as in fictional first-person narration; in this case, we suspect that readers maintain distinct representations of the author and the narrator. However, even here, readers may commonly feel that many of the characteristics or traits of the narrator may also be shared by the author. Thus, it is appropriate to think of the reader's representation of the author and narrator as overlapping. In addition, the reader's representation of the author may be affected by extratextual information concerning the historical author. Depending on the relationship between the reader's representation of the author and the narrator, such information may or may not affect the representation of the narrator. Similarly, inferences about the narrator drawn on the basis of the text may or may not influence the reader's view of the historical author: If the reader maintains independent representations of the narrator and the author, such textual inferences should have little direct effect on the view of the author, while such inferences could easily apply to the reader's view of the author if the two representations are seen as overlapping.

These relationships and the possible organization of the reader's representation of the source of the text are depicted in Figure 3.2. The text is viewed as being the words of the narrator, who is directing those words to the reader. The reader may also maintain a distinct

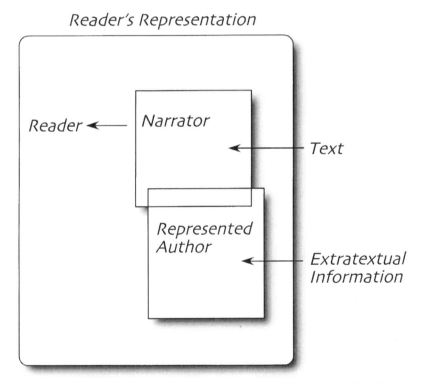

FIGURE 3.2. Relation between the narrator and the represented author.

representation of the author. Note, however, that what is illustrated in Figure 3.2 is the reader's *representation* of the author, not the historical author per se, and we use the term "represented author" to make this clear. The represented author in this case corresponds approximately to what is typically referred to as the implied author in narratological terminology. We have also indicated the source of the information used to construct these representations. The narrator is constructed on the basis of the text, while the author representation may also be influenced by extratextual information concerning the historical author.

   This diagram simplifies the communicative situation by reducing it to the immediate transactions and relations that seem to constitute the reality of the reading experience. One of the advantages of this analysis in terms of the reader's representation is that a distinction between the historical author and the representation of the author that might be inferred from the text is no longer necessary. From the perspective of the reader, they are in fact the same. As Toolan (1995) pointed out, this association was intended by Wayne Booth (1961) who coined the term "implied author" to convey a sense of how readers construct authors. Toolan added that the "pictures" we "conjure up" of different authors "are the only versions of the author we know, and there is *no* 'real author,' unitary, unchanging, standing behind these narrative-derived versions" (78). In the case of readers who actually know the authors personally, Toolan suggested that readers "still perform the same process of forming a mental picture or representation . . . of that author . . . as an integral part of the activity of knowing a person" (78). In trying to understand the reason for the use of a narrator with a given set of characteristics, readers are likely to infer the existence of a creative figure with a set of goals and plans. This is the represented author.

   Focusing on the link between readers and narrators has potent implications. Foremost among them is the notion that readers treat the narrator as a conversational participant. In particular, in conversation each speaker must of necessity maintain a representation of the other participant, together with certain aspects of their mental state for communication to proceed. For example, in conversation this representation must include information about the participant's physical perspective, so that one can understand deictic expressions such as "here" and "there." The representation must also include information about the knowledge and mental state of the participant, so that one can decide what information of one's own would be helpful to provide. The representation must include information about the intentions and goals of the other participant to understand the function of speech acts during the conversation. These and other requirements of the representation of the other participant have been discussed extensively in psycholinguistic analyses of conversation (e.g., Clark & Schaefer, 1989). Our proposal is that the same kind of representation is constructed in processing narrative and that similar processes are used to maintain it. However, in this case, that representation is a representation of the narrator, not a representation of an actual individual, and is inferred by the reader from textual features. We propose that, just as in conversation, the representation of the narrator consists of information concerning the narrator's knowledge, goals, and perspective.

Embedded Representations

Assuming that the reader represents the narrator (and the represented author) as conversational participants also provides a simple interpretation of the notion of the implied reader and the narratee. In conversation, a participant must represent not only what the other participant knows and intends but also what that participant believes about the first (e.g., Winograd, 1977). For example, in replying to the indirect request, "Can you tell me how to get to Jasper Avenue?", one might construct a representation of the speaker that included the belief that the addressee knew the layout of the city streets. Similarly, it follows that when the reader constructs a representation of the narrator, he or she would also construct an embedded representation of what the narrator knows or believes about the textual audience of the narrative, that is, the narratee. In other words, from a conversational perspective, the narratee is a representation embedded in the reader's representation of the narrator. By the same token, the represented author, to the extent that he or she is represented as distinct from the narrator, may be construed as having an embedded representation of his or her audience, the reader. These possibilities are depicted in

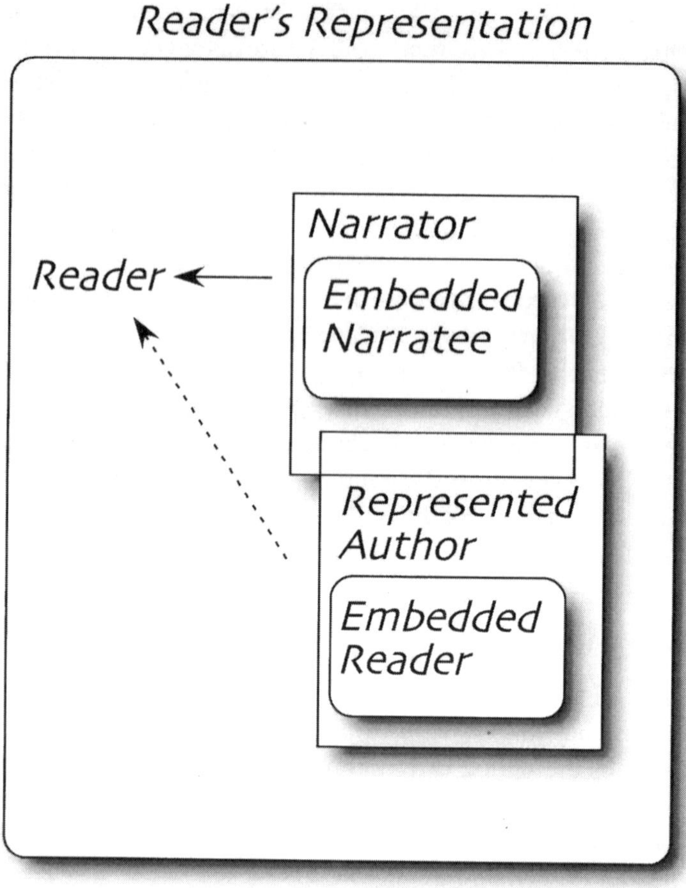

Reader's Representation

FIGURE 3.3. Embedded representations of the reader and narratee.

Figure 3.3. Of course, in the analysis we are proposing, these representations are normal components of the conversational process and do not have any special diegetic status. Moreover, these representations are presumed to exist in the mind of the reader, rather than being logical constructs based on the text, and as such are subject to empirical investigation and validation.

Unlike Toolan (1995), who also excluded the category of implied reader, we include it but embed it in the reader's representation of the author. As Toolan explains, the "implied reader" is simply "the inescapable *version* of a reader that we can assume an author to have in mind" (80). We prefer the term "represented reader" for the conceptual simplification it offers over the traditional term "implied reader." Just as the represented author may coincide in part with the real author, so may the represented reader coincide largely with the actual reader. Moreover, in many cases, we anticipate that there would be little reason for the reader to attribute personal characteristics to the represented reader other than those of his- or herself.

It is unlikely that readers can always distinguish among all the entitites identified by narratologists, and it is probably often the case that, in the mind of the reader, narratee and implied reader are one and the same thing. We agree with Toolan that it is best to correct this proliferation of communicative roles, especially since the distinction may have little explanatory power in understanding reading processes. In particular, in most narratives, the most salient and important representation is that of the narrator and the embedded representation of the narratee. We anticipate that many of the conversational processes we discuss later are limited to this representation. However, we allow the possibility that the more complex embedded representations we mention here may play a role for some readers under some circumstances.

A logical question ensuing from this supposition is what readers do if they perceive that the narrative is not addressed to them. There are various possibilities: They may reject the work and stop reading; or they may continue reading to get whatever they can from the narrative; or they may try to identify with their understanding of the intended reader, imagining how this individual might have understood the narrative; or they may continue to think of themselves as the intended audience, but decide that the author/narrator has misunderstood them. To illustrate this point, we can compare narrative communication with everyday oral conversation. At times, interlocutors perceive that the speaker has misunderstood them. For example, if a speaker relates the details of a baseball game with specialized vocabulary to someone who has no experience with baseball games, then that speaker commits an error in his or her representation of the knowledge of the interlocutor. As a result, the interlocutor may correct the speaker or continue listening and trying to understand anyway. Once again, these are empirical questions.

A related possibility that may arise in some texts occurs when an audience for the narrator is explicitly identified, as in the case of Joseph Conrad's *Heart of Darkness*. Conversation provides a good model for how this may be handled. In three-party conversations, one participant may address a second, but with a clear intent that the information should also be received and understood by a third. That third participant is a conversational side participant (e.g., Clark & Carlson, 1982). The side participant is a recipient of the message, and the speaker makes allowances for the side participant's knowledge and perspective, rather than simply leaving him or her out of the interchange. Explicit narratees in a text can be handled in the same way: Although the narrator is addressing someone other than the reader, the narrator presumably intends that message to also be received by the reader. Indeed, Gerrig (1993) argued that authors generally expect readers to function as side participants.

Processing the Narrator

In this section, we outline some elements of an account of how narrators are processed by readers. We begin by distinguishing two classes of textual features related to the narrator: explicit attributions and inference invitations. Then we discuss the notion of narrator–character associations and the problem of unreliable narrators.

Categories of Features

Drawing in part on earlier scholarship, we suggest that it is important to distinguish two broad classes of textual features pertaining to the narrator. We refer to these as explicit attribution and inference invitations. Explicit attribution occurs when characteristics, behavior, knowledge, or beliefs are attributed to the narrator explicitly in the text. The textual information might be produced by the narrator him- or herself, or it might be produced by others in the story world. Two cases need to be considered. The first concerns personal narrators. In intradiegetic narration, for example, the narrator is an agent in the story world and, as a consequence, is readily available for explicit attributions. A somewhat different situation arises with impersonal narrators. As we discuss later, in such cases the narrator may be associated with a character in the story world through a variety of means, and what may be relevant to the reader's representation of the narrator are the explicit attributions to that associated character.

Inference invitations, on the other hand, pertain to what is *not* said about the narrator and consist of those signs and signals that invite the reader to make inferences beyond what is stated in the text. Narratives may invite inferences pertaining to the narrator in a variety of ways. For example, an ironic tone might lead the reader to infer that the narrator harbors disdain for the subject under discussion. An important class of such implicit attributions is related to the interpretation of the narrator as a conversational partner. As we discuss later, when the narrative appears to flaunt conversational conventions, readers are invited to the draw narratorial implicatures, that is, inferences licensed by the assumption that the narrator is being cooperative.

As an example of how the processing of narratorial implicatures might proceed, consider the following description from John le Carré's *The Naïve and Sentimental Lover*:

Cassidy drove contentedly through the evening sunlight, his face as close to the windscreen as the safety belt allowed, his foot alternating diffidently between accelerator and brake as he scanned the narrow lane for unseen hazards. Beside him on the passenger seat, carefully folded into a plastic envelope, lay an Ordnance Survey map of central Somerset. An oilbound compass of the newest type was fastened by suction to the walnut facia. At a corner of the windscreen, accurately adjusted to his field of view, a copy of the Estate Agent's particulars issued under the distinguished title of Messrs Grimble and Outhwaite of Mount Street W. was clipped to an aluminium stand of his own invention. (1972:8).

This description provides an excess of information pertaining to how the character has arranged, positioned, and organized his immediate environment and, given that it is not relevant to the immediate events of story, violates the Gricean maxim of quantity. However, on the assumption that the narrator is being cooperative, one can infer that this extra information must actually be relevant given the narrator's attitude or belief, and one is invited to infer what that attitude might be. In this case, it may be plausible to suppose the narrator believes the character to be fastidiously careful and excessively organized. Such implicatures are, of course, reader constructions; however, the information in the text that signal such implicatures (in this case, the excessively detailed description) constitute a textual feature.

Narrator–Character Associations

An intuitively salient characteristic of many narratives is that a particular character may have a privileged status: The narrative may provide detailed information about that character's thoughts, feelings, perceptions, and behaviors. When such information is provided about a character consistently, we hypothesize that readers may assume that the character in some sense stands for the narrator. This gives the narrator a presence of sorts even when the narrator is technically absent from the narrative world. We use the term "narrator–character association" to refer to this form of construction. An association with a character makes the task of tracking the knowledge and perspective of the narrator much easier for the reader because he or she may simply assume that it is the same as that of the character. One of the implications of the narrator–character association is that the properties of one may be presumed to be true of the other. For example, the narrator is assumed, as in conversation, to be rational and cooperative; the same may be assumed of an associated character. Similarly, personal attributes of the character, such as age, gender, and social standing, may be presumed to apply to the narrator even when there is no explicit indication that this should be the case. Some evidence for these attributions is presented in several of the succeeding chapters.

Two kinds of textual features may lead to the formation of a narrator–character association. First, the narrator may provide descriptions of the character's perceptions while excluding those of other characters; this may be referred to as specific perceptual access. The role of perceptual access in associations is discussed in Chapter 6. Second, the use of free-indirect speech may suggest that the narrator's and the character's voices are intertwined. The use of this kind of technique and its effects are discussed in more detail in Chapter 7.

Unreliable Narrators

In classical narratology, an "unreliable narrator" is one "whose rendering of the story and/or commentary on it the reader has reasons to suspect" (Rimmon-Kenan, 1983:100). Examples of unreliable narrators would include young narrators, idiot narrators, and narrators with questionable value systems. The term implies that readers are less likely to believe such narrators or that they are more readily inclined to discount their authority. But this may not be the case at all. As Rimmon-Kenan herself acknowledged, it is not always easy for readers to conclude that a narrator is to be interpreted as unreliable. The fact that a narrator may be young and inexperienced, as the narrator of *The Catcher in the Rye*, does not necessarily lead the reader to find his account less authentic or meaningful. With respect to narrators of questionable values, the argument is that these values conflict with those of the implied author, and thus readers perceive the tension between the two, causing them to discount the narrator's authority. But Rimmon-Kenan recognized that the values of the implied author are "notoriously difficult to arrive at" (101). Complications such as possible irony, hyperbole, and allegory make decisions about unreliability all the more difficult.

From our perspective it is important to distinguish the reliability of the narrator's information concerning the story world from the narrator's presumed conversational competence. Even when the reader may have reason to doubt some of the information provided by the narrator, he or she may still assume that the narrator is cooperative and is abiding by the conversational postulates of Grice. Parallels are easy to find in everyday conversational interactions. One can speak with children and hold fluent conversations even though they may have a limited view of the world; one may converse with individuals who have an obvious vested interest in a particular perspective or conclusion; and so on. In situations such as these, one draws one's own conclusions concerning the topic of conversation without taking one's conversational partner's view at face value. A similar process may arise with unreliable narrators: Readers may draw their own conclusions regarding the events in the story world, taking into consideration the specific knowledge and goals of the narrator.

We argue that readers apply whatever knowledge, experience, and information they can to make sense of the narrator's perspective, inconsistent and "unreliable" as it may be. Hence, reading the narrative of a mentally unstable narrator may have the effect of increasing the reader's sympathy, tolerance, and understanding, placing the reader in the position of a privileged "psychologist." Even though readers may not approve morally of a narrator's behavior or attitude, they may derive pleasure at having gained insight into an abnormal psychology or extraordinary experience. From the perspective of a more reader-oriented framework, more knowledge does not necessarily translate into more authority or greater truth; readers understand that "truth" is a relative value, and that first-person narratives are true in a different sense. Furthermore, first-person narrators possess a perceived authenticity associated with eyewitness accounts that in some sense makes it greater and more powerful than the authority of third-person narrators. Faulty as an eyewitness account may be, it is still believed to be superior to hearsay, speculation, or pure fabrication.

An important empirical puzzle is the precise nature of the features in the text that lead the reader to interpret the narrator as unreliable. Intuitively, it seems likely that it is easier to signal that a narrator is unreliable in homodiegetic narration, that is, when the narrator is a character in the story world. Narratologists, for example, typically describe third-person narrators as more authoritative, and hence more believable, than first-person narrators. It is usually the latter who might be considered unreliable. However, not all third-person, impersonal narrators may be believed by readers. Feminist criticism is a powerful example of how one class of readers, namely educated, feminist-oriented readers, reject the ideology of certain omniscient narrators. For example, Judith Fetterley (1977) was not persuaded by the narrator of "Rip van Winkle"; she challenged outright the implications of his narrative perspective. Although this critic was not taking issue with the narrator per se, but rather the historical author, she did dispute the discourse of the narrator. As a reader, Fetterely treated the narrator as a conversational participant, drawing inferences about his communicational intent. Individual features of that narrator, for example his gender, were used to justify those inferences.

Identifying with the Narrator

A central tenant of our approach is that the reader treats the narrator as a conversational partner. This assumption in turn drives the narratorial implicatures that readers draw on the basis of implicit attributions found in the text. Narratorial implicatures may serve a variety of functions in narrative, but we suggest that a key one is the generation of identification with the narrator. In our view, readers may identify with the narrator by attributing their own knowledge and experience to the narrator in the course of drawing narratorial implicatures. In this section, we describe an experiment on one aspect of identification and demonstrate how it is related to the generation of narratorial implicatures.

Prior Research on Identification

Descriptions of identification in literary studies have been typically inscribed within the circular logic alluded to in Chapter 1: Features of different kinds of texts are described, and on the basis of these, correlative reader effects are posited so that features and effects reflect each other. For example, Jauss (1974) listed five categories of identification: "associative," "admiring," "sympathetic," "cathartic," and "ironic." Different kinds of literature correspond to each category of identification, and readers are implicitly assumed to experience a corresponding reaction. For example, corresponding to the "cathartic" identification category are tragedy and comedy. Presumably, the presentation of a hero in either a suffering or comic state produces a purging of emotions or affective states, thereby leading to emotional liberation for the reader/audience. Corresponding to the "admiring" category of identification are medieval and communist literatures; the allegation being that readers of this literature will experience admiration for the exemplary hero.

More than a decade later, the same circular logic was taken to an extreme by Frow (1986), who argued that "there can be no separation between an objective textual construct and something (desire) brought to it by a reader." Frow argued that character "is an effect of the self-'recognition' of a subject which is not preconstituted but which assumes a specific identity in the identification of and, hence, identification with the identity of a character" (Frow, 1986:238–9). Frow adduced complex psychoanalytical arguments to prove this point. For example, he argued that the "process of narcissistic dissemination of ego-libido" is "the basis of all historically specific regimes of identification" (243). Apart from the hypothesis that the reader's identity is altered as a function of identifying with literary characters, and that narcissistic strategies are at the basis of identification, such sweeping psychoanalytical generalizations and convoluted phrasing do little to advance our understanding of the complexities of the identification process of real readers.

In the early nineties, this type of text-based circularity still prevailed. Numerous critics understood the constructed nature of literary characters, as well as the real-world dependence of that construction, but continued to insist on the equivalence of features and construction. One example was Fishelov, who, while maintaining that "the core of this constructing activity is an attempt to 'match' the various details and patterns provided by the literary work with the conceptual network with which we perceive and apprehend the world" (425), then proceeded to describe the textual properties that might lead to richer or more schematic character constructions (Fishelov, 1990), thereby suggesting that the decoding of textual properties is the basis of better or lesser informed reconstructions of literary characters. Naturally, the more attention paid by readers to the particulars of the text, the more informed the interpretation will be, but our point is that even in the most "competent" readings, the interpretation will never be an exact replica of the textual figuration; rather, the interpretation will always be a construction that exceeds the text to varying degrees.

Two general themes can be identified in previous empirical work on identification. The first is the notion of similarity: A reader may identify with a character in a story to the extent that the character is perceived to be similar. An example of this general notion can be found in the work of Larsen and Seilman (1988). They propose the term "personal resonance" to refer to a reader's feeling that a literary work is profoundly relevant and meaningful to him or her. Personal resonance is hypothesized to occur when self-knowledge is activated in memory while reading a story. In support of this analysis, they asked participants to read a text and indicate which parts of the text generated a personal reminding. Later, participants were questioned concerning the role they played in the reminding. They found that narrative texts were more likely to produce remindings in which the participants played an active role, whereas expository texts were more likely to produce remindings in which the participants were passive. These results are consistent with the view that identification depends on the retrieval of active personal memories similar to those described in the text.

A second general theme is the view that identification is related to reader strategy. The idea is that identification is promoted or perhaps controlled by the strategy or processing mode adopted by the reader. The research of Cupchik, Oatley, and Vorderer (1998) provides an example of the general approach. In one experiment, readers were asked to adopt either a "sympathetic spectator" perspective or a "self-oriented" perspective for reading either an experience-loaded story or an action-loaded story. As a sympathetic spectator, readers were encouraged to view the events of the story as an outside observer; with the self-oriented perspective, readers were encouraged to relate the events to their own experience. The self-oriented readers rated the experience-loaded stories higher in personal meaningfulness than did the sympathetic-spectator readers. From this, they concluded that readers react most strongly to a story when they are encouraged to focus on their own thoughts and experiences when reading about those of the character. In general, these results suggest that identification may depend on the reader electing to process the text in a particular manner. Similarly, Oatley (1994) argued that readers adopt a character's goals and plans through a process of mental simulation and then experience emotions as those plans succeed or fail. Oatley's view of mental simulation is similar to our notion of a reading strategy in that mental simulation is active and intentional.

The concept of mental simulation is related to the general approach adopted by Gerrig (1993). He argued that readers are metaphorically transported to the narrative world by engaging in "participatory responses" to the narrative. A participatory response is like the response that might have been produced had the reader participated in the narrative world. Thus, the production of participatory responses depends on a kind of simulation of the events of the narrative, with the reader participating. Although Gerrig suggested that some classes of participatory responses are highly predictable, they would seem to be strategic in the sense that they depend on reader's intentional involvement in the story world. Moreover, the active nature of participatory responses seems to suggest that readers have some control over the nature or extent of their involvement.

Combinations of these themes can be found in a variety of sources. For example, Cupchik (1997) argued that "spontaneous identification" occurs when there are strong parallels between the circumstances of the character and those of the reader; this is clearly a process based on similarity. However, "instructed identification" can also occur when readers are told to be sympathetic toward a character or to imagine being the character; this form of identification seems to involve specific reading strategies. In the realm of cinema, Tan (1994) suggested that viewers engage in a process of imagining how the characters must feel and, by virtue of this process, experience emotions similar to those of the character. He argued that different viewers may have different propensities to identify with the characters. This analysis suggests that identification varies with properties of the viewer and is perhaps under intentional control to some extent, as we would expect for a reading strategy. However, Tan also suggested that the imagination process is greatly aided when the viewer is familiar with the concerns of the character. Thus, strategy and similarity may both be involved in producing identification.

Although these theoretical ideas are helpful in understanding what identification is and what mental processes it is related to, they provide relatively little insight into the role of the text itself in producing identification. Intuitively, it seems that narrative style and the manner in which a character is portrayed are important determinants of identification. Indeed, one might argue that the ability to produce identification with a character is a hallmark of a well-written narrative. However, the similarity of the reader to the character and the reading strategies that a reader uses seem to be unrelated to such textual properties. For example, in Len Deighton's *Berlin Game*, insightful evaluations and a wealth of detailed information about behavior is provided for the first-person narrator's colleagues and friends; in contrast, information about the narrator himself is sketchy and conveyed only indirectly through others' reactions. Despite this relative paucity of information, most would agree that identification is purely with the narrator's character. In contrast, if identification were determined by reader–character similarity, one might expect that different readers would identify with different characters in the narrative, depending on who seemed most similar to the reader. Similarly, if identification were determined purely by intentional reader strategies, one might expect that readers could identify equally well with many different characters in a story depending on preference or idiosyncratic inclination. The fact that such ambiguity concerning the object of identification is relatively rare suggests to us that important properties of the text determine how and when identification occurs, and that identification must involve other mechanisms besides similarity and strategy.

Transparency

We use the term "transparency" to refer to one aspect of identification: A character is transparent to the extent that readers believe that they understand the character and his or her feelings, thoughts, and behaviors. The various conceptions of identification generally entail that it depends on transparency in one way or another or predict that transparency should occur as a result of identification. Further, because narratorial implicatures often involve attributing the readers' knowledge and experience to the narrator, they provide a mechanism that might produce transparency in the narrator. Consider, for example, the following text fragment (taken from "The Office" by Alice Munro, 1968):

> But here comes the disclosure which is not easy for me: I am a writer. That does not sound right. Too presumptuous; phony, or at least unconvincing. Try again. I write. Is that better? I try to write. That makes it worse. Hypocritical humility. Well then? (301)

The attitude expressed by the narrator in this excerpt is superficially unreasonable because there is no reason a priori for one to be embarrassed or insecure about being a writer. However, based on the assumption of narratorial cooperativeness, the reader will generally presume that the narrator's attitude is reasonable and that the narrator is providing sufficient information for the reader to understand that attitude. As a consequence, the reader would attempt to draw inferences to resolve the apparent inconsistency. In particular, he or she may try to imagine experiences and life circumstances that would justify the narrator's insecurity and attribute those to her. When successful, this process can resolve the apparent inconsistency.

We argue that when drawing inferences concerning the narrator's attitudes and beliefs, a central component is likely to be the readers' own knowledge and experience. Readers intimately understand their own attitudes and beliefs and are likely to have readily available explanations and justifications for those attitudes. Consequently, because readers can find an attitude of their own that matches that of the narrator, it is easy to draw the necessary implicature by attributing an analogous explanation and justification to the narrator. In this particular instance, most readers are unlikely to have had experiences related to being a writer; however, they *are* likely to have experienced a similar form of insecurity concerning skill in some other activity or hobby. Consequently, the superficially unreasonable attitude of the narrator can be resolved by adapting whatever those experiences are to the situation of the narrator and the writing profession and attributing those experiences to the narrator. Our hypothesis is that this process of using one's own knowledge and experience in the service of constructing narratorial implicatures produces identification because the narrator is now seen to have the same kind of experiences as the reader. In effect, the text invites readers, through the use of narratorial implicatures, to construct a representation of the narrator that shares important elements of the readers' backgrounds and attitudes. This view is not dissimilar to that of Iser (1974), who argued that "the process of absorbing the unfamiliar is labeled as the identification of the reader with what he reads" (291). Our contribution is to describe the process whereby the unfamiliar is made familiar.

Empirical Evidence

Here we describe an empirical investigation in which we measured transparency as a function of the narratorial implicatures that readers draw.[1] In particular, we tested the hypothesis that transparency is produced by readers attributing their own knowledge and experience

---

[1] These results are based on a reanalysis of a subset of the data reported by Maria Kotovych in her Honors' thesis, *Identification in literature: Role of conversational processes and narratorial technique*, completed in 1999 at the University of Alberta under the supervision of Peter Dixon.

to the narrator in the service of constructing narratorial implicatures. The hypothesis was tested by making implicit attributions explicit. We started with a narrative that seemed to produce strong identification and isolated some of the information that was entailed by narratorial implicatures, that is, the implicit attributions. This information was then explicitly added to the text. Presumably, the modified version contained approximately the same information that readers would infer anyway, except that now that information was stated explicitly, and readers would not need to generate the inferences themselves. Thus, because much of the information needed to understand the narrator's attitude and beliefs was already provided in the modified version, readers should be inclined to construct fewer implicatures, and, by hypothesis, the narrator's transparency should be reduced.

The experimental materials were based on the story "The Office" by Alice Munro. The story is a first-person narrative about a woman who wishes to be a writer, but who has little support from her family and friends. She rents an office in which to do her writing and encounters interpersonal difficulties with her landlord. The initial portion of the story, before any plot events occur, is devoted to a description of the narrator's family, situation, and views on how others react to her desire to be a writer and the writing profession. We refer to this initial segment as the story's "preamble." To evaluate our hypothesis concerning the role of implicatures in identification, we created a second version of this preamble in which many of the inferences that were only implicit in the original version were stated explicitly. An excerpt of the original and the explicit preamble is shown in Table 3.1. The explicit preamble was contrasted with the original, implicit preamble under two conditions. In the single-preamble conditions, participants read either a version of the story with the implicit (original) preamble or a version with the explicit (modified) preamble. Our prediction was that less identification should occur with the explicit version. In the dual-preamble conditions, participants read stories containing both preambles but varying in order. According to our hypothesis, identification should depend on which preamble is read first: When the implicit (original) preamble is read first, implicatures will be necessary to interpret the narrator as cooperative, and identification should result; the subsequent, explicit preamble should merely confirm more or less what the reader has inferred already. However,

TABLE 3.1. *Example of Implicature Manipulation*

Implicit (Original) Preamble

But here comes the disclosure which is not easy for me: I am a writer. That does not sound right. Too presumptuous; phony, or at least unconvincing. Try again. I write. Is that better? I try to write. That makes it worse. Hypocritical humility. Well then? It doesn't matter. However I put it, the words create their space of silence, the delicate moment of exposure. But people are kind, the silence is quickly absorbed by the solicitude of friendly voices, crying variously, how wonderful, and good for you, and well, that is intriguing. And what do you write, they inquire with spirit. Fiction, I reply, bearing my humiliation by this time with ease, even a suggestion of flippancy, which was not always mine, and again, again, the perceptible circles of dismay are smoothed out by such ready and tactful voices – which have however exhausted their stock of consolatory phrases, and can say only, "Ah!"

Explicit Preamble

I feel embarrassed telling people that I am a writer because I have noticed that the typical reaction to such claims is one mixed with sympathy and amusement. It is almost like they want to ask me what I really do for a living. It seems to me that writers do not get any respect until they are commercially successful. I also get the sense that people do not take writers seriously, so this makes my admission of being one all the more uncomfortable to make.

when the implicit preamble is encountered second, after reading the explicit version, implicatures should not be necessary because the explicit preamble has already provided an appropriate background for the narrator's views.

Transparency was measured by asking readers to rate how appropriate and reasonable the character's actions and evaluations were. The items that were rated are shown in Table 3.2; these were embedded in a longer list of questions concerning the story, the writer, and the reader's attitudes. If readers attribute their own knowledge

TABLE 3.2. *Transparency Items*

The narrator's final impression of Mr. Malley was fair.
I think that asking for the office was an unreasonable request for the narrator to make.
The narrator judges her husband fairly.
I think that the narrator was justified in leaving the office.

and experience to the narrator, the narrator's attitude and behaviors should, as a consequence, be easier to understand. Between twenty-seven and twenty-eight participants read each version of the story and evaluated character transparency by responding to these questions on a five-point scale.

The results for transparency are shown in Figure 3.4. The figure shows that the explicit versions (in which the explicit preamble was presented alone or first) produced less transparency than the implicit versions (in which the implicit preamble was presented alone or first). The factor of single preamble versus dual preamble produced little effect. In this figure, the error bars indicate the size of 95% confidence

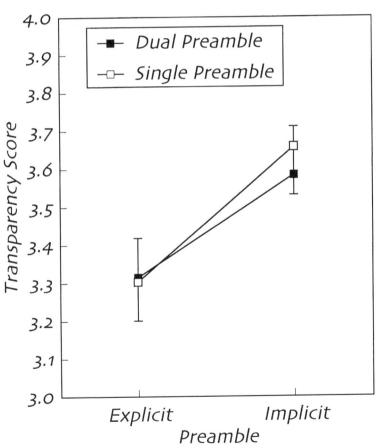

FIGURE 3.4. Transparency score as a function of type of preamble. Error bars indicate the size of 95% confidence intervals, adjusted for pairwise comparisons.

interval for the difference between implicit and explicit versions, adjusted for pairwise comparisons; thus, because the error bars for the two types of preambles do not overlap, one can be reasonably confident that the difference is greater than 0. Following the procedures outlined in the Appendix, we assessed the strength of evidence these results provide by fitting linear models to the data. A model in which it was assumed that the explicit preamble (either alone or first) produced less transparency than the implicit preamble (either alone or first) matched the pattern of means quite well. When this model was compared to a null model in which all means were assumed to be equal, the likelihood ratio was $\lambda = 107.03$, indicating clear evidence for an effect for type of preamble. We also assessed the fit of a model that included all possible differences among conditions. This model showed little improvement over the model with only an effect of explicit/implicit preamble, with a likelihood ratio of $\lambda = 1.16$. Thus, there is little evidence for an effect of single preamble versus dual preamble or an interaction.

The results were in accord with the hypothesis that transparency is produced when readers use their own knowledge and experience to construct narratorial implicatures. In particular, transparency was greater when participants read the implicit preamble (either first or alone) rather than the explicit version. Our interpretation is that the implicit preamble leads readers to generate a variety of implicatures that are not needed in the explicit version, and, as a consequence, readers have a greater opportunity to attribute their own experience to the narrator. The result is that the narrator's thoughts and behavior are easier to appreciate and understand. Paradoxically, this result occurs even though the implicit version of the text provides less information than the explicit version. In effect, the ability to understand the narrator is contributed not by the information provided in the text (as in the explicit version) but by readers themselves as they attempt to understand the narrative on the basis of the principle of narratorial cooperativeness.

In addition, there was little difference between the transparency found in the single-preamble conditions and that found in the dual-preamble conditions. This result conforms to our predictions. If implicatures are generated by readers when gaps or inconsistencies are encountered in the text, the second preamble in the dual preamble versions should have little effect. For example, when the explicit preamble follows the implicit preamble, the additional information should have no impact because the implicatures have already been generated at that point; when the implicit preamble follows the explicit preamble, no implicatures should be generated because the initial, explicit information provides an appropriate justification for the narrator's attitudes. The similar transparency in the single- and dual-preamble conditions also provides evidence that the explicit preamble was fairly consistent with the inferences that readers draw when reading the original, implicit version. For example, simply adding the explicit preamble to the text after the implicit preamble had little effect on transparency, and one cannot attribute the obtained effects to simply the nature of the information provided in the explicit version.

Summary

In this chapter, we have developed the concept of the narrator as a reader construction. Previous analyses of the narrator have focused on two characteristics: diegetic level and communicative function. The notion of diegetic level derives from the distinction between mimesis, that is, the story, and diegesis, that is, the discourse. Narrators can thus be classified in terms of their relationship to the story world. An extradiegetic narrator, for example, is outside of the story world; an autodiegetic narrator tells a story about him- or herself. The role of the narrator in the communicative function of a text is based on a hierarchical analysis of the interaction between the author and the reader. Embedded within the exchange between the author and the reader is a communicative interaction between an implied author and an implied reader; within this exchange is an interaction between the narrator and a narratee. However, there are a variety of difficulties with this "levels" analysis, and, in many cases, readers may not readily distinguish levels or the entities that embody them.

As an alternative, we argue that the narrator should be construed as a reader construction, that is, a representation in the mind of the reader. Based on previous analyses in narratology, we suggest two broad categories of features that are relevant for constructing such a representation: explicit attributions and inference invitations.

Explicit attributions are things that are explicitly said about the narrator; inference invitations are the cues that may lead readers to make inferences about the narrator. We hypothesize that based on these textual features, readers construct a representation of the narrator akin to that which they would construct of a conversational participant. A variety of implications follow from this approach. First, the narratological concepts of the narratee and the implied reader can be seen as corresponding to representations of the reader embedded in the representation of the narrator; such representations are a natural part of conversational interactions. Second, readers will commonly draw narratorial implicatures, that is, inferences licensed by the assumption of narratorial cooperativeness, in service of understanding the narrator. Third, the representation of the narrator and the characters can be influenced by narrator–character associations. Fourth, the notion of an "unreliable" narrator can be understood as an invitation for readers to draw their own conclusions about the story world rather than relying on the interpretations offered by the narrator; similar processes occur in conversation.

Evidence in support of our view of the narrator is found in the phenomenon of identification. The term "transparency" is used to refer to one aspect of identification, the tendency for the thoughts and actions of the narrator to be clear and understandable. It was hypothesized that transparency would be generated by narratorial implicatures invited by implicit attributions in the text. As a test of this hypothesis, we constructed different versions of a story in which the implicit attributions were made explicit. Even though the explicit versions in effect provided more information, readers saw the narrator as more transparent, that is, more rational, justified, and easy to understand.

4

Events and Plot

Perhaps the most salient and obvious characteristic of a narrative is its plot, that is, the temporal, causal, or logical sequence of events that provide the basis of the story: Most, when asked to describe a narrative, will respond with a summary of the plot. Attempts at characterizing the nature of events and plot go back at least as far as Aristotle, and it has been a central problem in the scholarship on narratology since the pioneering work of Propp (1968; originally published in 1928) on story grammars. Yet more than seventy years after the original Russian publication, our conceptual understanding of narrative events and plot is far from complete. In this chapter, we summarize some of the issues in the debates concerning plot structure. Our analysis is that at the heart of many of the controversies lies the issue of how the reader's experience of plot should be handled and, in particular, the problem of distinguishing textual features from reader constructions.

There is a surprising similarity among the debates that have gone on in literary studies, discourse processing, and artificial intelligence concerning the appropriate starting point in the analysis of plot. In all these domains, an important question has been whether it is more appropriate to analyze plot structure based on the manner in which the story is told, that is, as a property of the discourse, or as reflecting properties of the story world itself. We first elaborate on this distinction between discourse and story, and then describe some of the attempts to describe plot in terms of either one or the other. Following this review, we discuss an approach in which plot structure is attributed to the reader, and we discuss some of the advances that accrue from distinguishing features and constructions.

Story versus Discourse

The parsing of the narrative into the levels of the telling (the discourse) and the told (the story) can be attributed to Aristotle, who distinguished between logos – "the imitation of a real action," or the story itself – and mythos – the "selection and possible rearrangement of the units constituting logos" (Prince, 1987:56). Since Aristotle, scholars have coined other terms for similar ideas. The Russian Formalists distinguished between fabula, or events in their chronological order, and sjuzet, or events in the order in which they are presented in a narrative. Forster differentiated between the story, or "narrative of events with an emphasis on chronology," and the plot, or "narrative of events with an emphasis on causality" (Prince, 1987:72). Other accounts distinguish between *what* is told and *how* it is told, or between the content and the expression, the narrated and the narrating, or the fiction and the narration (Prince, 1987:91).

As we argue later, the story/discourse distinction may not sufficiently delineate the parameters of plot construction because it excludes from consideration the reader's experience of plot. Further, as numerous narratologists have pointed out, distinguishing between story and discourse elements is often difficult because story and discourse features can refer to inseparable elements of the text, and both story and discourse can refer to representations in the reader's mind. As a consequence, separating story and discourse can sometimes seem counterintuitive, and an exclusive reliance on this distinction may not be fruitful. Nevertheless, we believe that there is a clear distinction in the scholarship of different fields between analytical efforts that begin with the text itself and attempt to derive a description of the structure of the story as it is told, and those that begin by describing the relationship among events in the story world, regardless of how those events are described in the text.

In the former case, the goal is to reconstruct the actions and sequence of events from the text as it is presented. Although it is clear in this approach that a variety of transformations, rearrangements, or inferences may be required to identify that plot structure, the starting point for such analyses is the text itself. As we discuss later, the notion of a story grammar is the most common conceptual tool in this form of analysis. We characterize such an approach as an attempt to find plot in the discourse. In the latter case, the manner in which information is presented in the discourse is largely ignored; it is the information concerning the actions and events itself that is deemed important, not how it is presented in the text. In other words, the starting point for this approach is the elements of the story world themselves, not the words of the text. We refer to this approach as an attempt to find plot in the story. Because the information concerning the story world in fact comes primarily from the text, these two approaches in some cases can provide very similar analyses. However, we believe that the difference in starting point – beginning with the text itself versus beginning with a description of the events of the story world – indicates an important difference in orientation, and the distinction is useful at least for organizing our discussion of various approaches.

Plot Structure in the Discourse

The main conceptual tool in deriving the structure of the plot from the text itself is the notion of a grammar for stories. Such a grammar allows one, at least in principle, to find the essential structure of the story as reflected in the text. In most approaches, the notion of a story grammar entails the notion that readers possess a corresponding grammatical competence so that they can apprehend the structure of the story. We review both notions in more detail later. After this discussion, we describe some of the empirical evidence suggesting that at least some aspects of the structure identified by story grammars are understood and used by readers. Finally, we outline what we feel are the shortcomings of this approach.

Story Grammars

The notion of a grammar for stories derives from an analogy with the linguistic description of sentence structure. The central assumption in this approach is that stories have a consistent structure, evident in the text, that can be described by formal or quasi-formal grammatical

rules. Thus, an appropriate set of rules would capture, at different hierarchical levels, the obligatory and optional constituents of stories
and their mutual dependencies. An influential early work in this regard was that of Propp (1968; originally published in 1928) on Russian
folktales. Working on a corpus of 115 Russian fairy tales, Propp isolated thirty-one invariable and sequentially fixed functions that he
believed are fundamental to the action structure of all fairy tales.
For Propp, functions were categories of meaningful acts that have a
specified role in the story. For example, the first three consisted of
absentation (a family member leaves home), interdiction (the hero is
faced with an interdiction), and violation (the interdiction is violated;
Prince, 1987). A given act may have different roles in different stories.
For example, finding a treasure chest may be a reward in one story,
but a delusion in another if the antagonist had previously found and
emptied it. Although not all functions are found in any one story, they
always appear in the same order. For example, it would be inconceiv-
able that any of the last four of Propp's functions – the exposure of the
villain, the donning of the hero's new appearance, the punishment
of the villain, and the hero's marriage and ascension to the throne –
appear anywhere but at the end of the story. Also, in Propp's theory,
a character can assume different functions within the same story; for
example, a person the hero meets on his quest to capture the villain
can be both a helper and an opponent. As Propp explains, Baba Yaga
begins as an opponent by fighting the hero Ivan but involuntarily becomes a helper when she shows him the path to the other kingdom
(Propp, 1968).

A related approach was that of Roland Barthes (1977). Barthes
developed an analytical scheme that was much more complex than
Propps'. In it, the category of functions was divided into several sub-
categories, including cardinal functions, which are the main articu-
lations or vertebrae of the story, and catalysers, which connect the
vertebrae. He also identified the category of indices, which refer to
the characters and the setting without moving the plot forward. These
were further subdivided into indices proper (those that are relevant
or significant) and informants (those that merely add detail).

Claude Bremond (1966) developed a model intended to account
for the potential logical outcomes that arise at every step of the story.
The function was still the basic plot unit for Bremond. However,

whereas Propp demonstrated how each function leads logically to the following one, Bremond showed that each function exists in a state of potentiality with two possible outcomes. It can be actualized or not, and if it is actualized, that process can be successful or not. For example, at the beginning of the classical play *Oedipex Rex* by Sophocles, King Laius is alive, married, and enjoys good fortune and security. This initial state has the potential for two possible outcomes: the state can either be sustained or deteriorate. Functions are further combined into a variety of simple and complex sequences. The most basic of these functions is the triad, consisting of an opening possibility, a process, and an outcome. What ensues in the play is a deterioration process consisting of several stages and actions, and the ultimate outcome is that he loses both his wife and his life.

Van Dijk (1976) developed a set of distinctions for the analysis of narratives based on concepts from the philosophy of action. In his analysis, naturally occurring narratives consist of a sequence of action descriptions at various levels. In turn, each action description is defined in terms of behavior, intentions, mental states, and circumstances in the world. Natural narrative is analyzed as a conversational speech act subject to a variety of pragmatic constraints; natural narrative should, for example, be relevant to the conversation and provide new information. The logic of presenting a narrative in conversation entails that it consists at least of an initial exposition, in which the circumstances, agents, and instruments are introduced; a complication that makes the narrative conversationally relevant; and a resolution, in which the agent reacts to the complication. Artificial narratives (including literary discourse) are assumed to build on this structure with the additional problem that they are not embedded in a conversational interaction. This means that they may be more complex, with a variety of possible transformations and embeddings, but there are additional pragmatic requirements that derive from the lack of a common conversational context.

The notion of story grammars has had a substantial impact on psychological investigations of narrative comprehension. This influence can be traced to Rumelhart (1975), who proposed essentially a "systematization of Propp's (1968) analysis of Russian folk tales" (235). Rumelhart and many others used the formalism of rewrite rules to capture the combinatorial regularities. For example, rules such as the following have been suggested:

1. Story → Setting + Episode
2. Episode → Event + Reaction
3. Event → {Episode | Change-of-State | Action | Event + Event}

In other words, a story consists of a setting followed by an episode, an episode consists of an event followed by a reaction, and an event consists of either an (embedded) episode, a change of state, an action, or an embedded sequence of events. When such rule systems are elaborated sufficiently, they provide a systematic basis for characterizing a wide range of ways in which constituents may combine. For example, the rewrite rules proposed by Mandler (1984) can be used to describe a variety of what she terms "traditional" stories, including those with lengthy and complex combinations of episodes. Johnson and Mandler (1980) described how their rewrite rules generate stories in which episodes are embedded as the beginning of other episodes, the endings of other episodes, and the outcomes of protagonists' actions.

Competence

Regardless of their details, the various grammatical approaches share a common dependence on the notion of competence: Readers are assumed to have the competence to identify the structure of a story in accordance with the grammar. By analogy with Chomsky's (1957, 1965) description of language competence, it is often assumed that the competence for understanding stories is innate and universal across cultures and language groups. This view was explicitly described by Jonathan Culler (1975a), who indicated that theories of plot structure "can only be evaluated by their success in serving as models of a particular aspect of literary competence: readers' abilities to recognize and summarize plots, to group together similar plots, etc. This intuitive knowledge constitutes the facts to be explained" (127). It seems to us that in many cases, the essential goal of characterizing readers' "competence" is to rescue a formal analysis of the text from the vagaries of the specific collection of skills and knowledge that individual readers may have. By characterizing the nature of some general competence, one need not be concerned that a given reader may or may not be sensitive to a given aspect of the plot or sequence of events or its implication. Thus, one is free to pursue a more formal analysis of the text and its constituent plot on the assumption that readers are generally competent to process it.

However, we suspect that the notion of an *innate* competence for understanding narrative plot may be difficult to sustain. Even with respect to sentence structure, the notion that all people have an innate universal grammar has been hotly debated (e.g., Bates, 1979; Sinclair-de Zwart, 1973; Whitehurst, 1982), and many of the strongest arguments in its favor do not readily apply to the appreciation of story structure. For example, in support of a universal grammar for sentences, it has been noted that the human acquisition of language is virtually universal (e.g., Lenneberg, 1967), that there is a stereotypic pattern of acquisition across language groups (e.g., Pinker, 1994), that species-specific brain regions seem to be critically involved (Dingwall, 1975), and that language use has a clear adaptive value from an evolutionary point of view (e.g., Pinker, 1994). Many of these arguments have much less force when applied to the knowledge of story structure: Stories are understood and spontaneously generated at a much later age, there is much more variability in stories and the use of story structure across individuals and cultures, there is no evidence to our knowledge linking story use to neural function, and the adaptive significance of story telling is much more obscure. Our view is that, on balance, the argument for an innate knowledge of story structure is not compelling.

Toolan's (1995) revision of the concept of competence is somewhat more palatable. Toolan restricts competence to the "acquired and developed ability of a group of readers, rather than some universal mental ability, comparable to the near-universal ability to walk or subtract" (29). Anticipating an argument that will be elaborated later by Fludernik (1996), Toolan argues that plot-summarizing competence develops because it is a valued skill in society. Further, we suspect that readers acquire plot competence mainly by reading narratives. Rimmon-Kenan's understood this when she wrote that competence is acquired "by extensive practice in reading and telling stories" (1983:8). Toolan is more concerned with cultural-group-specific competence and describes this preoccupation in terms reminiscent of Stanley Fish's "community of readers." Because competence is a function of culture in a limited, group-specific sense, Toolan argued that individuals "get good at identifying what, relative to their own framework of world knowledge and cultural assumptions, is the 'main' point of a story" (29–30).

This perspective, in its simplest form, is troublesome because it is difficult to know to whom, precisely, one should attribute this knowledge. On one hand, one would not want to assume that all readers possess precisely the same knowledge because it is likely that different individuals' exposure to narratives and plot structure varies. On the other hand, it does not seem profitable to simply assume that each individual's knowledge of story structure is completely idiosyncratic. This dilemma is reminiscent of the tension between the description of general and specific readers discussed in Chapter 2, and one may be able to resolve it by applying the notion of the statistical reader we developed in that context. However, if one then admits that competence varies with reading groups or communities, that it may be acquired over time with experience with different narrative forms, or that it is sensitive to levels of expertise, then the concept loses its logical force. In that case, one must consider the particular knowledge that readers may or may not have, and a formal analysis based purely on the notion of a general competence may easily be irrelevant to a given reader's processing.

The Psychological Reality of Story Grammars

Formal characterizations of story grammars have enjoyed a certain amount of success in accounting for aspects of readers' processing. For example, story grammars specify a canonical order for the various constituents: Settings precede episodes, reactions follow events, and so on. A common result that is often cited in support of the psychological reality of story grammars is that stories are better recalled when they are presented in this canonical order rather than in a random arrangement (e.g., Glenn, 1978; Thorndyke, 1977), and that constituents are read more slowly when they are moved from their appropriate position (Mandler & Goodman, 1982). Further, readers are more likely to recall outcomes and important actions from story episodes rather than elaborations or details (e.g., Black, Turner &

Bower, 1979; Omanson, 1982). A more critical result is that errors in story recall typically match the story grammar, even when the content is incorrect. For example, readers may sometimes add constituents that match the grammar but were actually omitted in the narrative. Similarly, confabulations tend to conform to the appropriate story grammar constituent; for example, readers may make up a character reaction where a reaction is called for by the grammar, even if they do not recall the reaction that was in the text (Mandler, 1978; Stein & Glenn, 1979).

Related to the notion of story grammars is the so-called "levels" analysis of Meyer (1975). In this framework, textual elements are classified as general, "high-level" statements or specific, "low-level" statements or at various levels in between. Although there are several interpretations of the best way to define various levels, they generally depend on some form of embedding: Low-level statements are finer-grained descriptions of events or actions that are embedded in the high-level statements. For example, a high-level statement might indicate that the hero of a story seeks revenge; low-level statements might indicate the nature of the revenge, how the revenge is planned, problems that arise in the execution of the plan, and so on. From our perspective, what is interesting about these approaches is that what determines whether a particular event is high- or low-level is the precise manner in which it is expressed in the discourse. Thus, like story grammars, a levels analysis provides a basis for using the discourse to identify what may correspond to the hierarchical structure of the plot.

When analyzed in this way, levels have been shown to be related to various aspects of reading behavior. In Meyer's analysis of expository prose, high-level statements were better recalled than low-level details. Kintsch et al. (1975) verified this result for short paragraphs. Several authors have attempted to apply this analysis to narrative texts. For example, Thorndyke (1977) found that high-level statements in a story were better recalled than low-level statements. Similarly, Bower (1976) reported that high-level statements in a narrative were rated as more important than low-level statements. However, one difficulty with the approach is that it can be unclear how to assign statements to levels. For example, in a narrative consisting of a sequence of episodes, a high-level description of the story might correspond to the last episode, the first episode, or all the episodes in some combination. Johnson and Mandler (1980) suggested that a levels analysis predicts memorability because the high levels of the hierarchy typically correspond to important story-grammar constituents. For example, a high-level description of the Cinderella story might include "Cinderella's fairy godmother helps her go to the ball." However, this statement pertains to important categories such as attempt and outcome rather than less memorable categories such as reaction or ending. Consequently, one may view the evidence for an effect of levels on readers' processing also as evidence for an effect of some form of story grammar.

Problems with Story Grammars

Despite the evidence that story grammars are related in some ways to comprehension and memory, it is clear that rewrite rules by themselves cannot provide a complete description of plot or story structure. For example, Propp (1968) himself intended his work as a study of Russian fairy tales, and his model would clearly have difficulty when applied to stories that are unrelated to the original corpus. Rumelhart (1975) found it necessary to include a set of semantic rules that indicated how a formal arrangement of constituents should be interpreted. For example, a sequence of two events specified by the story grammar should be interpreted semantically in terms of causal relations: The first event may cause or enable the second. Johnson and Mandler (1980) distinguished between the deep structure of a story and its surface structure: The deep structure contained all the story grammar constituents in the appropriate order, while the surface structure could be derived from the deep structure by applying rules that delete or move these constituents. The surface structure may present an outcome before the preceding event, for example, or may omit a character's reaction.

More generally, Black and Wilensky (1979) argued that the formal systems that have been used for characterizing story structure are inherently inadequate for anything other than an artificially limited set of narratives. The essence of their argument has the following form: Only very powerful grammatical formalisms are adequate for characterizing the structure of sentences (e.g., Chomsky, 1959); even simple stories have a much more flexible organization than individual sentences; therefore, an adequate story grammar formalism would have to be much more powerful than the simple rewrite-rule systems that have typically been proposed.

This argument does not rule out the possibility of using more powerful grammars to specify the structure of stories. An obvious enhancement of the rewrite-rule approach is to add transformations such as movement and deletion rules, as is commonly done in the theory of sentence grammar. This would allow story grammars to be applied to a wide range of possible narratives. However, such transformations can make the grammar *too* powerful and allow it to identify "story structure" in any arbitrary sequence of sentences. Although it may be possible to constrain the application of such transformations, the problem, as Black and Wilensky argued, is that it is in fact the required constraints that embody the interesting aspects of structure and plot, not the story grammars themselves. For example, Johnson and Mandler (1980) suggested that beginnings, reactions, and endings can be deleted only if they can be inferred from the surrounding context. However, such inferences are often drawn on the basis of narrative structure and story–telling conventions that the story grammar was intended to characterize in the first place.

Beyond the precise formalism used to represent story grammars, there is the question of the content of the grammar; that is, what is the nature of the underlying structure and regularity that is being expressed in the grammar? Both linear (temporal) chronology and causality have been adduced as structuring principles, but not all agree on their relative importance. It is clear to narratologists that linear chronology alone "is neither natural nor an actual characteristic of most stories" (Rimmon-Kenan, 1983:17), and for this reason some reject temporality as a necessary condition of plots. Causality is presumably the element that converts stories into plots; however, as narratologists have pointed out, causality is of many different types and, therefore, is a far-from-simple concept to infer. For example, in modernist narrative where the entire narrative is an interior monologue, there is no action and thus no causality at the level of the narrative. Rimmon-Kenan concluded that "causality can either be implied by chronology or gain an explicit status in its own right. But the very notion of causality is by no means unproblematic" (1983:17). The source of these difficulties, we argue, is the theoretical requirement that causality provide a coherent organizational scheme for the analysis of plot. The alternative view that we develop subsequently is that plot should be thought of as reader construction. Although information concerning causality in the text contributes to this representation, it need not be the sole organizing principle.

A more general difficulty with the story grammar approach is that the grammars do not readily generalize to new plot structures. Story grammars following in the tradition of Propp were clearly intended to be specific to the corpus from which they were derived, and they would not necessarily be expected to provide a universal description of plot. More seriously, though, such models shed little light on the understanding of genre or work-specific plots with which the reader may be unfamiliar. Our intuition is that new story structures are readily understood, even if that structure deviates substantially from one's expectation. Although it might be argued that well-known story grammars might provide a basis or starting point for the understanding of unfamiliar plot structures, the story grammar itself does little to illuminate the flexibility and creativity with which readers would seem to adapt to novel structures that they have not encountered previously.

Also, story grammars, by themselves, say little concerning process. Even if it were granted that a given grammar provided an adequate description of the structure of a story and that readers implicitly understood that structure, there is a wide range of unanswered questions concerning how that structure is or is not involved in comprehension. At one extreme is the possibility that the story grammar has no involvement in processing at all: Readers may be able to recognize and label the grammar constituents (and perhaps differentially rehearse them for later recall), but such recognition may occur only after the story has been processed on the basis of quite different principles. At the other extreme is the possibility that the grammar is essential to the processing and organization of the textual information. In other words, readers might be unable to form a coherent representation of the events of the story without implicitly applying a grammar of some sort. Simply identifying an adequate grammar does little to constrain the possible processing alternatives.

Plot Structure in the Story

An alternative to viewing plot structure as reflecting the manner in which a narrative is told is to view it as reflecting the structure of the story itself. Situating events and plot strictly at the level of the story makes intuitive sense. In naturally occurring (i.e., real-world) narratives, the events of a story are commonly part of the world we live in, are experienced as such, and then are later recounted as narrative discourse. Fictional narratives differ, of course, in that they are not transparently related to real events that precede the telling; thus, the "events" of a fictional narrative are created by, and therefore dependent upon, the discourse. The narrator can rearrange and select the events to be described at will and can decide whether to use a thorough or brief description of those events. Nevertheless, events are told as if they had occurred, and this suggests to the reader that the story elements exist in some pure form, independent of narratorial embellishments and reorganization. A general approach to understanding plot is to assume that it is the relationship among these story elements in the story world that constitute the plot.

Events and Event Structure

An initial hurdle in locating the plot structure in the story world is simply identifying the basic story elements. Unlike the story-grammar approach, which begins with the words of the text, there is no unambiguous indication as to what is in the story and what is not. Moreover, it is not always easy to determine if particular elements of the narrative belong strictly to the story or the discourse. Toolan points out that "even as we attempt to specify the allegedly core events and characters of stories...we find that *content* still remains" (Toolan, 1995:14). In other words, there would seem to be important information for the interpretation of the narrative beyond any delineation of the events, actions, and characters of the story world. However, in spite of this difficulty, one senses intuitively that the text does contain indices of elements that constitute a plot; certain things are said to happen to the characters, who are also said to perform certain actions. The real problem is determining which actions and events do in fact count as relevant plot elements. As Monica

Fludernik points out, while falling in love may clearly be considered an event, so might "sudden mental realizations on the part of a character," or even a character's "tiny gestures" (Fludernik, 1996:335).

An intuitive starting point for this kind of analysis is to identify chronological sequence, and the most basic element of such chronology is the event. Clearly, the text indicates something about events, but there is not always a direct and obvious relationship between elements of the text and the events they presumably describe. Toolan defined an event as "a change from one state to a modified state" (1995:14). Prince's definition is more elaborate: "a change of state manifested in DISCOURSE by a PROCESS STATEMENT in the mode of Do or Happen. An event can be an ACTION (when the change is brought about by an agent . . .) or a HAPPENING (when the change is brought about by an agent . . .)" (1987:28). A point of contention is the role of states in the constitution of events. Rimmon-Kenan prefers not to insist on the opposition between state and event (1983:15). Trabasso and Sperry (1985) argued that an event can be identified when a set of statements describe an entity (the patient) that changes in state as a result of actions or processes generated by another entity (the agent). Although these various approaches seem to capture important aspects of our intuition about what constitutes an event, the detailed formal analysis of the textual features for an event would seem to run into the some of the same kinds of difficulties that confronted formal story grammars. In particular, it may be difficult to find a set of rules that can be guaranteed to apply to all texts in all circumstances for all readers.

Further, narratologists have not been able to agree on how many events constitute a story sequence and what kind of events these must be. For Prince, a

minimal story consists of three conjoined events. The first and the third events are stative, the second is active. Furthermore, the third event is the inverse of the first. Finally, the three events are conjoined by conjunctive features in such a way that (a) the first event precedes the second in time and the second precedes the third, and (b) the second causes the third. (1973:31)

Rimmon-Kenan disputes this, and claims that temporality is a sufficient criterion for the constitution of events into a story (1983:18). More generally, stories of any length have many more than three events, and a useful account of plot would need to describe not only their order but also their organization into hierarchically related sequences. How this is to be done provides a major challenge to the general approach, and, we suspect, it will be difficult to accomplish based on purely formal grounds.

Stereotypic Experience

A central argument in the view that structure exists in the story world is that the story world reflects the real world, and events in the real world have structure. Sometimes this structure is described in terms of habitual sequences of events. The pioneering work of Schank and Abelson (1977) on scripts is a good example of this approach. They argue that people possess a vast quantity of scripts, that is, generalized information concerning specific sequences of events that are commonly encountered in the world. Scripts are specific in the sense that they contain information about events that occur in particular situations, but they are also generalized in the sense that they represent an aggregate of a wide range of experience in situations of that type. Scripts indicate the causal connections between events, common variations in the sequences, and nature of the goals that actors have in the situation. Although the notion of scripts is useful in a theory of world knowledge, in fact the problem to which Schank and Abelson applied their ideas was a computational model of story comprehension. They argued that the interpretation of many events in a narrative is only possible against a background of scriptlike knowledge of typical event sequences. Support for the role of scripts in the processing and memory for stories was obtained by Bower, Black, and Turner (1979). In a narrative description of a scripted activity, comprehension was faster when events were described in their stereotypic order. In later recall, participants often misremembered reading typical script events that had not actually been stated. These and other results (see, for example, Mandler, 1984) suggest that readers use their knowledge of stereotypic experiences in understanding and representing narratives related to those experiences.

Representations of stereotypic experience by themselves do not provide a particularly helpful vehicle for the description of plot, however, since most stories do not conform to commonly experienced scripts. For example, one might describe a script for a detective story that involved encountering a crime, identifying clues and suspects, and then finding the culprit. Although this would seem to be a plausible depiction of a wide range of such stories, it would be difficult to argue that this is a scenario with which all readers have had direct experience. As a consequence, characterizing a plot in such terms has more in common with the story grammar approach than the analysis of "scripted experience." In particular, if readers have knowledge of the general sequence of events in different genres, then that knowledge must have been acquired from the processing of narrative rather than through direct experience, and any regularities in that sequence cannot be ascribed to experienced regularities in the world. Further, such an account fails to provide much insight into the processing by individuals who do not have prior experience with the genre. Even the argument that scripts can help process isolated scenes in narratives is weak, as the power of fiction resides to a great extent in its ability to arouse interest in situations and experiences totally removed from the reader's field of experience. Although an analysis along these lines may be relevant in some cases, our impression is that at best the approach is of limited applicability.

Character Plans

An alternative to stereotypic sequences is the view that plot structure is based on the interpretation of characters' plans. The view is that in understanding human behavior in the world, we typically attempt to infer the plans that people have and how those plans map onto the circumstances of the world. The comprehension of characters and their actions in a story world is no different, so the argument goes. Indeed, a central ingredient in the approach Schank and Abelson (1977) used for comprehending stories involves the development of representations of character plans, particularly as they pertain to scripted event sequences.

According to this analysis, human behavior in the world is planful: Individuals have goals, and goals typically are achieved by generating a sequence of subgoals, each of which resolves some obstacle to the superordinate goal. The execution of plans needs to be monitored and revised as required by the circumstances. Actions can be understood in terms of their relationship to such hierarchically organized plans. In the classic example of Schank and Abelson, the action of going to a restaurant is understood as a plan for achieving the goal of satisfying one's hunger; looking at a menu is a plan for achieving the goal of selecting the meal; and so on. The argument is that because narratives are generally about human behavior, the same process can be used to interpret and represent narrative plots. Notice that, in this approach, the representation depends purely on the story world; the narrative is assumed to be simply a window on events as they occur in that world.

Causal Chains

An even more basic notion is that our perception and understanding of events in the world are organized around causation. Our understanding of plot in a story, then, reflects this interpretation just as our understanding of the world does. An important formal analysis of causal chains in stories is that of Trabasso and Sperry (1985).

Based on the work of Mackie (1980), causal chains are identified on the basis of the criterion of "necessity in the circumstances." The circumstances are the conditions that one may assume exist in the story world. A given event is classified as a cause or enabling event of a second event if it satisfies a counterfactual test: Would the second event not occur if the first had not? Causes are classified as motivation, (unintentional) psychological causation, physical causation, and enablement (Warren, Nicholas & Trabasso, 1979). Enablements are events or states that are necessary (according to the counterfactual test) but not sufficient; that is, simply adding the event or state to the conditions of the story world does not by itself lead to the second event.

Based on this definition of causation, Trabasso and Sperry defined the notion of a causal chain in a narrative. Opening events are those that "introduce the protagonist(s), set the time and locale, and initiate the story's action" (1985:605). Closing events are those that pertain to the final disposition of the protagonist's goal. The causal chain consists of all those causal links that lead from the opening to the closing; other events are classified as "dead ends." Causal chain analysis allows one to predict a variety of indices of comprehension.

For example, Trabasso and Sperry found that the rated importance of an event was related to whether the event was on the causal chain and by the number of causal links to the event; Trabasso and van den Broek (1985) found that the causal chain variables also predicted recall and summarization.

Lehnert (1982) provided a related analysis based on the causal connections between events that have affective valence for characters and the mental states related to those events. She defined a system of fifteen primitive plot units based on the different types of possible causal relationships between a pair of positive events, negative events, or mental states. For example, a "success" plot unit is defined as a mental state actualizing a positive event; a "resolution" is a positive event terminating a negative event. These primitive plot units are combined to form complex plot units for narratives involving single or multiple characters, and the overall structure of the plot is derived from the resulting causal connection graph structure. This theoretical analysis provides the basis for an artificial intelligence system that would summarize simple stories. Lehnert's approach is similar to that of Trabasso and colleagues in that it ties plot to the causal connections among events in the story world. However, Lehnert attempts to draw much more meaning and structure purely from the form of the network of causal connections than does Trabasso.

Problems with Chains and Plans

An essential difficulty with the description of plot in terms of causal chains and character plans in the story world is that one cannot count on information concerning chains and plans being in the text of the narrative. Although many events and actions are signaled directly in the text, many are not; instead, they must be inferred in some manner by the reader. Thus, the plot structure, to the extent that it exists in the story world, must be in the reader's mental representation of the story world, rather than exclusively in objective indicators in the text. Situating formal plot analyses at the level of story cannot explain what elements of the fictional world and the discourse readers will select as relevant and combine to construct a plot. Moreover, since what readers infer can vary over individuals, one cannot be certain what that representation is. The result is that there is no metric or analysis one can apply to identify events and their relationship consistently.

Consider, for example, the definition of causes proposed by Trabasso and Sperry (1985). They point out that the notion of cause can only be identified when the conditions of the story world are known, and such conditions must generally be inferred by the reader. Although some of these inferences are relatively consensual, many are not, and they may vary from one reader to another. Similarly, it is likely to be difficult to find agreement concerning psychological causes and motivations with narratives of any complexity. As a consequence, far from providing an objective analysis of plot structure, the notion of a causal chain is critically dependent on the details of the reader's representation of the story world and its characters, and in many cases, such representations will vary significantly over readers.

Even further difficulty might be expected if the theoretical analysis requires that events be catalogued according to types, as in Lehnert's affective-valence scheme. In extended narratives, reactions are often mixed or confused and cannot be easily qualified as negative or positive. In addition, the identification of events and their relationship to characters depends on the nature of the reader's knowledge. For example, most have little difficulty in understanding this event described in "The Wife's Story" by Ursula Le Guin:

Lodge Meeting nights, more and more often they had him to lead the singing. He had such a beautiful voice, and he'd lead off strong, and the others following and joining in, high voices and low. (1983:244)

However, the interpretation of what this event entails is quite different when one knows that the characters are wolves, and readers would not normally realize this on first reading. One of Toolan's (1995) critiques seems particularly poignant and important to us: He argued that what readers deem important in a text is an interpretative activity that depends on what readers believe is important generally and what they think the author considered important, both of which are determined by cultural background. In accord with this view, the "events" that readers isolate as salient are subject to variability.

Even accepting that plot must pertain to reader constructions, a further problem with assuming that plot structure should be located in the story world is that it ignores the potential impact of the discourse on how readers represent that structure. It does not explain, for example, what the effect might be of presenting events in flashback, the role of temporal gaps in the narrative, and so on. In particular, it seems clear that the attitude and emphasis of the narrator plays a crucial role in how readers identify plot structure, and it is likely that events and actions that the narrator implies are important are more likely to be processed more extensively than comparable events in which the narrator is uninterested. Consider, for example, a sentence from "The Father, the Son, and their Donkey," a story used by Trabasso and Sperry (1985): "They had not gone a great distance, when they met a group of pretty maidens who were returning from the town." Trabasso and Sperry argued that the proposition corresponding to "returning from town" is an example of the kind of information that readers rate as unimportant because it has few causal connections and is off the causal chain. However, it is also the case that the narrator does not mark this information as important in any way. In contrast, the same information might be presented with much more narratorial emphasis, as in the following:

They had not gone a great distance, when they met a group of pretty maidens. The girls were traveling on the same road as the father and the son, on precisely the same day, but they had already been to town and were now returning to their homes.

Our conjecture is that this emphasis is likely to lead to a higher importance rating for this information, even though the causal relationships are unchanged.

Plot Structure in the Reader

The Role of the Reader

While narratologists have not been concerned with the experience of plot per se, it would be incorrect to say that they have been insensitive to the issue of the reader's perception of the story. Plot, wrote Prince, refers to "the situations and events as presented to the receiver" (Prince, 1987:71). Rimmon-Kennan had already described the story as an abstraction of the text, or "part of a larger construct, referred to by some as the 'reconstructed' ... world", which as such "is not directly available to the reader" and therefore had to be inferred and constructed (Rimmon-Kenan, 1983:6). O'Neil claimed that the story, even at its most basic level, is a readerly construct (O'Neil, 1994) and by virtue of that "is riddled with instabilities and uncertainties" (34). Fludernik argued that "it is not temporality per se that makes narrative, and that temporality relates more to the reading process than to the context of the story" (1996:21); as a consequence, what is important is the reader's interaction with the plot. Hochman argued that readers reduce plots, or sequences of events, to what they take to be their essential meaning, or their animating principle (1985). Furthermore, narratologists have often noted that the perception of plot is dependent on an individual's competence, acquired through the experience of reading. However, apart from these glimpses of insight regarding the importance of the reader's role in the construction of story, narratological theories of plot have typically been formalist in nature. As such, and in keeping with formalist concerns, they have focused not on issues of reception and response but rather on issues related to the temporal, causal, and teleological laws governing the structure of events (Bremond, 1973; Chatman, 1978; Culler, 1975a; Forster, 1974; Genette, 1980; Propp, 1968).

Plot and Experience

A step in the direction of a more rigorous method for incorporating the experience of plot within the realm of narratological inquiry can be found in Fludernik (1996). Building on the work of Chafe, Tannen, Wolfson, and Harweg, she grounded narrativity in experience on the assumption that a similar cognitive experience underlies all narrative, be it oral or written, simple or complex, traditional or contemporary. As a general statement, this insight is sound and probably indisputable. However, it does not significantly advance our knowledge of how particular kinds of knowledge and experience interact with specific texts. Consider, for example, her discussion of postmodernist fiction. Such works pose a problem for her view that the experience of plot in narrative is comparable to the experience of the world since the narratives often seem to be deliberately constructed to make the link between the narrative and the real world difficult to discern. Fludernik addressed this problem by merely assuming that given

texts with irreconcilable, impossible plots, or absent plots that produce an "erosion of real-world parameters" (273), readers respond an-
thropomorphically by enforcing "a minimal holistic (cognitive) story
shape on what is threatening to become unreadable, unshapable textual fluidity" (274). In other words, where the story world does not
map onto anything familiar, the reader tries earnestly to make it somehow conform. Besides being an untested intuition, this does not tell
us anything about the particular representation that readers generate
to accomplish this nor what the effects of such works might be.

Similarly, Fludernik argued for a correlation between the reader's
experience of the texts' actants (character functions), and real people's experience of human action. The reader's experience of the
text characters, she claimed, involves the recognition of personal and
world knowledge as represented cognitively in frames, schemata,
and scripts (Fludernik, 1996). In other words, people have stereotypic knowledge regarding aspects of human behavior, and these
are tapped in the interpretation of literary character. This position is
comparable to the previously discussed proposals that plot pertains
to the representation of character plans or to scripted event sequences
(e.g., Schank & Abelson, 1977). Our critique is similar: Although it
is plausible to assume that a reader's representation of characters' actions is comparable to that of individuals in the world, it is important
to consider as well the impact of the discourse on that representation.
Frames for interpreting characters' actions are likely to be affected
by the attitude of the narrator and the manner in which events are
presented in the text. In other words, readers do not experience the
characters of the story world directly as they do in the real world,
but only indirectly by way of the words of the narrator. To our way
of thinking, this mediation is crucial in understanding how readers
generate a representation of the plot.

In fact, Fludernik suggested a form of mediation that is not unlike
our arguments concerning the role of the narrator. She argued that
plot structure is not to be equated simply with causality and temporality but needs to be approached "from a higher level semantic perspective which one could picture as the narrative's over-all structure"
(1996:22). This structure is supplied not by the structure of the plot
events per se, but by "the implied author's shaping intentions"
(22). In other words, the significance of the plot derives from its

dependency on the overall conceptual plan from which it is derived. Although she viewed this process as akin to immediate, as opposed to mediated, experience, the dependence on the conceptual architecture of the implied author is in fact a form of mediation. We would not deny that the readers' reaction to the implied author is important in this context. However, we think that, in many cases, the narrator is more critical for the reader's representation of plot than the implied author.

Textual Features for Plot

As indicated in our review, a central problem with viewing plot as based on the discourse is that it is difficult to find a general and consistent algorithm for identifying the crucial elements of the plot from the words of the text. On the other hand, viewing plot as based on relations in the story world would seem to discount the importance of the discourse and the manner in which the information about the story world is presented by the narrator. Our psychonarratological approach addresses both problems by assuming that the reader processes the text on the assumption that the *narrator* is signaling events and causal chains. In other words, what readers understand about the sequence of events is not what is implied by the text, but what the narrator invites the reader to infer. To carry out this analysis, we distinguish features of the text from constructions on the part of the reader. Our view is that the difficulty with many approaches to plot typology is that they attempt to deal in a uniform manner with both features and constructions. Take for example the central notion of an event. In many cases, an event might be explicitly described in the text and would constitute a textual feature. However, in other cases, events might not be described in the text at all but rather be inferred by the reader; such events would be reader constructions. Thus, an overriding difficulty in using the concept of an event in a formal analysis is that only some events are actually in the text; others may only exist in the mind of the reader. Further, readers may or may not infer any particular event depending on their knowledge and goals. As a consequence, one cannot reconstruct the plot from the text without involving readers, and what readers do in any given situation is an open, empirical question.

That being said, it is also clear that *some* plot elements can be found reliably in the text. In the next section, we provide a short summary of what we take to be essential ingredients of plot-related textual features. In many cases, we draw heavily from previous attempts at plot typology, and, indeed, we believe many of these approaches are valuable as long as one is careful to read them as descriptions of what may be found in the text rather than as a complete description of everything a reader might understand concerning plot. For ease of exposition, we distinguish two broad classes of features: those that provide information about the story and those that pertain to the discourse.

Plot Features in the Story

Story features are features of the text that provide some indication of what happens in the story world. Following the terminology of Greimas (1971), we use the term "existants" to indicate the places and things that are referred to in the text. Previously, the corresponding term "actants" has been used to refer to individuals who play a fundamental role in the structure of the plot. However, such a definition would seem to beg the question of what that plot structure is, and in our view this definition would be difficult to sustain as an objective definition based solely on the text. Consequently, we use a more neutral definition of actant, namely, any individual who, on the basis of the text, can be seen to engage in planful, intentional behavior. Corresponding to the definition of Trabasso and Sperry (1985), we define a (textual) event feature as a set of statements that indicate existants or actants have changed in some way. The text also provides information about how events are related to one another. However, as indicated earlier, there are difficulties in limiting potential causes to those that can be identified explicitly in the text itself because what one may infer about the causes of various events is shaped by the potentially variable details of readers' constructions. Thus, as we discuss later, we assume that causal chains are reader constructions, not textual features. A different conception is needed to identify causal information in the text.

We argue that what the text provides is information about causal *event contingencies*. An event contingency is textual information that indicates that a given textual event causes another textual event given some collection of assumptions concerning the story world. This is similar to the method used to identify causes developed by Trabasso and Sperry (1985); however, we do not assume that all the assumptions concerning the story world that might be necessary for a coherent causal inference are generally available as textual features. Our definition of a contingency is only that if some set of assumptions *were* to be made about the story world, the causal inference would follow based on the text. Because the assumptions about the story world are potentially variable, the contingencies might license different inferences for different readers. However, our point is that the contingencies themselves, which provide the information for those inferences, can be reliably identified in the text.

An example may make this distinction more clear. Consider the following fragment (from William Faulkner's "Honor"):

There was a fellow named White lost a thousand one night. He kept on losing and I wanted to quit but I was winner and he wanted to play on, plunging and losing every pot. He gave me a check and I told him it wasn't any rush, to forget it, because he had a wife out in California. (1950:562)

A likely causal inference in this set of events is that the narrator's winning is a cause of the poker game continuing, despite the fact that the narrator wanted to quit. However, this inference is not in the text. Instead, it must be drawn by the reader and, consequently, should be viewed as a reader construction. In particular, the inference can only be drawn if the reader assumes that in the story world it is socially unacceptable for the winner to deny the loser a chance to recoup his or her loses. Thus, the contingency in this case is that there would be a causal relationship between winning and the game continuing if some assumptions concerning social norms in the story world were made. A variety of other event contingencies can also be found in the excerpt given other possible (but perhaps less likely) assumptions. For example, the fact that White had a wife in California might be a cause of White's wanting to play on if it were assumed that he was in desperate financial straits, that he needed money to support her, and that poker was the only way in which he could get a suitable amount of money. Similarly, "plunging" might be inferred to be a cause of losing, if it were assumed that some styles of poker play are more effective than others. In each case, the contingency refers to the potential relationship that may or may not be causal depending on the assumptions that one brings to the analysis. In theory, there are a limitless number of possible event contingencies that one could identify. However, because event contingencies are only relevant if readers consider them, we need only be concerned in practice with those that are based on assumptions about the story world readers are likely to harbor.

Character goals are a special type of cause. They are internal, psychological events that provide a cause of other subgoals and events in the story world. We analyze the textual features relevant to goals in the same way: Sometimes the causal link is specified in the text, but more often than not, it must be inferred. The causal contingencies among goals and between goals and character actions provide the information that readers can use to make such inferences. Consider, for example, the following excerpt from "Miss Bracegirdle Does Her Duty" by Stacy Aumonier:

> She could do no good in the room. She could not recall the dead to life. Her only mission was to escape. Any minute people might arrive. The chambermaid, the boots, the manager, the gendarmes ... visions of gendarmes arriving armed with swords and notebooks vitalized her almost exhausted energies. She was a desperate woman. Fortunately now she had not to worry about the light. She sprang once more at the door and tried to force it open with her fingers. The result hurt her and gave her pause. If she was to escape she must *think*, and think intensely. She mustn't do anything rash and silly; she must just think and plan calmly.
>
> She examined the lock carefully. (1974:35)

In this case, one may analyze the character's planning as follows: The character has the goal of escaping from the room; this provides a cause for the action of trying to force the door open with her fingers; when this attempt fails, the goal provides the cause for a subgoal of thinking and planning calmly, which in turn is a cause of examining the lock carefully. However, all these causal relations require a set of background assumptions concerning the story world. For example, interpreting the action of forcing the door open with one's fingers as an attempt to escape from the room entails assuming that in the story world there are no other obvious methods of escape and that the design of the door is such that it might plausibly yield to an attempt.

Of course, in many cases some of the assumptions that support a causal contingency can be found elsewhere in the text. For example, in "Miss Bracegirdle Does Her Duty" there is an explicit description prior to this excerpt of how the doorknob comes off the door, which is crucial for understanding the action of trying to force the door. Similarly, causal relationships are also indicated explicitly in some cases using, for example, words such as "because," "since," or "consequently." In our terminology, we identify such relationships as causal contingencies in which no additional assumptions are necessary. It is also clear that a large number of events and causal relations have no explicit mention in the text. For example, in the excerpt from Faulkner's "Honor," one presumes that the game being played involved a sequence of events such as shuffling cards, dealing hands, and betting money. However, since such events and their relations are inferred by the reader, we treat them as reader constructions rather than textual features. Some hypotheses concerning important aspects of such constructions are discussed in a subsequent section.

Plot Features in the Discourse

Aspects of the discourse also can be found in the text. We discuss two such features will be central to our hypotheses concerning reader constructions. First are what we refer to as *epistemic features*. These features indicate what the narrator knows or believes about the events and plans in the story world. Sometimes epistemic features take the form of explicit evaluations of those events. Consider, for example, the following excerpt from Le Carré's *The Tailor of Panama*:

There are several ways for a large-bodied young man with a blue-and-white bookmaker's brolly to get out of a small car in pelting rain. Osnard's – if it was he – was ingenious but flawed. His strategy was to start opening the umbrella inside the car and reverse buttocks-first in an ungainly crouch, at the same time whisking the brolly after and over him while opening it the rest of the way in a single triumphant flourish. (1997:26)

The narrator in this case provides an explicit appraisal of Osnard's manner of getting out of the car: "ingenious but flawed." In other cases, the narrator's evaluations may be conveyed implicitly by the choice of words or phrasing. For example, the vocabulary "triumphant flourish" implicitly provides an evaluation of the manner in which the act was performed and the character's demeanor at the time. In either case, the critical distinction is that such information pertains to the narrator's cognition and interpretation rather than to the events of the story world per se.

Index features indicate what the narrator expects the reader to know or understand concerning the plot. These function similarly to inference invitations discussed in Chapter 3: Although the inferences that readers may draw concerning the plot are not properly thought of as being a feature of the text, the invitations to draw those features are. Many of such inference invitations take the form of implicatures, that is, inferences that are licensed by the assumption that the narrator is rational and cooperative. Examples can be found in this excerpt from "The Office" by Alice Munro:

> Several times after this I found notes on my door. I intended not to read them, but I always did. His accusations grew more specific. He had heard voices in my room. My behaviour was disturbing his wife when she tried to take her afternoon nap. (I never came in the afternoons, except on weekends.) He had found a whiskey bottle in the garbage. (1996:310–11)

The final sentence invites the inference that one of the notes falsely accused the narrator of drinking whiskey in the office. Although the inference that the note pertained to the whiskey bottle might be drawn on the basis of local coherence processes (cf. Graesser et al., 1994), an implicature is required to identify this accusation as false. In particular, if the narrator *did* consume the whiskey, that fact would clearly be relevant to the interpretation of the accusation. Because a cooperative narrator would provide such relevant information, one can infer that the narrator did not consume the whiskey and that the accusation is false. In this context, the sentence, "He had found a whiskey bottle in the garbage" is the textual signal that enables such processes to unfold. In particular, the sentence is an index feature because it indicates what the narrator expects the reader to be able to understand.

Reader Constructions for Plot

Following our general approach to psychonarratology, we propose that one of the most important processes coloring readers' construction of plot is that readers treat the narrator as a conversational participant. In particular, we hypothesize that readers represent not the plans and events of the story world, but rather that which the narrator seems to convey concerning those plots and events. What this means is that readers are not directly concerned with the what happens in the story world, but instead with what the narrator implies is important or interesting about what happens.

There are some important limitations to this proposal. Certainly, many aspects of the story world are portrayed explicitly in the text but do not seem relevant to the narrator's apparent intent or message. Readers may process such features, and they may have some impact on their interpretation of the story, separate from narratorial importance or intent. Consider the following sentence from "The Office":

So I got up and went to the window and looked down into the empty Sunday street through the slats of the Venetian blind, to avoid the accusing vulnerability of his fat face and tried out a cold voice that is to be heard frequently in my thoughts but has great difficulty getting out of my cowardly mouth. (Munro, 1996:306)

The fact that there was a Venetian blind on the window, that the street was empty, and that it was Sunday do not have an obvious relationship to the message the narrator appears to convey, but it could easily have some impact on the reader's interpretation of the situation in the story world. However, our suggestion is that, under most circumstances, such information is processed only in the service of understanding the narrator. That is, the reader is generally interested in what the narrator is trying to say, and if such details are not relevant to that understanding they may have little direct impact on the reader's constructions.

Another important exception is related to unreliable narrators. In this case, the narrator's description and perception of the story world may be suspect, and readers may be led to devise their own account of the story world, independent of what the narrator implies is relevant or important. In "Haircut" by Ring Lardner, for example, the narrator describes a character in superficially positive terms, but the reader is led by the events of the story world to generate a quite negative appraisal of that character and his actions. Related to this are narrators with limited knowledge of the story world. Often in such cases, the reader may be invited to attend to or draw inferences concerning the story world that go beyond the knowledge that the narrator professes. Mystery stories, in which clues may be found in the text even though they are ostensibly unnoticed by the narrator, provide one such example.

Story Lines

Corresponding to the notion of causal chains developed by Trabasso and colleagues, we hypothesize that readers typically attempt to identify a sequence of events in the story world that link the important events of the story world in order to make a point. We refer to this as the represented story line. Crucially, though, readers attempt to identify the point that the narrator is trying to make, not a point that might be evident from an objective depiction of the events in the story. For example, in Douglas Adams's *A Hitchhiker's Guide to the Galaxy*, the protagonist narrowly escapes when Earth is destroyed by an alien race. Those events by themselves might suggest an overarching message involving revenge, triumph over adversity, or sentimental attachment to our world. However, in this case, the narrator is clearly making a humorous point regarding the intractability of bureaucracy, and we suspect that these other ideas are unlikely to occur to the reader.

Character Plans

A similar distinction can be made with respect to goal structures and plans. Readers may generate a representation of the plans possessed by various actants in the story world. However, what is important in this regard is what the narrator highlights with respect to such plans, not what might be plausibly inferred from behavior of characters in the story world. For example, in "The Office," the protagonist is a housewife and writer who plans to rent an office in which to do her writing. From the circumstances of her life and the events of the story world, one might infer that the goal of this plan is to find an environment for writing that is free of noise and interruptions. However, the narrator implies that the goal is somewhat different and instead relates to a need for a personal space devoted specifically to the task of writing. Our hypothesis is that under most circumstances readers would be more likely to represent the latter goal rather than the former.

Empirical Evidence

As a demonstration of the central role of the narrator in the interpretation of plot, we report a simple study of the effect of narratorial point on the processing of characters' plans.[2] The essential point of this study is that readers' representations of plans do not depend purely on what information about a character's plans are provided in the text, but also on what readers infer the narrator wishes to communicate about such plans. The manipulation was simply to vary what the narrator said was important concerning events in the story world, and we measured the effect this had on readers' interpretations of the described events and plans.

In this study, the materials we used were artificial and based on those used by Richards and Singer (2001). The experimental materials consisted of twenty short passages with the same simple structure: Two characters have a common goal and carry out a coordinated plan for achieving that goal. An example is shown in Table 4.1. In this case, the common goal was to arrange a trip to Banff, and this would be achieved if each character succeeds in his part of the task. In particular, Phillip has to borrow a car, and Andy must reserve a room. We refer to the overarching, common goal as the superordinate goal and each character's part in the plan as a subgoal. The main part of each passage consisted of two episodes, each devoted to a character's attempt to achieve his or her respective subgoal. To disguise the stereotypic structure of the experimental passages, they were interspersed among eighteen other passages with an entirely different structure. Sentences were read one at a time on a computer screen. After each passage, readers answered a simple yes/no comprehension question.

There were four conditions in the study, constructed by manipulating two sentences, the leading "passage point" sentence and the "succeed/fail" sentence at the end of the first subgoal episode. The passage point sentence could indicate that the narrator wished to

---

[2] These data were previously reported by Dixon and Bortolussi (2000).

TABLE 4.1. *Example of Narratorial Point and Subgoal Manipulations*

	Sentence	
Sentence Type	Superordinate Point	Subordinate Point
Passage Point	It seemed like Philip and Andy always ran into obstacles whenever they tried to take a holiday together.	At some times of the year, it can be really difficult to find a hotel room in Banff.
Introduction	Once, Philip and Andy wanted to go away for spring break.	
Introduction	They had saved up enough money to drive to Banff.	
Introduction	They both were avid skiers and were looking forward to the trip.	
Subgoal 1	Philip planned on borrowing a car.	
Subgoal 1	He asked all of his friends but nobody could lend him one.	
Subgoal 1	At the last minute, he asked his father if he could borrow the family car.	
	Subgoal 1 Succeeds	Subgoal 2 Fails
Succeed/Fail	Philip's father said the car has just been fixed, so he could take it.	Philip's father said the car would need to be fixed before he could take it.
Subgoal 2	Andy needed to book a hotel room in Banff.	
Subgoal 2	He called several motels, but they were all full.	
Subgoal 2	He eventually got an accommodations guide and found several inns that he didn't know about.	
Subgoal 2	Andy was able to book them a room at a small motel right downtown.	
Target	Andy packed his bag and waited out in front of his house.	
Conclusion	Andy had also packed a lunch for the long trip.	
Conclusion	They planned to rent all their ski equipment in Banff.	
Conclusion	The weather report said that Banff had just received 20 cm of new snow.	

make a point about the superordinate goal (in this example, that Phillip and Andy often have problems taking vacations together), or it could suggest a point concerning only the second subgoal (here, that Banff hotel rooms are hard to come by). The succeed/fail sentence could indicate that the initial attempt at achieving the first subgoal either succeeded or failed. The critical question was how readers would react when the first subgoal failed. Consider what should happen when the narrator emphasizes the superordinate goal. In this case, if the first subgoal attempt fails, readers should need to make further inferences concerning how the superordinate goal will be achieved. We assume that normally this involves hypothesizing a further attempt at accomplishing the subgoal; in the present example, readers may infer that Phillip would have to get the car fixed before going on the trip. Next, consider how readers may react when the narrator's point is related only to the second subgoal. In this case, the entire episode concerning the first subgoal is largely irrelevant to the narrator's point, and the reader need not be especially concerned about whether the subgoal succeeds or fails. Consequently, we would not necessarily expect readers to spend additional effort drawing inferences about further subgoal attempts.

To assess whether readers make such inferences, we examined reading time at the point in the narrative when the episodes need to be reconciled. In Table 4.1 this is indicated as the target sentence. To make sense of this sentence, readers would typically need information about the outcome of the first episode. For example, to understand why Andy is waiting outside, readers would have to retrieve information about the car that Andy had planned to borrow. Reading time provides an index of how available the information from the first subgoal was. Relatively fast reading times indicate that readers had little difficulty integrating the information from the subgoal episodes, and by implication, that the outcome of the first episode was readily available. On the other hand, slower reading times imply more difficulty, presumably because the information from the first subgoal episode was less available. If readers draw additional inferences concerning the fate of the first subgoal, that additional processing should make information concerning the first subgoal more accessible (e.g., Craik & Lockhart, 1972; Craik & Watkins, 1973), and, as a consequence, reading time for the target sentence should be relatively fast. In sum, we predict that when the narrator emphasizes the superordinate goal, the target sentence should be read more quickly following a failed first subgoal; when the narrator emphasizes only the second subgoal, there is no reason to expect a difference in reading time.

The results are shown in Figure 4.1. As anticipated, when the superordinate goal is emphasized, reading time for the target sentence

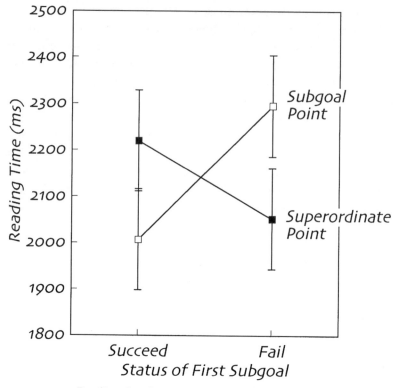

FIGURE 4.1. Reading time for target sentence as a function of first subgoal status and narratorial point. Error bars indicate the size of 95% confidence intervals, adjusted for pairwise comparisons.

is substantially faster following a failed attempt of the first subgoal. We attribute this to the additional processing that is needed to infer how the subgoal is ultimately achieved and the consequent increase in availability of that information. Similar results were reported by Richards and Singer (2001). The passages in that study were similar to those used here, except that there was no narratorial-point sentence at the beginning of the passage. Without any other indication, readers may assume that the narrator's point is related to the superordinate goal and process the subgoal failure accordingly. However, Richards and Singer had a somewhat different interpretation of this effect: They hypothesized that readers only needed to integrate the information concerning the two subgoals when the first subgoal succeeded, not when it failed, and that the additional reading time in the "succeed" condition was attributed to this process of integration.

Surprisingly, when the narrator's point is related to the second subgoal, readers took more time following a successful attempt of the first subgoal. One possibility is that the successful outcomes are more obvious and predictable than the failures, and, as a consequence, are easier to retrieve when the information needs to be integrated during the comprehension of the target sentence. The superordinate goal, for example, might provide a basis for retrieving successful subgoals but not unsuccessful ones. Alternatively, readers may need to draw some inference concerning how the first subgoal is achieved while reading the target sentence. In any event, the critical result from our perspective is that a change in the narratorial point leads to a clear difference in how readers process information about the characters' goals and plans.

To evaluate the strength of the evidence provided by the data in Figure 4.1, two models were fit to the results. The first incorporated additive effects of the first subgoal factor and the narratorial-point factor; the second included the interaction as well. The likelihood ratio was $\lambda = 72.48$ in favor of the model including the interaction. Thus, there is clear evidence that the effect of the subgoal varies as a function of the narrator's point.

Summary

As a heuristic for discussing various approaches to narrative plot, in this chapter we distinguished analyses that begin with the words of the discourse from those that begin with the events of the story world. A typical discourse approach is the development of story grammars: formal analyses of the narrative that identify the constituent elements of a story and their relationships. Our review suggested that story grammars may not be sufficiently general, may not in themselves capture the most interesting regularities in stories, and have an uncertain relationship to the processing and competence of actual readers. In story-world approaches, the relationships among events in the story world are assumed to be comparable to relationships among events in the world, and readers are assumed to process both similarly. A principal difficulty in such approaches is that events are often not stated in the text and must be inferred. In addition, locating plot in the relationship among story-world events would seem to neglect the impact of the discourse itself.

The solution we propose is to locate plot in the reader, rather than in the text or the story world, and to distinguish carefully features of the text that provide information about events and the constructions readers build to represent those events. In particular, we assume that the narrator has an important role in this process by signaling which events or relationships are relevant or important. We proposed event contingencies as the important source of information about the story world, and epistemic and index features as providing information about the narrator's evaluation of those events. We assumed that, based on this information, readers construct representations of story lines and character plans. The results from a reading time experiment were used as evidence that the narrator's point affects how readers process characters' coordinated goals.

5

Characters and Characterization

After plot, the most intuitively important aspect of a story concerns the characters. For example, in some simple stories, characters create the plot: The villain creates a problem that the hero must overcome. In some complex, literary narratives, characterization would seem to be an overriding motivation of the implied author, with the events of the narrative merely serving to provide information about the characters. Not surprisingly, then, character and characterization have been a productive area of scholarship in narratology and literary studies. Important work has also been done in linguistics and discourse processing. Our view is that work in personality and social psychology is also directly relevant to understanding character in narrative, although the connection has not always been made in discourse processing research. In this chapter, we review some of the work in these disciplines. We then discuss some categories of features that are relevant to character in narrative and provide a general framework for how these might be used by readers. Finally, we provide some evidence on the use of characterization features by readers.

Theories of Literary Character

Theories of literary character can be situated on a continuum ranging from traditional to contemporary and more radical models. (For an excellent coverage of these theories, see Margolin, 1989, 1990b). The central issue in this debate has been the relationship between literary character and real people. Traditional theories treated literary characters uncritically as analogues of real people. However, these models came to be deemed inadequate for their excessive "psychologizing," that is, the tendency to analyze the personalities, deduce the motivations, and fill in the unwritten histories of purely indeterminate, fictional entities. Underlying this criticism is the logic that narrative characters are not real people and formally cannot be treated as such. Instead, more contemporary approaches treated character as an aggregate of textual signs (e.g., Fisch, 1990; Hamon, 1977; Tomachevsky, 1965). This approach has the value of directing attention to those features in the text that actually provide the information concerning the characters. However, from the point of view of the reader, such an approach seems incomplete because of the undeniable tendency of both sophisticated and naïve readers to respond to literary characters as real people. Thus, a variety of theorists have emphasized the role of readers' real-world knowledge and expectations in the interpretation and understanding of literary character. Each of these theoretical positions will be described in turn.

Characters as People

Critical approaches that analyze characters in terms of their psychological personality traits typically tend to fill in the textual gaps with hypotheses about the motivations, conscious or unconscious, that drive characters' actions. Psychoanalytical criticism, which falls within this category, focuses sometimes on the character and sometimes on the author, whose work is considered to contain clues or signs about his or her own personality and psychology. An intriguing example of the latter is Jean-Pierre Richard's (1954) analysis of some stylistic features of Flaubert's novel *Emma Bovary*. After observing that food and eating recur frequently in the novel, Richard attempted to shed light on the author's psychology through an analysis of the metaphorical function of food consumption in the novel. Activities related to eating, such as absorption and digestion were said to correlate to spiritual impulses, such as the desire or appetite for learning; the nausea caused by food was associated with the sense of impotence in the pursuit of knowledge; and so on.

A story whose heroine has been analyzed in a similar fashion is Borges's "Emma Zunz." The story is about a young woman who, after hearing about the death of her father, commits the perfect crime, murdering her boss in the belief that he has wronged her father and thereby caused him a lifetime of suffering. Omitting descriptions of thought processes unrelated to the murder plot itself, the narrative focuses predominantly on the action and provides only a very schematic depiction of Emma Zunz. Yet some critics have interpreted her murder as the result of an Oedipus complex. In this vein, Ortega (1971) claimed that Emma sees her father in his boss, Lowenthal, concluding that by murdering the employer, she succeeds in killing her incestuous instinct. Similarly, Kushigian (1989) argued that Emma sees her father in the sailor with whom she has sex prior to murdering Lowenthal, and Murillo (1968) inferred that Emma had actually had incestuous relations with her father (1968:148). Brodzki (1985) concluded that the story is about the recovery of the female self, and Kushigian (1989) maintained that Emma didn't kill Lowenthal to avenge her father at all but rather to punish men, thereby affirming her independence as a woman. In a similar vein, Norman Holland (1987) concluded that the character Miss Emily, in Faulkner's "A Rose for Emily," is driven by Oedipal and anal unconscious motives. In particular, he explains her murder and retention of her lover's corpse as motivated by Miss Emily's identification with her father, which leads her to take on "his iron will, his strength, and his brutality, regressing from the little girl's Oedipal wish to have her father to the pre-oedipal, phallic wish to be her father" (297).

Suffice it to say that these interpretations have been advanced in the absence of any supporting evidence in the text. Instead, the characters are assumed to have coherent, fully developed, and consistent personalities. Like real people, they are assumed to have psychological motives and unconscious drives. On the basis of this assumption, critics supply whatever information is missing from the text to construct a cohesive image and persuasive narrative about the character in question. The underlying motives and drives are assumed to be accessible through the inferential procedures of personality theory and psychotherapy.

Characters as Textual Signs

Rebelling in part against the excessive lengths to which this speculative psychologizing often lead, analytical models inspired by French Structuralism emphasized rather the textual signs that constitute characters. One of the most prominent of these studies was Philip Hamon's article "Pour un statut sémiologique du personnage" (1977). On the assumption that the sense ("signifié") of the characters is accessible through systematic analysis, he devised several tables or charts in which specific categories of information are listed as column headings, and the absence or presence of each category with respect to different characters is tallied by plus or minus symbols in the corresponding cells. The categories of information included semantic axes (sex, geographic origin, ideology, money), functions (reception of a helper, order, acceptance of a contract, reception of information, reception of a benefit, victorious combat), modes of determination (single qualification, reiterated qualification, single virtuality, reiterated virtuality, single action, reiterated action), and so on. Although Hamon's complete analysis was much more complex, the essence of the approach is to conceive of characters as a checklist of signs. Although Hamon recognized that character is as much a reconstruction of the reader as a construction of the text ("autant une reconstruction du lecteur qu'une construction du texte"; 119), he understood by reconstruction a process that evolves gradually over the course of the reading and that consists of piecing together all the encoded textual signs.

However, purely formal models of this sort have their own limitations. In particular, numerous scholars openly acknowledged that such approaches are unintuitive in their disregard for the natural, default tendency of readers, professional and amateur, to respond to literary characters as if they were real people. That is, the processing of literary characters in terms of real-life models would seem to be a natural response, and many literary theorists have acknowledged this to some extent (Chatman, 1972; Frow, 1986; Gergen, 1990; Harvey, 1965; Hochman, 1985; Knapp, 1997; Phelan, 1989; Richardson, 1997; Walsh, 1997b; Werth, 1995). Chatman argued that "the understanding of character – our chief pleasure in reading modern fiction – depends, and depends radically . . . on outside knowledge," adding that the "inferences that are necessary to the recognition of character traits can only be formed by reference to the real world" (Chatman, 1972:78). Quoting from Martin (1986), Margolin remarked that "our sense that fictional characters are uncannily similar to people is not something to be dismissed or ridiculed, but a crucial feature of narration that requires explanation" (1989:10). Baruch Hochman stressed that fictional characters are both configured by the text and generated in the minds of readers who interpret them in terms of real-life models, so that they both take root in and transcend the text (1985). These admissions constitute an advance over previous research in their recognition of the constructed nature of literary characters. Intuitive and undeveloped as they are, they mark a theoretical turning point in literary studies, exercising a decisive blow to prescriptive and normative formalist and poststructuralist theories that advocated against "naïve" anthropomorphizing responses to character.

However, this conceptual advance raised an important philosophical question: If literary characters are not the same as real people nor merely an aggregate of textual signs, what are they? In this debate (e.g., Hochman, 1985; Margolin, 1989; Pavel, 1986), some have concentrated on the basic differences between literary characters and real people, while others have focused on the similarities, both drawing conclusions about how these similarities or differences affected the reader's response to characters.

A proponent of the first approach was Margolin (1989). Margolin stressed the fundamental distinction between "non-actual" and real people. A central element of this distinction is the fact that literary characters are unlike real humans in that they are "ontologically thin," incomplete, and schematic in nature, existing only as "a series of discontinuous states or phases," possessing no "continuity or identity over time," and failing to "conform to any pattern of ontological regularity or even consistency," as required by logic (Margolin, 1989:10–11). Presumably, this makes the interpretation of literary character more ambiguous than that of real people. A subtext of this conclusion is that because logical ambiguity is an essential property of literary characters, speculative and externally motivated gap filling to create consistent constructs is unwarranted and misleading. In contrast, a proponent of the similarities between literary and real characters is Pavel (1986). Pavel rejected the belief that literary characters are "reducible to clusters of definite descriptions" (36) and argued instead that in speaking about literary characters, people think of them as "individuated objects, independent of the objects' properties" (37). As a consequence, he concluded that "there is no detectable difference between nonfictional and fictional proper names" (37). If literary characters are like real people in fundamental ways, then it appears legitimate to bring real-world knowledge and expectations to bear on the process of making sense of literary characters.

One important consequence of this debate is that it paves the road for future studies on the importance of extratextual considerations that are relevant in the construction of character. However, in essence these studies typically remain within the confines of text-based approaches and do not advance our knowledge of how real-world knowledge is used by real readers. For example, Margolin (1989) conceded the importance of reader inferences in the processes of interpreting characters but described character inferences as a fundamentally rule-bound activity regulated by cultural and inherent literary rules. Consequently, he argued, the insertion of characters in a literary context obligates us to process them in terms of interliterary norms and conventions. This faith in the regulative function of textual features led him to the conclusion that readers cannot apply their own world view if it clashes with the generic or aesthetic rules of the text. Indeed, character inferences are not given in isolation, but in relation to other characters, and are thus processed in relational terms. Margolin also pointed to the importance of reader inferences in the process of supplying information to fill in the gaps left open by the text. Noting that textual features provide only a schematic presentation of characters, he rightly concluded that readers fill in the missing information through inferential procedures. However, because his approach is driven by a "textually oriented theory of character" (20), his conceptualization of the inference process accounted only for those inferences that are constrained by textual and literary conventions. What is not included, as he acknowledged, is the "reader's comprehension process and its stages" (20). This process, as well as the nature and specificity of the readers' construction of literary characters, can only be properly understood through an empirical investigation of readers' cognitive processes activated during reading.

Some linguistic analyses are relevant to understanding character as textual signs. For example, Catherine Emmott (1997) dedicated a chapter of her book *Narrative Comprehension* to the reader's mental creation of character representations. But as mentioned in Chapter 1, Emmott's objective was to describe the conditions necessary for competent comprehension – in other words, what readers need to do to achieve coherence and make sense of narrative texts. In particular, she was interested in how readers interpret pronouns and how they use grammatical clues throughout the text to interpret them. However, her description does shed light on the mechanics of mental character representation. Based on the common-sense intuition that different information about characters appears at different points throughout the text, she rightly concluded that "only a subset of the total information that we know about a character is true at any one time," and that this subset "needs to be held in the entity representation of that character so that it can be separately drawn on" (81). In her view, entity representations consist of overlapping subsets of information that are foregrounded separately at different times throughout the text. This framework would seem to provide a sound basis for the empirical investigation of memory cuing and retrieval processes during comprehension of extended texts. However, Emmot herself does not advance this program beyond this initial intuitive analysis.

Characters as Constructions

While it is indisputable, as Margolin (1989) argued, that literary characters cannot be considered real people from a logical point of view, from a *cognitive* perspective, there is more to the story. If we consider how real people actually perceive and interpret individuals in the world around them, the distinction between real people and literary characters is less apparent. For one, no individual in the world is known to any other in his or her totality (that is, in all his or her states or phases) because the available information about others around us is necessarily discontinuous, schematic, and incomplete. Commonly, whole aspects of an individual's life are unknown to even those closest to him or her. For example, a wife may know few details of her husband's childhood, close associates at work may know little of each other's home life, and so on. Stanley Fish had a similar idea in mind when he wrote that we don't know real people any more directly than we know characters in a novel (Fish, 1989). Baruch Hochman (1985) endorsed the same position, arguing that although real people are more ontologically complete, we can never fully get to know them. In contrast, although literary characters are more schematic, we often have the sense that we know them better than real people and that they have more unity and consistency.

Our view is that even though literary characters and real people are ontologically distinct, they are processed in much the same way. In other words, literary characters are processed *as if* they were real people, and real people are processed in terms analogous to the categories brought to bear on the interpretation of literary characters. There are three aspects to this position: (1) the relationships used to understand literary characters are similar to those used with real people; (2) the codes and conventions of description are similar; and (3) the nature of the inference processes is similar.

Similarity in Relationships

Margolin (1989) argued that literary characters must be interpreted in relation to other characters because these relations are charged with significance in the narrative. Certainly authors can create accessible and meaningful relations among characters (symmetry, opposition, analogies, etc.). However, real individuals too are perceived as deriving at least a part of their identity from their sphere of personal and social interactions and relationships, as well as from the social circles and general context in which they conduct their lives. Although the relationships among real individuals may not be as clear or unambiguous as those found among literary characters, there is no reason to think that readers process these relationships differently.

Similarity of Codes and Conventions

We argue as well that real people are just as susceptible to being interpreted from the perspective of "codes...conventions, stereotypes, clichés" as literary characters, and many times the codes and conventions are the same. We have heard of someone's behavior described as conforming to the "Oedipus complex" or in terms of epithets such as "anal," or literary adjectives such as quixotic, faustian, bovaresque, and donquanesque. No one would deny that in their interpretation of others, real people tend naturally to construct other individuals on the basis of previously held notions, stereotypes, and experience. In fact, one could argue that this is an inevitable mental activity given the constraints of human perception and knowledge. We suspect that in our analysis and interpretation of other individuals, we are no less guided by conventionalized knowledge and stereotypical patterns of thought than we are in our response to literary characters. Indeed, in some cases, literature may supply the stereotypes that are applied to real-world characters. Therefore, the same literary and cultural conventions that Margolin described as constraining factors in the construction of literary characters also constrains the perception of people in real life.

Similarity of Inference Processes

Finally, we argue that in processing both fictional characters and real people, we draw on the same knowledge base of experience with people and situations. Restricting inferences concerning literary characters to textual properties understates the role of real-life knowledge in readers' inferential processes, and it presupposes the existence of purely hypothetical, ideal readers who can decode textual signs in a programmatic fashion. One of the fundamental premises of this book is that such an ideal-reader framework fails to account adequately for real readers' processing of texts. With respect to the processing of character, it underestimates the potent influence of the real-world knowledge. As we develop later, the actions, thoughts, and beliefs of characters in the story world do not transparently provide information about characterization. Instead, that behavior must be interpreted as signs, and the reader's knowledge of people in the world is what allows those signs to be decoded.

Social Cognition

Research in the field of social psychology known as "people perception" provides evidence that, from the perspective of human perception, literary characters and real people are processed in terms of similar sense-making strategies. Philosophy, literary studies, and psychology have come a long way in their theorizing about the individual, or "self," and the developments in each field have evolved along parallel paths. Some of the predominant conceptual frameworks for defining human nature and behavior include trait theory, role theory, and humanistic theories (Potter & Wetherell, 1987). Very succinctly, trait theory regards the individual as being composed of a set of consistent, identifiable, and quantifiable personality traits (e.g., extroverted versus introverted); role theory considers the conscious or unconscious roles that people assume in the course of their social interactions; and humanistic or romantic theories presuppose the existence of an essential, central, or authentic self that may be lost, hidden, forgotten, and needs to be recuperated through a questlike search. We will not attempt to assess the relative strengths and weaknesses of these approaches. The important insight, though, is that variants of any or all of these views might be used by individuals in trying to make sense of their own and others' behavior. We suggest that similar sense-making strategies may be applied by readers attempting to interpret and judge the behavior of literary characters.

There are many possible determinants of the strategies that people use. Some of these include the values imparted through past child rearing and educational practices, personal beliefs and preferences, dominant patterns in one's immediate social circles, and so on. In general, we suppose that people apply those sense-making strategies with which they are familiar, drawing on real-life experience to supply the mechanisms they need to make sense of individuals and characters in a wide variety of different contexts. As research in social psychology has indicated, the application of these strategies is not always consistent, and different theories and frameworks can be applied to different people (Wilder, 1978). A similar conclusion regarding the variability of reading strategies was reached by the literary critic George Dillon, who observed that processing strategies are probabilistic in nature: "They are based on expectations and likelihoods; they are not categorical" (Dillon, 1978:xxvi). They belong to the realm of performance, not competence.

Attribution Theory

Although it is clear that people have a range of strategies for interpreting the behavior of others, much of the theoretical analysis in the field of social cognition has been based on the notion of traits. A trait is assumed to be a relatively stable internal disposition that is related to certain classes of behavior. An important theoretical framework for understanding how people use traits in reasoning about behavior is attribution theory. According to the influential analysis of Kelley (1967), an individual's behavior might be attributed to characteristics of the situation or role in which the individual is, characteristics of the object to which the behavior is directed, or enduring dispositions of the individual. Consistency over time provides the primary tool for making such attributions. For example, if a given individual is observed to be friendly on many occasions, one would be able to infer a stable trait of friendliness. On the other hand, if people all behave similarly in a given situation, then one would be able infer that the behavior is caused by the situation, not enduring dispositions.

However, often attributions are based on a single observed behavior in a single situation. In that case, observers must use their prior knowledge of the range of behaviors people are likely to produce in that situation and decide, for example, whether that behavior should be attributed to the situation or the person. Under such circumstances, people often make what has been termed the "fundamental attribution error" of attributing the cause of the behavior to the individual even when there is good reason to suspect situational causes (Ross, 1977). For example, Ross, Amabile, and Steinmetz (1977) randomly assigned participants to two groups: one was to create difficult "quiz-show" questions, and the other group was to attempt to answer the questions. Observers watching the performance of the groups rated the questioners as higher in general knowledge even though they were informed that assignment to groups was random. The error in this case was to attribute the performance to an internal disposition (general knowledge) rather than to the situational constraints (it is easier to make up questions than to answer them).

Jones and Davis (1965) examined the relationship between behavior and inferred traits. A correspondent inference occurs when observers take a behavior at face value and assume that the individual has a corresponding trait. For example, inferring that an individual is friendly because he or she engages in a friendly act would be a correspondent inference. A correspondent inference would characterize an individual as either high or low on a given trait relative to the average on the basis of the distinctive effects of the action. The distinctive effects of the action mean that observing those actions leads to a gain in information about the individual.

Building on the concept of correspondent inferences, Reeder and Brewer (1979) identified several different inference schemas that might be used to identify the relationship between dispositional traits and behaviors. They conceptualized traits and behaviors as continuous dimensions that vary in degree or magnitude. In their terms, a "partially restrictive schema" indicates that a given level of a trait may be associated with a range of behaviors of similar levels. For example, an intermediate level of the trait of friendliness may be associated with a range of behaviors from moderately high to moderately low in friendliness, but very friendly or very unfriendly behaviors would be unlikely. A "hierarchically restrictive schema" indicates that a given level of a trait is associated with behaviors of the same or lower level. Skills and abilities would fall into this category, so that an individual with an intermediate level of skill may sometimes display performance below that of which he or she is capable, but would be unable to perform at levels higher than his or her ability. Reeder and Brewer described how such relationships may be modified by situational constraints and how such schemas would be used to identify traits on the basis of observed actions. Their analysis highlights the fact that actions are not transparently related to traits; instead, traits can only be inferred by using prior knowledge of the particular trait in question and its relationship to various possible behaviors.

Kenny (1991) used Anderson's (1981) weighted-average model to describe consistency and consensus in impression formation. In the weighted-average model, behaviors provide information about internal dispositions. Each behavior has a scale value that describes the implication of the behavior with respect to a given trait. For example, the behavior of spontaneously engaging a stranger in conversation would have a positive scale value for the trait of friendliness. The information from a range of behaviors is integrated by taking a weighted average of the associated scale values. Kenny used this basic idea to describe the consensus and accuracy with which traits are evaluated by different individuals. The essential idea in his analysis is that because different observers have different but overlapping sources of evidence, their evaluations of an individual's traits will be similar but not identical. However, Kenny considered the additional complication that observers may communicate their evaluations to each other, and that such evaluations may become another source of information. Kenny's model is important for our purpose because it provides a quantitative description of how trait information derived from behaviors might be integrated with explicit evaluations.

In many of the experiments on person perception, situations and behaviors have been presented as simple narrative. Consequently, the evidence on the process of inferring traits from the behaviors is directly relevant to our concerns. For example, Uleman et al. (1996) found evidence using a memory-probe technique that some inferences about traits were made immediately in the course of comprehension. In this paradigm, participants read a narrative in which a character engaged in a sequence of actions. Periodically, a probe word was presented, and participants decided whether that word had been presented previously in the text. Participants were slower to reject the probe when it was consistent with an immediately preceding action than when there was no related action. The authors argued that this effect implies that readers immediately infer traits whenever relevant actions are encountered in the text. However, this effect was small and not always observed in the reported experiments. Thus, it seems plausible to suppose that such trait inferences are not inevitably made in reading narrative, but rather are made only in the service of other interpretive processes.

In sum, attribution theory provides a number of concepts that can be applied to the understanding of characterization in narrative. Behavior of individuals can be used to make inferences about underlying dispositions or traits – that is, a behavior can be attributed to that trait. However, that inference depends on prior knowledge of the likelihood of the behavior and the trait, and a variety of relationships are possible depending on the nature of the behavior and the trait. More generally, the evidence from a range of behaviors and other sources would typically be combined in order to assess internal traits and dispositions. Although there is some evidence that such inferences can be made whenever the relevant actions are encountered, it seems more plausible to assume that they are generally made at need or during later interpretive activity.

Bayesian Analysis

A number of authors have cast the mechanics of attribution theory in terms of Bayes' theorem (e.g., Ajzen & Fishbein, 1975; Trope & Burnstein, 1975). The advantage of this approach is that it provides a uniform and consistent framework for describing how prior knowledge is used in assessing the evidence for traits, and we will use it in our subsequent discussion of character constructions. Bayes' theorem is a basic element of probability theory that allows one to manipulate conditional probabilities. In applying the theorem to attribution theory, we denote a characteristic of the situation, person, or object as T, and the action to be explained as A. Bayes' theorem can then be stated as

$$P(T \mid A) = \frac{P(A \mid T) P(T)}{P(A)} \qquad (5.1)$$

The notation $P(T \mid A)$ indicates conditional probability, that is, the probability of T given that A is true. Using $\overline{T}$ to refer to the *lack* of a given characteristic, this can be rewritten in terms of odds ratios:

$$\frac{P(T \mid A)}{P(\overline{T} \mid A)} = \frac{P(A \mid T)}{P(A \mid \overline{T})} \frac{P(T)}{P(\overline{T})} \qquad (5.2)$$

The left-hand term, $P(T \mid A)/P(\overline{T} \mid A)$, is the posterior odds of the characteristic, that is, the odds that the characteristic is present after observing the behavior. The right-hand term, $P(T)/P(\overline{T})$, is the prior odds, that is, the odds of the characteristic a priori, before observing the behavior. The middle term, $P(A \mid T)/P(A \mid \overline{T})$, is the likelihood ratio; it indicates how likely the behavior is when the characteristic is present relative to how likely it is when the characteristic is absent. In words, then, this can be rewritten as

$$\text{Posterior odds} = \text{Likelihood ratio} \times \text{Prior odds} \qquad (5.3)$$

The likelihood ratio is critical in this formulation because it describes how diagnostic the behavior is of the characteristic. For example, the behavior of spontaneously engaging strangers in conversation is diagnostic of the trait of friendliness. This means that such behavior is likely when an individual is friendly (i.e., $P(A|T)$ is large), not very likely when the an individual is not friendly (i.e., $P(A|\overline{T})$ is low), and the likelihood ratio would be substantially larger than 1. Thus, applying Equation 5.2, one could update one's prior odds of an individual being friendly to a new, larger value after observing this diagnostic behavior.

Ajzen and Fishbein (1975) described how this analysis could be used in understanding a variety of previous research on the attribution. For example, it has been found that observers are more likely to attribute behavior to an internal disposition when that behavior is displayed consistently. This result follows directly from a Bayesian analysis. For example, if an individual has a trait of friendliness, he or she is likely to display friendly behaviors consistently. Thus, the probability of displaying a consistent string of friendly behaviors, given the trait, should be much higher than doing so in the absence of the trait. This means that the likelihood ratio for the consistent behaviors would be very large, and people should be very likely to change their belief about the trait after observing such consistent behaviors. Trope and Burnstein (1975) demonstrated that in-role behaviors (that is, behaviors appropriate to the situation) are much less diagnostic of dispositional traits than out-of-role behaviors, consistent with a Bayesian analysis.

Applications to Literature

Several authors have pointed out that the mechanisms of attribution theory can be applied to understanding literary characters. For example, Pollard-Gott (1993) argued that the nature of the information provided in a novel can determine the reader's dispositional attributions. By describing a character's behavior under a variety of circumstances, a work provides information about the consistency or lack of consistency of a behavior, which in turn affects the tendency to attribute dispositional traits as causes. Pollard-Gott hypothsized that under some circumstances, the available information may bring about an "observer–actor shift," in which the reader comes to "appreciate the myriad circumstances that seem to govern the character's behavior" (506). In general, one would expect that access to a character's thoughts and feelings would lead to less of a tendency to assume that the character's behavior is determined simply by corresponding traits. Correspondingly, there would be a greater tendency to see that behavior as determined either by the situation or by an interaction between the situation and dispositional characteristics.

Some cognitive psychologists interested in literature have also taken up the issue of literary character. Gerrig and Albritton (1990) argued that readers construct characters by supplying real-life knowledge and experience. They wrote: "readers actively participate in the construction of literary worlds, and thus, literary characters. Rather than being passive recipients of information, readers venture beyond the text to explain and predict aspects of the unfolding story" (380). Gerrig and Allbritton developed three insights from the perspective of attribution theory. The first is that the fundamental attribution error predisposes readers to ignore the formulaic nature of many fictional situations. Because readers are biased to believe that character's behavior is determined by internal attributes, they fail to attribute actions and outcomes to the conventions of the genre. Thus, readers would attribute the success of a protagonist to the character's heroic traits rather than the conventional nature of the narrative. Second, Gerrig and Allbritton discussed how the mechanics of impression formation operate in a narrative work. A reader is likely to form an initial impression of a character by assimilating him or her into well-known categories. With further information and involvement, the reader may have to reorganize his or her representation to allow for complex, less stereotypic analysis of the character. Finally, Gerrig and Allbritton point out that the representation of characters may be mediated by the process of "immersion," in which readers seem to reexperience the events of the story world as if they were part of that world (cf. Gerrig, 1993).

Raap, Gerrig, and Prentice (2001) examined the role of character traits in understanding and predicting narrative events. In one study, participants read two-episode stories. In the first episode, a character acted in a manner consistent with a particular trait. At the conclusion of the second episode, readers rated a subsequent action as more expected when it was consistent with that trait. Evidence from reading times suggested that the inferences regarding traits were made as soon as the trait evidence was available. However, the trait inferences were relatively specific and did not generalize to other traits of the same general valence. These results provide general validation for the view that readers attribute traits to characters on the basis of their behavior in the story world, just as they might for individuals in the world.

Characterization Features

Previously, we argued that purely formal models of character are incomplete because characters are more than simply a collection of textual signs. However, dispensing with formalist analysis entirely would be absurd because readers' point of departure is always the clues provided by the text. How readers use their prior knowledge, expectations, and beliefs in interacting with those clues is what needs to be investigated. The first step in such an understanding is to determine the textual features of characterization, some combination of which readers encounter in any given reading. As we develop later, we argue that a central problem in characterization is how readers attribute traits to characters and how those traits evolve over the course of a narrative. To this end, we are concerned specifically with the textual information readers use to find those traits. We can distinguish three broad classes of information: story-world actions by the character, evaluations by the narrator and other characters, and indications of character change. (See also Margolin, 1989, for an elaboration of textual characterization signs.)

Story-World Actions

The simplest analysis applies to story-world actions. The idea here is simply that what a character does or says provides information about what that character is like. We assume that the inference processes in this regard are the same in nature as those that are applied to interpreting real people. In particular, readers have knowledge concerning what traits go together with what actions in the world; this is used to infer traits based on character actions. It is important to note, however, that actions do not have meaning in isolation, and can only be interpreted in the context in which they occur. In turn, this creates an inherent ambiguity in identifying the features of the text because the "situation" typically involves important constructions on the part of the reader. Indeed, the social psychology research reviewed earlier suggests that the failure to represent important aspects of the situation as possible causes of behavior is a critical determinant of attribution errors. This ambiguity is precisely the same difficulty we discussed in Chapter 4 concerning causal connections: Possible causal relationships depend on what the reader knows or represents about the circumstances of the story world and so cannot be thought of as purely textual features. Our conceptual analysis of the actions is thus comparable: We describe the available information about possible situational causes of a character's behavior using event contingencies. As described in Chapter 4, an event contingency is information that would allow a causal inference given some set of background assumptions about the story world; in this instance, of course, we are concerned with possible causes of the character's behavior.

To be precise, then, features of story-world actions consist of the observed actions given the event contingencies. As described later, we assume that these actions-plus-contingencies are used in identifying character traits. In principle, a large number of contingencies relevant to an action could be identified as textual features. Which of these are used by the reader in any instance in identifying character traits is a separate, empirical question concerning reader constructions.

Evaluations

Evaluations consist of cases in which trait descriptions are explicitly attributed to a character, either by the narrator or by another character. Evaluations by the narrator are particularly important because they may invite narratorial implicatures. As described earlier, when the narrator provides an evaluation for which there is scant support in the text, this invites the reader to attribute knowledge and experience to the narrator that would justify that evaluation. Such inferences would be based on the conversational assumption that the narrator is cooperative and providing necessary and sufficient information for understanding. Thus, when the narrator provides a seemingly unjustified evaluation of a character, the reader may infer other actions by the character that would justify that evaluation. Consider the following example from Aumonier's "Miss Bracegirdle Does Her Duty":

In the sleepy cathedral town of Easingstoke, from which she came, it was customary for everyone to speak the truth. It was customary, moreover, for everyone to lead simple, self-denying lives – to give up their time to good works and elevating thoughts. One had only to glance at little Miss Bracegirdle to see that in her were epitomized all the virtues and ideals of Easingstoke. (1974:26)

The narrator provides an evaluation – that Miss Bracegirdle led a simple, self-denying life – without any supporting evidence. The reader is thus invited to attribute to the narrator knowledge of the character that would make such a judgment reasonable. For example, the reader might infer that the character dresses conservatively, goes to church regularly, and so on. The complexity in this instance is that the extreme nature of the evaluation also invites the inference that the narrator is satirizing the virtues and ideals of Easingstoke, which in turn invites a range of further inferences. Evaluations provided by other characters can also be an important source of information about a character, although such evaluations are less likely to be reliable than those originating with the narrator and need to be interpreted differently depending on the source of the information.

Indications of Character Change

Another category of features concerns character change. In literary works of any length, characters inevitably grow or change, and identifying such changes is an essential part of the reading process. Later, we propose an analysis of character change in terms of discrete events that signal a discontinuity between the traits of a character before and after the event. In keeping with this analysis, we suggest that it may be possible to find events, character reactions, or narratorial comments that signal that such a discontinuity has occurred. Although we do not have a complete analysis of how to identify signals for discontinuities in texts, at least some examples are intuitively clear. For instance, in *Life during Wartime*, by Lucius Shepard, the narrator indicates:

Halfway through the telling of his story, Mingolla had realized he was not really trying to offend or shock Debora, but rather was unburdening himself; and he further realized that by telling it he had to an extent cut loose from the past, weakened its hold on him. For the first time he felt able to give serious consideration to the idea of desertion. (1987:66)

Here, the character explicitly realizes that the dispositions that applied in the past may not apply in the future; thus, one type of discontinuity signal must be explicit statements. At other times, character changes may be signaled more obliquely by the narrator. For example, in William Gibson's *All Tomorrow's Parties*, a character returns to her home after a long absence to find that a close friend has died and left her a valuable knife:

She zips her jacket. "Thank you for keeping his knife." Whatever history it was she'd felt herself dodging, she hasn't found it. She just feels tired now; otherwise, she doesn't seem to feel.

"Your knife. Made it for you. Wanted you to have it. Told me." Looking up from beneath his sparse gray dreadlocks now. And gently says: "Asked us where you were, you know?"

Her fit with history, and how that hurts. (1999:162)

In this case, our intuition is that a discontinuity is signaled by strong change in emotional reactions ("doesn't seem to feel" versus "how that hurts"), the indications that the passing of the knife is significant, and the suggestion of a reconciliation ("[w]hatever history it was she'd felt herself dodging" versus "[h]er fit with history"). However, the precise nature of the discontinuity and to which dispositions it applies are only hinted. We suspect that a careful delineation of such textual cues would allow one to treat such discontinuities as a textual feature.

A Framework for Character Constructions

A theory of literary characters and characterization must provide a framework for understanding the processes or operations that effect the passage from mere textual markers to "images of possible individuals with properties above and beyond those that can be ascribed to the narratorial text itself" (Margolin, 1990b:457). Readers by default assume that they will encounter real-life characters and make a concerted effort to fill in the schematic gaps to produce human-like constructs. In fact, we believe that the constructive operations of readers are so significant that they render it difficult, if not impossible, for readers to distinguish between what is actually said about characters in the text and what they themselves have supplied. Moreover, we believe that consistency building is probably one of the most important aspects of this gap-filling activity. Because it is impossible for any reader to maintain in working memory all the behavior and attributes associated with a character in any literary work, only some of these are retained and organized into a coherent image or interpretation (cf. Emmott, 1997). The ultimate goal of a cognitive, empirical model must be to help us understand the principles underlying the selection of some and the omission of other features, as well as the mechanism of their combination.

It is entirely conceivable that some readers impose on the text character constructions that are discordant with the text. At the same time, there is no objective and reliable method for measuring the degree of consonance between the textual configuration and the construction, other than common sense and communal consensus. In a sense, all constructions are representations that exceed the text, for they supply information that is absent from it; yet this does not suggest that constructions are invalid operations. Understanding character constructions should therefore not be confused with hermeneutic, evaluative activities regarding the validity of any construction. From a cognitive perspective, the important issue is the interaction between textual features, the reader's knowledge and beliefs, and the reading context, in other words, what features of the text are processed how and under what conditions. Once again, these are empirical questions that cannot be answered by theoretical blanket statements.

The key to unlocking this empirical puzzle is to identify the link between the kinds of constructions readers generate and their prior knowledge. In particular, because we argue that narrative characters are represented much as real people are, readers must use their real-world knowledge and beliefs concerning the relationship between dispositions and people's behavior. To make this relationship clear, we build on the Bayesian analysis of traits discussed by Ajzen and Fishbein (1975) and others. This framework embodies a normative account of how information about behavior should be used to make inferences about internal dispositions. Although we doubt that readers would always be normatively correct, it seems sensible to expect that readers' inferences will often be approximately correct, subject to the constraints of working memory and long-term memory retrieval. Thus, the Bayesian approach is likely to reflect some of the kinds of things that people do in attempting to understand narrative characters, and it provides a framework for discussing a wide range of influences and processes. In what follows, we use the Bayesian framework to discuss reader constructions based on characters' actions, evaluations by narrator and other characters, and constructions concerning character change.

Constructing Traits from Actions

As a working hypothesis, we suggest that readers' prior knowledge determines *naïve personality theories*. The essential notion is that people assume that other people's personality can be described by a list of traits (such as friendly, morose, or domineering) and that readers expect such traits to be related to how people behave in a variety of contexts. The processes involved in identifying the causal relationship between a trait and a particular action is likely to be complex and depend on the interaction of experience, memory retrieval, and reasoning processes. However, as a shorthand for these processes, we can conceive of the relationship between traits and actions as joint probabilities. In particular, we use p_{ij} to refer to the probability that a character has a trait i and engages in act j, and $\overline{p}_{ij}$ to refer to the probability of a character not having trait i and engaging in act j. By summing over all possible actions, one can find the marginal probability of the trait: $\sum_j p_{ij} = p_{i.}$ and $\sum_j \overline{p}_{ij} = \overline{p}_{i.}$ There are a large number of possible traits and a very large number of possible actions, so clearly we are not suggesting that people have any kind of explicit representation of such probabilities. Rather, we assume that readers have a range of knowledge and processes that allow them to make the judgments about characters and story-world actions that follow from such probabilities. Brown (1995), for example, noted how such frequency estimates depend on a range of heuristics and memory retrieval strategies. We use the joint probability formalism simply as a conceptual tool for analyzing how traits may be attributed to characters based on their actions and the readers' knowledge.

Although there is undoubtedly broad consensus in the population concerning how traits are related to actions, we emphasize that the details of this relationship vary from person to person based on knowledge and personal experience. Moreover, although we stress the continuity between the implicit personality theory that people apply to the real world and that which they apply in understanding narrative, we also anticipate that there are significant differences and that these differences may vary with narrative genre. For example, in reading a detective novel, the marginal probability of someone committing a murder is likely to be much higher than in the real world, in romance novels the marginal probability of dramatic love affairs is likely to be higher than in life, and so on. In other words, the characters and actions in a narrative are usually not ordinary, and readers often have expectations about the manner in which the likelihood of traits and actions in narratives may depart from that in real life. Despite these differences, we argue that the conceptual analysis of how traits are related to actions is the same for narrative and real worlds.

One of the elements missing from this theoretical analysis is an account of how the features of the text interact with readers' memory processes. In general, we allow for the possibility that readers' estimates of the probabilities of traits and behaviors will vary with recency, retrieval strategies, salient memory cues, and other factors known to affect memory. However, it seems clear that there is a role in the text for such processes. The material in the text might, for example, call to mind a variety of experiences in which otherwise unfriendly, asocial people engaged strangers in conversation; this in turn would bias the probability estimates used in one's personality theory and, in this example, alter the extent to which a character displaying such behaviors is viewed as friendly. In this way, readers' assessments of characters would depend jointly on both their experience and the manner in which information is presented in the text. Unfortunately, we do not have much insight into such interactions other than to simply note their likely importance.

The link between trait constructions and this conception of naïve personality theories is provided by Bayes' theorem. In the form that is most useful for our purposes, this states

$$\frac{P(T \mid A \wedge H)}{P(\overline{T} \mid A \wedge H)} = \frac{P(A \mid T \wedge H)}{P(A \mid \overline{T} \wedge H)} \times \frac{P(T \mid H)}{P(\overline{T} \mid H)} \tag{5.4}$$

Here, T signifies that the character has the trait; $\overline{T}$, that the character does not have the trait; A is the action in question; and H is the reader's prior evaluation of the character with respect to that trait. In other words, this means that the posterior odds of a trait (given one's prior evaluation and a new action) is the likelihood ratio for that action times the prior odds of the trait (from one's previous evaluation of the character).

This formulation makes it clear that what matters in changing one's impression about a character's trait is the second term, the likelihood ratio. In words, the likelihood ratio indicates how likely the action is given the trait relative to how likely it is when the trait is not present. If the reader's personality theory is stable (that is, does not change appreciably when new actions are encountered) and if actions are evaluated independently, the likelihood ratio will be independent of the prior evaluation of the character and can be derived from the joint probabilities of the actions and traits that constitute the readers personality theory. In particular,

$$\frac{P(A \mid T \wedge H)}{P(A \mid \overline{T} \wedge H)} = \frac{P(A \mid T)}{P(A \mid \overline{T})} = \frac{p_{ta}/p_t}{\overline{p}_{ta}/\overline{p}_t} \tag{5.5}$$

Thus, the likelihood ratio depends on readers' estimates, based on their prior knowledge and experience, of the joint frequencies of the behaviors and traits.

A more intuitive analysis can be obtained by taking the logarithm of both sides of Equation 5.4, yielding expressions in terms of log odds. Log odds can be thought of as evidence, and the log of the likelihood ratio denotes the amount of information that action provides about the trait. Using this terminology, the updating process can be written as

$$\begin{array}{ccc} \text{Posterior evidence} & = & \text{Informativeness} \\ \text{for trait} & & \text{of action} \end{array} + \begin{array}{c} \text{Prior evidence} \\ \text{for trait} \end{array} \tag{5.6}$$

Thus, the updating process amounts to saying that a reader's evidence for a trait, after observing a given action, is the information about the trait provided by the action plus the prior evidence for that trait (based on the history of that character). The informativeness of the action is based on the reader's personality theory, which in turn is a product of the reader's knowledge, experience, and genre-specific expectations. Notice that, in this form, the Bayesian updating procedure is analogous to the weighted-average model of information integration proposed by Anderson (1981), except that here we assume that weights placed on observed actions derive from the reader's estimates of the joint probabilities of traits and actions.

Constructing Traits from Evaluations

A comparable analysis can be given for evaluations, except that the evidence for a trait comes not from what a character does but from what the narrator and other characters say about the character. In this case, the same updating procedure would be written as

$$\frac{P(T \mid E \wedge H)}{P(\overline{T} \mid E \wedge H)} = \frac{P(E \mid T \wedge H)}{P(E \mid \overline{T} \wedge H)} \times \frac{P(T \mid H)}{P(\overline{T} \mid H)} \tag{5.7}$$

where E is the evaluation. Because the evaluation is in fact a direct expression of the trait in question, the likelihood ratio is really an index of reliability. If the source of the evaluation is very reliable, the evaluation would be produced only when the character has the trait and the likelihood ratio would be high. If the source of the evaluation is unreliable, the evaluation might be produced even in the absence of the trait, and the likelihood ratio may be much smaller. Thus, in words, the updating procedure for evaluations would be

$$\begin{array}{c} \text{Posterior evidence} \\ \text{for trait} \end{array} = \begin{array}{c} \text{Reliability of} \\ \text{evaluation} \end{array} + \begin{array}{c} \text{Prior evidence} \\ \text{for trait} \end{array} \tag{5.8}$$

When the narrator provides evaluations of other characters, we assume that readers will generally assume that the evaluation is reasonably reliable. However, reliability of the evaluations can change in predictable ways: An omniscient narrator would be expected to have more reliability than one with limited knowledge; a narrator with mental access to a character may be seen as more reliable than one without; and so on. If there are good reasons to think of the narrator as unreliable (e.g., if the narrator is insane or delusional), then readers may uniformly discount the reliability of the narrator's evaluations. Evaluations provided by other characters in the story will similarly depend on how reliable that character is expected to be. In this case, a variety of conversational processes intervene between the evaluation and the reader's attribution of evidence. For example, the character may or may not be telling the truth, or his or her interpretation of the character's behavior may be incomplete or biased. Under some circumstances, it may become clear that the personality theory used by the character to generate the evaluations may not match that of the reader. Similar processes may occur when the narrator provides evaluations of him- or herself, as may happen in autodiegetic narration. In this case, the labels that the narrator applies to him- or herself would be interpreted in light of their view of the narrator's communicative intent. For example, the narrator may be viewed as boasting, exaggerating, or self-serving. Alternatively, the reader may decide that the narrator is being politely modest or understating his or her case. In our analysis, all of such considerations would be subsumed in the "reliability" term in Equation 5.8.

Character Change

Identifying the processes that are involved in constructing representations of character change is a critical problem in theories of character and one on which there has been very little previous work. Our own analysis in this regard is thus very tentative. As described earlier, we assume that readers accumulate evidence for a character's traits from actions and evaluations, and that such evidence is simply pooled to form an aggregate impression, as in Equations 5.6 and 5.8. At some points in the text, however, readers may identify discontinuities; a discontinuity is an event or reaction that potentially changes a character's trait and, as a consequence, qualifies the import of the accumulated evidence. The form of Bayes' theorem we use to describe the impact of discontinuities is similar to that used previously:

$$\frac{P(T \mid D \wedge H)}{P(\overline{T} \mid D \wedge H)} = \frac{P(D \mid T \wedge H)}{P(D \mid \overline{T} \wedge H)} \times \frac{P(T \mid H)}{P(\overline{T} \mid H)} \tag{5.9}$$

where D is the discontinuity. Assuming that the discontinuity is independent of the trait and using the definition of conditional probability, the likelihood ratio can be rewritten as

$$
\begin{aligned}
\frac{P(D \mid T \wedge H)}{P(D \mid \overline{T} \wedge H)} &= \frac{P(D \wedge T \wedge H)/P(T \wedge H)}{P(D \wedge \overline{T} \wedge H)/P(\overline{T} \wedge H)} \\
&= \frac{P(D \wedge T \wedge H)}{P(D \wedge \overline{T} \wedge H)} \times \frac{P(\overline{T} \wedge H)}{P(T \wedge H)} \qquad (5.10) \\
&= \frac{P(D \wedge T \wedge H)/P(D)P(T)}{P(D \wedge \overline{T} \wedge H)/P(D)P(\overline{T})} \times \frac{P(\overline{T} \wedge H)/P(\overline{T})}{P(T \wedge H)/P(T)} \\
&= \frac{P(H \mid T \wedge D)}{P(H \mid \overline{T} \wedge D)} \times \frac{P(H \mid \overline{T})}{P(H \mid T)}
\end{aligned}
$$

The right-hand term in this derivation is the *inverse* of information provided by the prior history; the left-hand term is the information provided by the history given the discontinuity. Thus, incorporating a discontinuity in one's aggregate impression of a character's trait means replacing the old information with new information in light of the discontinuity. In the limit, if the character is an entirely new person after the trait discontinuity, none of the prior actions and evaluations of the character would matter, and the reader would have to start over in evaluating evidence for the trait.

Although the Bayesian mechanics in this approach are straight-forward, the corresponding psychological processes are not. In particular, our analysis suggests that identifying a discontinuity allows the reader the opportunity for reevaluating the evidence for character traits, but we are uncertain of the processes that determine how much reevaluation takes place. In general terms, this is likely to depend on the various indications in the text as to the extent or depth of the character change, along with the reader's prior knowledge and expectations concerning how traits evolve and change over time. A more detailed analysis, however, must await further research.

Traits and Behavior

The evidence readers accrue concerning traits can be used to understand and predict actions and evaluations. In principle, the information readers have concerning the odds of various traits could be combined to construct an estimate of the probability of any action in any given situation. However, the details of such calculations are complex because traits cannot be assumed to be independent of one another. Further, there are likely to be a large number of possible traits for which there is little evidence one way or the other, and it is unlikely that readers would systematically evaluate all possible evidence in the course of comprehension. Instead, we expect that readers will usually consider character actions against a backdrop of only a few traits that seem to be relevant to the current situation. Which traits the reader is concerned with are likely to be largely dependent on specific cues in the text, but there may be a role for strategic memory processes on the part of the reader.

Informativeness of Story-World Actions

One of the central assumptions of our approach to character constructions is that story-world actions provide evidence for traits, and that these actions are combined with information from evaluations to arrive at an assessment of the character traits. Although this simple idea is uncontroversial, the contribution of the present analysis is to separate the reader constructions from the features of the text and to describe how the former depends on readers' knowledge of the world. In particular, we argue that story-world actions and evaluations are textual features; these in turn are interpreted in terms of readers' personality theories based on their knowledge and experience; and this information is used to construct traits for the characters. Thus, although story-world actions can be found in the text, what causes them to be informative is the knowledge readers have of how real people behave in the world. We next describe a simple demonstration of one piece of this analysis.

Empirical Evidence

In this section, we show that adding actions and evaluations to a literary narrative changes readers' assessments of relevant traits. The general approach was to add actions and evaluations to a story that were consistent with a given trait. For example, for the trait "friendly," the character might be described as engaging in social interaction or spontaneously talking to strangers, or the narrator might describe the character as friendly or sociable. After reading the story, readers simply rated the character on a number of traits including the manipulated one. We anticipated that readers would rate the character higher on the target trait after reading the story with trait-consistent actions and evaluations than after reading the original version.

This prediction is probably self-evident in general outline; indeed, comparable manipulations are commonly used with artificially constructed narratives in research on people perception and attribution theory. However, any number of complexities might compromise the ability to demonstrate effects of story-world actions in this instance. First, the impressions of characters generated by well-written literary texts might not respond to the addition of a few relatively isolated actions. The original stories by themselves might succeed in clearly evoking a coherent impression of the character that is impervious to minor variations in the events of the story world. Second, when such manipulations are used with artificial materials, there is typically little else of interest for readers to focus on in the text; consequently, it is not surprising that readers in those studies notice and react to the trait-relevant actions. In our study, the manipulations were all orthogonal to the theme and main events of the story, and readers may simply not notice the additional actions in the face of much more central story developments. Third, there may be unpredictable interactions among traits. Although the framework developed earlier for character constructions allows for the possibility that evidence for traits interact, at present we have few analytical tools for identifying the potential for such interactions in real literature. For these reasons, the present study should be regarded as exploratory, despite the eminent plausibility of its motivating hypothesis.

We selected four short stories and for each identified a trait that, in our judgment, was largely orthogonal to the main events of the narrative. The stories (and traits) were "A Day's Wait" by Ernest Hemingway (1927) (friendliness), "In Another Country" also by Hemingway (humor), "In the Hills" by Christine Craig (1990) (dreaminess), and "Marbles" by Jamaica Kincaid (1990) (curiosity). In addition to the original, three versions of each story were created by adding three actions consistent with the target trait, adding a narratorial evaluation of that trait, or both. Because the stories were related in the first person, the evaluations were of the narrator him- or herself. An example from "In the Hills" is shown in Table 5.1.

TABLE 5.1. *Example of Evaluation and Action Manipulations*

Years before, I had left the heat and the noise and the warring of the city to build my small house here on my mother's land. *[evaluation: It was hard for me because by nature I am not a handy person, more of a thinker rather than a doer.]* The land had been new and difficult to work, but now it was yielding up its crops regularly and I had become part of the cycle of planting and weeding and watering and reaping. *[action: Even now, though, I would sometimes catch myself in wistful daydreams, not tending to chores.]* My nearest neighbour was some few chains away down the hill. A silent old man who kept a few cows and walked the two miles to the village to sell his milk.

Four adjectives were selected for each trait, two suggesting high values on the trait dimension and two suggesting low values on the dimension. Forty-eight participants read one version of each of the stories in a counterbalanced order. Across participants, each version of each of the stories was read an equal number of times. After reading each story, participants rated their agreement with sixteen statements of the form, "The writer is...," filled in with one of the sixteen adjectives selected for the traits.

A preliminary analysis of the results indicated that some of the adjectives did not correlate with the others selected for that trait. This suggested that our original intuitions concerning what labels were related to the manipulated traits were incorrect. As a (post hoc) remedy for this difficulty, we constructed indices for the target traits using only those adjectives that had substantial intercorrelations. The adjectives we used for each trait are shown in Table 5.2. For each story, an index of the target trait was constructed by changing the

TABLE 5.2. *Trait Adjectives*

Story	Trait	Positive Adjectives	Negative Adjectives
A Day's Wait	Friendliness	Friendly Sociable	Hostile
In Another Country	Humor	Humorous Comical	Serious
In the Hills	Dreaminess	Dreamy Scatterbrained	Practical Down-to-earth
Marbles	Curiosity		Uninterested

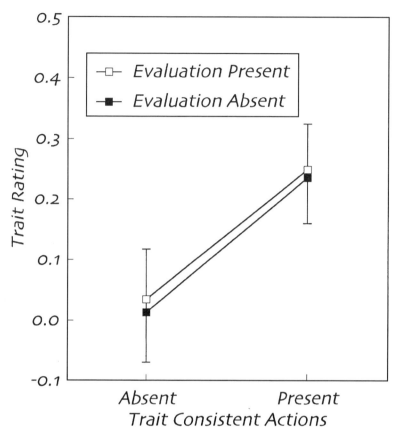

FIGURE 5.1. Trait rating as a function of the presence/absence of trait-consistent actions and narratorial evalutations. Error bars indicate the size of 95% confidence intervals, adjusted for pairwise comparisons.

participants' ratings to Z-scores and then averaging the ratings for the selected adjectives.

The trait index for each version of the stories is shown in Figure 5.1. There was a clear effect of adding the actions to the story: Participants were more likely to agree that the character had the trait when they had read a version with trait-consistent actions than one without those actions. This demonstrates that readers' evaluations of characters can be influenced by characters' story-world actions even with literary narratives in which (one might suspect) the characters are portrayed in a coherent and compelling manner, and even when those actions are not central to the theme or central events of the narrative.

In contrast, there was very little effect in adding the narratorial evaluations. We offer two possible explanations for the failure to find this predicted effect. First, only one evaluation statement was added to the narratives (in contrast to the three actions that were added). It is possible that these statements were not sufficiently salient, and participants simply failed to notice or remember this information in the course of reading the story. Second, readers may be unwilling to accept evaluations of the narrator at face value when the narrator is evaluating him- or herself. Even though the narrator may be accepted as cooperative and generally reliable, self-evaluations may be seen as a special case. Intuitively, there would seem to be a similar reticence to accept self-evaluations at face value in conversation; even though a conversational participant may be trusted to be generally truthful, one might discount self-evaluations as self-serving, self-effacing, or even ironical. From this perspective, one might expect larger effects of narratorial evaluations if we had used stories with impersonal, heterodiegetic narrators.

To provide evidence for the apparent effect of trait-consistent actions, we fit three linear models to the results. The first can be termed the null model and incorporated the assumption that all the means were equal; in the second model, we assumed that there was only an effect of adding actions; and in the third model, we assumed an effect of adding actions, an effect of adding an evaluation, and an interaction between the two. The action-only model fit substantially better than the null model, yielding a likelihood ratio of $\lambda = 20.54$; adding the effect of evaluation and the interaction produced only a minor improvement in fit, $\lambda = 1.02$. Thus, we conclude that there is clear evidence for an effect of action and little evidence for either the effect of evaluation or the interaction.

Summary

We began this chapter by describing the prior work in literary theory on characters. This work has been dominated by the tension between treating characters as real people versus treating them as a collection of textual signs. Our synthesis of this debate is that the information concerning character is not merely whatever clues can be garnered from the text but that readers commonly create representations of characters that are based on the same processes that are used for real people. Such processes have been extensively studied in the domain of social cognition, and we assume that many of those findings apply to the understanding of narrative character as well. We suggested that features for character consist of story-world actions, evaluations by the narrator or other characters, and cues for character change. We assume that the evidence provided by actions and evaluations is interpreted in terms of prior knowledge and experience and then pooled to identify character traits. However, cues for character change provide the reader an opportunity to reevaluate that evidence. Derivations from Bayes' theorem were used as a formal framework for describing these processes. Empirical evidence was reported confirming that character actions in a literary narrative do contribute to the traits reported by readers. In this study, self-evaluations provided by the narrator failed to produce such an effect.

6

Perception and Focalization

In this chapter, we discuss the role of perceptual information in narrative and its role in identifying the narrator and his or her knowledge of the narrative world. In the traditional narratological scholarship, the role of perceptual information is only one small part of the broader problem of focalization. First, we illustrate several specific problems that have arisen in the theory of focalization as a result of the unresolved tension between a formal description of the text and a subjective description of what readers may do with that text. Second, we discuss some of the psychological evidence on perspective and spatial representations. Third, based on some of these ideas, we propose a psychonarratological solution to the problems we identify in the theory of focalization. This approach enables us to step out of the circular logic relating the text to ideal readers and vice versa. Fourth, we present some new ideas concerning the nature of the representations pertaining to focalization that readers construct. Finally, we describe some empirical evidence consistent with our framework and hypotheses.

Narratological Approaches to Focalization

Among scholars who have engaged in the narratological dialogue on focalization, there seems to be a relatively clear understanding about the theoretical goals: A theory of focalization should provide an account of the source of knowledge and perception within the text based on the relationship between the narrator and the characters. Obviously, from the perspective of the reader, it is of crucial importance if a narrator appears to see, know, or say more than, as much as, or less than the characters; if the narrator has access to a character's thoughts; if the events are seen from the perspective of a single or multiple agents; or if the perspective is static or constantly shifting. Such information determines inferences readers draw about narratorial authority in the text and will influence readers' understanding and interpretations. In this respect, Genette's initial insight regarding the necessity of distinguishing between *who sees* and *who speaks* was fundamental, for the agent enunciating a statement in the text may not be the source of knowledge, perception, and hence authority (Genette, 1980). It is possible, for example, that an utterance is enunciated by the narrator but presented from the point of view of a character, so that the character is the agent of the seeing and the narrator of the telling. In other words, it is possible for the narrator to "present a character's vision without letting the character narrate" (Sanders & Redeker, 1996:292). In this way, distinct points of view can be embedded in the narrative discourse. Sanders and Redeker defined focalization as "the embedding of a subject's point of view in the narrator's discourse reality" (291). Given that the goal of narratology in general is "the study of forms and features" of narrative (Prince, 1987:65), one would intuitively assume that the distinction between speech and perception would be easy enough to make and that one would have only to rely on a detailed typology of text features that signal speech or perception.

Regrettably, however, and much to the chagrin of Genette himself, neither the term he coined nor the distinction between narration and perception it was intended to facilitate, were sufficiently clear to secure a general understanding and consensus. Part of the problem has to do with the paradox inherent in the very distinction between who sees and who speaks. As Sanders and Redeker explained, "the nature of (narrative) texts is such that in order to represent vision, one needs narration. In order to represent perception and thought *one needs a voice* – how else can perception and thought be verbalized?" (1996:292). This is only one of the numerous problems with which scholars must contend. Disconcertingly, no exhaustive typology of focalization forms exists in narratological theory (although it has been attempted by some linguists, e.g., Banfield, 1981). In fact, the theory of focalization has developed into a seemingly irreconcilable variety of frameworks and debates, suggesting that the initial intuitive distinction is anything but simple to apply. If anything, it would appear to prove that the identification of focalization in text is subject to much idiosyncratic interpretation. This of course raises the question of just how accurately textual forms can be described, and what kinds of methods are required to ensure maximum objectivity.

In our opinion, the confusing state of focalization theory today stems from the lack of a clear distinction between the text and its formal description on one hand, and the reader and the reading process on the other. This is not to suggest that all narratologists have been insensitive to the need to account for the reader. However, even though many have noted the role of the reader in general, very few have explicitly incorporated the reader in a theory of focalization. A notable exception was the approach of Patrick O'Neil (1992). He emphasized the general importance of the reader's role in the construction of narrative features, including focalization. Another exception was that of Monica Fludernik (1996), who recognized that "the category of focalization is an interpretative one and *not* exclusively a textual category" (345). Yet neither of these theorists elaborated on the role of the reader in any detail. In general, to expand on what might plausibly be attributed to the reader, narratologists and reader-response theorists have generated a hypothetical description of readers' knowledge and inferences with little grounding in objective evidence. As discussed in Chapter 1, the result has been a purely speculative positing of a competent, ideal, implied, model, informed, or super reader (Culler, 1975b; Eco, 1979; Fish, 1970; Iser, 1974; Riffaterre, 1966) whose very image emerges from a specific, formal description of the characteristics of the text. The result is a circular kind of logic: The characteristics of a text provide evidence for various narrative competencies, and the existence of a particular competence provides the evidence for a particular characteristic of the text.

To reiterate a general argument in this book, we suggest that the best way out of this circularity is to study not hypothetical "ideal" readers, but actual, real readers, and to ground one's analysis of the reading process in empirical evidence on how readers process narrative forms. For example, consider O'Neil's conclusion that readers interpret "a character-focalizer's perspective...as being subjective," and an "external focalizer's vision as entirely objective" (O'Neil, 1992:334). Our view is that this is a speculative hypothesis that cannot be proven or disproven by argument or by the intuitive analysis of texts and their properties. Instead, one needs to identify verifiable implications of this analysis and then evaluate empirically whether such implications actually hold with real readers.

Problems in the Theory of Focalization

We discuss here three related issues that have been central in the theoretical debate on focalization: the nature of focalization, that is, what constitutes focalization; the agent of focalization, that is, the Focalizer, or who can focalize; and the mode of focalization, or how something is focalized.

The Nature of Focalization

As Gerard Genette understood and lamented, much of the confusion about the nature of focalization stems from the visual connotations of the term, which he himself found too restrictive. Narratologists' speculations about Genette's real intention in coining this term contradict each other, but in a systematic way, ranging from what we refer to as a "maximalist" to "minimalist" positions.

At the minimalist end is Bronzwaer (1981), who, like Mieke Bal (1983), believed that the term "focalization" should exclude psychological data, but who took the reduction in scope one step further by limiting it, as did Jost (1983), to spatio-temporal positioning. Situated somewhere in the middle of the spectrum is Chatman (1986), who suggested that Genette preferred to extend the usage of the word beyond mere vision to include "the whole spectrum of perception: hearing, tasting, smelling, and so on" (192). At the maximalist end of the spectrum is Rimmon-Kenan (1983), who argued in favor of an even further expansion of the definition to include "cognitive, emotive, and ideological orientation" (71). The metaphoric association of the verb "to see" with the cognitive operations of understanding, concluding, judging, believing, rationalizing, knowing, and so on, makes understanding the maximalist position easy. (For a good description of these metaphoric connotations, see Chatman, 1986.) However, the problem with including all cognitive, emotive, and ideological perspectives in the definition is that only some of this semantic content will have any objective basis within the text, and much of it will inevitably be reader-dependent, relying on the inferences readers draw about the narrator and character's mental perspectives. Such inferences are subject to the variable and potentially idiosyncratic knowledge and beliefs of different readers. On the other hand, the problem with a minimalist position may be that it is too limited, and important phenomena related to focalization may be arbitrarily excluded.

The confusion arising from the inability to agree on what focalization is and what should be included in the term has led some, like Seymour Chatman (1986), to reject the term altogether. Arguing that if a narratological term is fraught with inconsistencies, it should be either redefined or replaced with a more appropriate one, Chatman's solution was to replace the term "focalization" with the term "filter," which he understood as the character consciousness from or through which a narrator chooses to tell a story or part of a story. The difficulty with this conceptualization is that it implies the same kind of maximalist logic as Rimon-Kenan's, with all of the same implicit problems. In particular, the character's consciousness per se is not in the text but is rather inferred or constructed by the reader. As Barry Stampfl explained, "a character's consciousness is an imaginative construct arrived at by speculation and (is) always therefore more or less problematic. Readerly speculation constructive of such consciousness is put into motion" (1992:390). Chatman's model does not allow us to specify with any technical precision the textual forms that signal "filter." Consequently, anyone interested in using Chatman's theory may conclude that the only recourse it leaves is the use of purely speculative descriptions of hypothetical readers and their reading. Chatman further argued that other narrative functions previously implied by the traditional term "point of view," and for which he coined the terms "slant" (the attitude of the narrator), "center" (the privileging of a given character), and "interest focus" (the intellectual or emotional perspective, or interest of a character) are, in his opinion, to be excluded from the semantic content of the term "filter."

The vagueness of these terms and the confusing nature of this terminological classification have been critiqued by several narratologists (Edmiston, 1989; Nelles, 1990; Stampfl, 1992).

However, there is perhaps an even more serious problem with Chatman's radical model: The entire aspect of spatio-temporal positioning is simply omitted. Thus, it does not recognize the crucial role that spatial positioning plays in narrative discourse and neglects the traditional, intuitive wisdom that a story is always told from some physical, spatial vantage point, be it the narrator's or a character's. As Edmiston aptly pointed out, Genette's reliance on Pouillon's concepts of "vision par derrière" and "vision avec" already implied this spatial dimension (Edmiston, 1989). The complete exclusion of this aspect has serious consequences. For example, we sense that spatial positioning provides vital information regarding slant, filter, interest focus, and so on. Rather than reject the term "focalization" altogether, it would seem more appropriate to integrate Bronzwaer's and Chatman's views. Our approach is to use the term "focalization" to refer to any perceptual information, retaining the crucial role of spatial location that such information provides. With respect to the *nature* of focalization then, we propose a revision of the term, restricting it to the perceptual information provided by the text.

The Agent of Focalization

The issue of who can focalize has given rise to an apparently irresolvable debate that has resulted in dividing narratologists into two main schools of thought. Representatives of the first, such as Bal (1983), Rimmon-Kenan (1983), and O'Neil (1992), accept a distinction between internal and external focalization based on the agent of perception and that agent's corresponding diegetic level. According to this conceptualization, internal focalization is that of a character within the story world, and external focalization is that of a narrating agent outside the story world (also referred to as "zero focalization"). Whereas the former can include the characters and a narrator who participates in the story world, the latter can only refer to an omniscient narrator. (The terms "external" and "internal" focalization have also been used to refer to the object of focalization. External focalization refers to that mode of presenting information that is restricted to characters' speech and behavior; internal focalization, to that mode that conveys the contents of the mind. In other words, characters are seen from the outside or from the inside (Prince, 1987).)

However, this fundamental distinction between internal and external agents of focalization was challenged by others like Chatman (1986) and Prince (1987), the main representatives of the second group. Taking Genette's important distinction between who speaks and who sees in a text to its logical conclusion, they argued that a narrator can only speak, not see; only characters can see. To quote from Chatman: "the narrator can only report events, he/she does not literally 'see' them" (Chatman, 1986:193). To this he added:

The narrator cannot perceive or conceive things in that world, only about that world, since for him the story-world is already "past" and "elsewhere." He can report them, comment upon them, and even (figuratively) visualize them, but always and only from outside, in his/her imagination or memory. The logic of narrative prevents him/her from literally seeing or thinking them from a post within the confines of the story-world. (Chatman, 1986:197)

Fludernik upheld this position, maintaining that "the narrator does not *see* the story, 'she' or 'he' *produces* the story. What the narrative focalizes on the story level is therefore the result of *selection* and not the result of *perception*" (Fludernik, 1996:345). However, Fludernik's distinction between the small-scale focalization at the story level, where characters observe, and the "macro-focalization" of the whole story (344) seems to undermine her argument by suggesting that the story, which is produced, can be focalized.

We believe that the argument that narrators cannot focalize is problematic for at least three reasons: (1) it is based on an ontological distinction between narrator and characters that is inherently flawed, (2) it is mired in the "anthropomorphic fallacy," and (3) it is a distinction that loses much of its relevance when related to the cognitive operations and reading practices of real readers. Each of these points will be taken up in turn.

The Ontological Distinction Argument
From the perspective of ontological logic, it is true that an external narrator does not literally belong in the fictional world, so he cannot

"see" in it in the same sense as the characters. If one chooses to re-strict vision to this literal level, stripping it of all metaphoric value as Chatman does, then it makes sense to disqualify the narrator as a fo-calizer. Someone who is situated outside the story world cannot "see" the characters and their story world except metaphorically in his or her imagination or mind. One could thus conclude that this kind of "seeing" is not equal to that of the inhabitants of the fictional world.

However, this argument could be taken to its logical conclusion and applied to narrators of all diegetic levels. For example, if we consider the case of narrators situated within the story world who engage in retrospective narrating acts about themselves, it is obvious, as shown by Vitoux (1984) and Edmiston (1989), that the narrating self of such autobiographies is external to the world of the experienc-ing self, distanced from that self in time, space, and thus, ontological level. We arrive at the same conclusion when we consider the case of narrators who are secondary characters within the story world en-gaging in retrospective narrative acts, such as Watson in the Sherlock Holmes novels; clearly, they are also situated at a different ontological level. Watson, for example, is removed from the Holmes of the story world, and thus can only "see" inside that world as an omniscient narrator "sees" inside the created fictional world, namely, in his or her imagination. Perhaps we can conclude that the same is true of all past narration, and that the only kind of narrative in which the narra-tor actually sees the events, characters, and objects of the story world are those that are narrated in the present, giving the impression that the acts of seeing and narrating are simultaneous. However, limiting focalization to only this single contrived convention would seem to make the concept almost useless.

Chatman's rejoinder to this conclusion is that the narrating self conceptualizes that earlier self's perceptions, who in turn perceives as a character. This explanation amounts to saying that autobiograph-ical narrators perceive in their mind's eye. Such a capacity would seem to make arguments regarding ontological levels moot because virtually all references to perception in a text would have to count as focalization in this regard. In our view, the approach also seems convoluted; what counts for the reader is likely to be simply that someone in the story perceives, and it would be sensible to attribute this focalization to the narrator. Readers may therefore construe the narrator as writing *as if* he or she were actually seeing, even though the narrator is (technically) at a different ontological level.

The Anthropomorphic Fallacy

Chatman's argument is prey to a further misconception: His tendency to accord ontological primacy and "vision" to participants in the story world is mired in what we refer to as the anthropomorphic fallacy. The anthropomorphic fallacy is perhaps the source of much of the confusion about focalization. Narratological terminology such as the words "narrator," "speaks," "sees," point to an ingrained tendency to anthropomorphize narrator and characters and to speak of them as a persons, whereas in fact there is no such person in the text. The narrator and the characters are no more than an aggregate of textual signs on the basis of which readers construct representations of the narrator and character personae and their knowledge. Characters themselves do not exist independently of the act of narration; they do not see any more than narrators speak; they are said to see, as narrators are made to speak. More specifically, the focalizer, as O'Neill explained echoing Bal (1983), is neither a person nor an agent, but "a chosen *point*, the point from which the narrative is perceived as being presented at any given moment" (O'Neill, 1992:333).

Lack of Reader Relevance

Chatman's fine-grained distinctions between subtle variations in ontological level, while useful in a meticulous analysis of narrative form, is unlikely to be functional for most readers reading most texts. For example, if we are told that a town measures ten miles across and that all around it enemy aliens are lying in ambush, then as far as the reader is concerned, it is the narrator's physical vantage point that allows him or her to "see" the entire scene. Or, if the pattern of the tiles on the top of the dome of a cathedral are described in a narrative, then there is an undeniable implication of an overhead vantage point. Little does it matter to the reader that this perception may be only metaphorical or ontologically distinct from that of any possible character.

Further, Chatman's model eliminates the notion of a spatial position in the text from which perception occurs. Yet, as mentioned earlier, the pre-Genettian, so-called optical metaphors revealed a great degree of intuitive insight regarding not only the nature of narrative, but of reception as well. Stories are always understood to be told from a given perspective or spatial frame of reference. Indeed, the old maxim that there can be no narrating without some perspective is too soundly intuitive to reject. The spatial positioning implied by perceptual descriptions is an essential component of the narration for the reader and should not be minimized. Unfortunately, the term "perspective" came to be used in many different and contradictory ways in the theory of focalization (ideological perspective, emotional perspective, etc.), creating the need to replace "perspective" with other terms. However, an understanding of what the reading process involves for real readers is not well served by terminological distinctions that ignore the obvious salience of spatial positioning. We suggest that the subtle delineation of ontological levels is not usually relevant for most readers; information concerning spatial position is.

The lack of reader relevance is a criticism that can be applied to accounts of focalization other than Chatman's. Erlich (1990) and other narratologists and linguists have devoted astonishing effort to determining the "origin" of the seeing, and to pinpointing minute change in focalization in limited portions of text. Our belief is that such precision is unnecessary and unproductive, at least as far as the reader is concerned. To begin with, readers are unlikely to be able to systematically track and retain in working memory the innumerable perceptual shifts that can occur in literary texts. O'Neil perceptively understood this in suggesting that readers are only "fully aware of the most *recent* focalizations" (O'Neil, 1992:343). We agree with O'Neill's conclusion that it is, after all, the reader who has to make decisions about how to deal with complex or compound focalizations, although not necessarily with his conclusion that readers recall only recent focalizations; this, once again, is an empirical question. He concluded that the reader is thus a focalizing agent who "has to *decide* which of the[se] multiple focalizations need to be seen as more important and which can afford to be discounted or even disregarded, at least provisionally" (345). Our view is slightly different: From our perspective, what matters is likely to be the global impression readers construct regarding the position of the perceptual agents.

In sum, then, with respect to the *agent* of focalization, we argue that the question of who sees cannot be resolved simply on the basis of the text. Although a perceiving agent located at particular point may be implicit in the textual descriptions, it may be difficult or impossible to find such an agent in the narrative. Consequently, as we discuss later, the agent of focalization should properly be understood as being a construction in the mind of the reader.

The Mode of Focalization

Mode of focalization refers to how entities are focalized. Generally speaking, there are two possibilities: An entity can be viewed externally, or, if it is a person, the internal contents of his or her mind can be exposed. Lanser (1981) preferred the terms "internal vision" and "external vision" to avoid the confusion created by the words "internal" and "external" focalization. This classical distinction may be useful in identifying different modes of character presentation, but it is plagued by some of the same kinds of interpretational difficulties as other aspects of focalization. For example, internal focalization may be construed much as a maximalist metaphorical interpretation of "seeing," including not only perceptual information but information that would result from other aspects of the contents of a character's mind, such as how that character feels, reacts, interprets, and thinks. Conceptually, this distinction corresponds roughly to Chatman's "center" and "interest focus." However, there is very little that cannot be subsumed under the general heading of "character reaction," rendering the concept of internal focalization hopelessly broad. Certainly, the essential element of spatial positioning we discussed earlier is largely lost in such a construal.

At the same time, there is little in the definition of internal versus external focalization that would allow one to identify with any precision when each is being used. For example, a narrative fragment that attributes a perceptual experience to a character (e.g., "Frank watched the workmen in amazement") might be viewed as external focalization because the narrator merely describes what the character is doing; on the other hand, it might be termed internal focalization because it depicts the perceptual experience of the character. Presumably, then, the distinction between internal and external focalization is not local, but rather built up over an extended body of text. What is missing, though, is an account of how this is done and what information is used. To anticipate, we argue that a coherent account of mode of focalization thus requires a systematic consideration of what readers do with the text and cannot be based simply on the text itself.

Fludernik's (1996) approach to the mode of focalization was somewhat confused. First, she suggested that the concept of focalization should be limited to the following narrative situations: (a) a first person describes his or her own story, (b) a reflector-mode or "internal focalization" where the story is presented as perceived by a character, and (c) a combination of omniscient and reflector modes. Rather than think of these situations as instances of focalization, Fludernik claimed that her approach constituted a shift to a "receptional frame," that entailed thinking in terms of telling, action-oriented, or viewing / experiencing frames and their parameters (345). Fludernik's goal was to subordinate all "visual and perceptional parameters" to the "presentation of consciousness" (345). However, it is not clear that she succeeded in shedding the nuances and difficulties that have plagued the narratological theory of focalization. For example, each type of frame was argued to imply different kinds of focalization : "TELLING frames and ACTION frames afford some kinds of focalizations, VIEWING frames quite different kinds of focalization"(345). It is not clear in this approach, though, whether these distinctions were intended to reside in the reader or in the text. As textual distinctions, they seem comparable and no more precise or objective than those made in the traditional narrratological scholarship. As distinctions among forms of reader representations, they are not compelling: They are not clearly connected to either particular features of the text or to verifiable processes or effects on the part of the reader. Our analysis is that the approach, while insightful, does not address the central problems we have identified.

In our view, many of the tensions and confusions in the narratological theory of focalization arise because of a failure to distinguish between features and constructions. One should not really say, for example, that all readers always distinguish who sees and who speaks because it is obvious that there are readers, even well-trained readers of literature, who do not under some circumstances. Instead, hypotheses concerning constructions should be understood as statements about tendencies or averages and must be carefully delimited with respect to the type of reader, the nature of the text, and pragmatics of the reading context. We attempt to follow this approach in the psychonarratological approach we discuss in a later section.

Psychological Approaches to Perspective

Psychological research in discourse processing has commonly not been concerned with the specific problems of focalization that have occupied the field of narratology. We suspect that this is because text is commonly held to be a form of communication between a writer and a reader, and the writer is assumed to have a particular perspective (either real or imagined) on the world he or she is describing. In this conception, the writer is the source of focalization regardless of the particular signs that may be found in the text. As a consequence, in this conception the issues of the nature, agent, and mode of focalization are moot. Nevertheless, there are several lines of research in discourse processing and psycholinguistics that have some implications for how perceptual information is conveyed in narrative and how it is understood, and some of this research is reviewed here. We first describe work on the use of perspective in language production, followed by a more general discussion of the nature of spatial representations generated during comprehension. Finally, we describe some of the psychological and linguistic evidence on spatial reference frames.

Perspective in Production

The use of perspective in spatial descriptions is studied most naturally in the context of spontaneous oral production. An important investigation of this general sort was conducted by Schober (1993). People were asked to describe a visual array to a conversational partner separated by a visual barrier. He found that people commonly cooperated with their partners and collaborated in finding a common understanding of the spatial relationships. Speakers adopted with facility either their own egocentric perspective or that of their partners. However, the choice of perspective was not always explicit in any given utterance, and the exchange typically continued until there was a common understanding of that perspective. Tversky

(1996) described an extension of Schober's paradigm in which some of the variables that control the choice of perspective were examined. Generally, a personal perspective (either the speaker's or the addressee's) was used less often when spatial arrangement could be described in terms of external coordinates or landmarks. Related results were obtained by Levelt (1989) in a well-known series of studies. He asked people to describe a complex link-node diagram so that it could be reconstructed by a hearer. He found speakers typically adopted a consistent system for describing the spatial arrangements, but that the details of the system were not always explicit. Unlike Schober's paradigm, there was no opportunity for interaction, and miscommunication was not uncommon.

A common strategy for describing large-scale environments is to describe routes or tours. For example, Linde and Labov (1975) found that people commonly described apartment layouts in terms of the path one might follow on a tour, and that such descriptions could be described by a formal grammar. Taylor and Tversky (1996) found that the use of route descriptions was influenced by the nature of salient landmarks and prior exposure to the environment, among other factors; in many cases, "survey" descriptions were used in which the overall spatial arrangement was indicated. Overall, these results demonstrate that speakers (and presumably writers of narrative) have a range of methods for describing spatial relationships but that these perspective systems are not always clearly signaled in a particular utterance. In extended conversation, the choice of perspective system must be explicitly coordinated or miscommunication can result.

Spatial Representations

As discussed in Chapter 1, it is commonly assumed in discourse processing that readers construct mental representations of the situation that is described by the text. Representations of this general sort have been termed situation models, referential representations, or mental models depending on the particular properties and uses that have been ascribed to them. One line of research is motivated by the hypothesis that such mental models have an intrinsically spatial character and that they support a variety of spatial operations and inferences. For example, Morrow et al. (1987) had participants read a narrative describing a character moving through a series of rooms in a building with a known layout. The mental representation of the narrative world was probed during the narrative by presenting the names of two objects in the building and asking readers to decide whether they were located in the same or different rooms. In keeping with the view that readers maintain a mental representation of the spatial layout surrounding the protagonist, responses to the probes were fastest when the objects came from the protagonists' current location, and became slower as the distance from the protagonist increased. Morrow, Bower, and Greenspan (1989) showed that this result also applies to rooms that the protagonist must have traveled through (but which were not mentioned in the text) and rooms that the protagonist was merely thinking about. In general, the results suggest that readers maintain a representation of the spatial layout that is relevant to a character's goals and actions in the story world.

One potential limitation of these results is that readers are assumed to be already familiar with the layout of the story world before reading the text. For example, participants in the studies by Morrow and colleagues had to first memorize a map of the building before reading the narrative. The requirement to answer spatial probe questions may have also encouraged readers to maintain detailed and accurate spatial representations. For example, Wilson et al. (1993) concluded that the reader's spatial representation depends on the task demands and the reader's goals; often, it may not include detailed information concerning spatial relationships. The results of Hakala (1999) suggest a similar conclusion: Readers may not draw some kinds of inferences pertaining to location unless they are told to attend to spatial information in the text.

However, other evidence indicates that at least some spatial information is maintained about the story world even in the absence of extratextual task demands. Glenberg, Meyer, and Lindem (1987) demonstrated a distinction between objects that are spatially associated with a main character and those that are not: Associated objects are foregrounded along with the main character and are more accessible in recognition probes and as pronoun antecedents. O'Brien and Albrecht (1992) measured sentence-reading time and found that inconsistent spatial information was associated with comprehension difficulties. As in the research of Morrow and colleagues, the presumed mechanism involves tracking the spatial layout surrounding the main character during comprehension. However, an explanation of these results does not require that readers maintain detailed representations of the spatial layout and geometry; readers could be using much coarser or fragmented spatial representations.

From these considerations, it seems reasonable to suggest that the amount of detail and geometrical precision that readers maintain in spatial representations is variable. In keeping with our thesis in this book, we suggest that the reader's understanding of the narrator's conversational point is likely to play a crucial role in this regard. As one example, Levine and Klin (2001) found that the tracking of spatial information was affected by how elaborately situations were described in the text. Such elaboration can be interpreted as a (conversational) cue that the location is important for the narrator's purpose; thus, readers may be more likely to represent the details of the spatial layout at that location and to track more carefully movements of characters to and from that location. More generally, though, there is no strong reason to believe that spatial representations constructed during comprehension are necessarily faithful to any underlying spatial geometry, and in many cases the spatial information readers have about the story world could easily be incoherent or piecemeal. However, it might be argued that these spatial representations are of the same *sort* as those constructed with deliberate memorization and instruction, albeit with less detail and fidelity. Thus, the literature on spatial mental models of the narrative provide information about what readers can represent based on spatial descriptions; the variables that determine what they do represent under a given set of circumstances remains largely unexplored.

Reference Frames

In psycholinguistic analyses, it is typically assumed that spatial descriptions entail a referent, a reference object, and a reference frame. The referent is the object whose spatial position is being described;

the reference object is used to identify the relative spatial description; and the reference frame dictates how directions and distances are described. For example, in the statement, "The chair is north of the table," the chair is the referent (the object being described), the table is the reference object (the chair's location is relative to it), and the reference frame is the canonical north-south-east-west coordinate system. It is common to identify three types of reference frames: intrinsic, relative, and absolute (e.g., Levelt, 1996). In an intrinsic reference frame, the parts or orientation of the reference object dictate directions, as in the "The engine is at the rear of the car"; here, it is the orientation of the car that determines where "the rear" is. In a relative reference frame, the coordinate system is determined by the observer, as in the "My car is the one on the left"; in this case, it is position of the speaker (or possibly the addressee) that dictates which side is left. Finally, in an absolute reference frame, the directions are taken from the environment. The north-south-east-west coordinate system is a prototypical example, but absolute reference frames would also include the gravitational axis of up-down. The detailed analysis of reference frames and how they are expressed linguistically can be complex (e.g., Levelt, 1996), and, in isolation, any given utterance may be ambiguous.

Several researchers have investigated the role of frames of reference in discourse. Franklin and Tversky (1990) had people read second-person narratives with a wealth of perceptual information described using predominantly relative reference frames; the readers' memory was then probed for information in various directions. Generally, information was most accessible when it corresponded to a vertical, head-foot axis and least accessible when it corresponded to a left-right axis. The researchers concluded that people construct representations of the described world in terms of what they termed a "spatial framework," and that such frameworks allow access to some information more readily than others. Our interpretation of a spatial framework is a mental representation of spatial arrangement based on a specific frame of reference. Bryant, Tversky, and Franklin (1992) extended the method to examine spatial frameworks in third-person narratives. In this case, information in front of the potential observer was accessed more quickly than information behind the observer. Franklin, Tversky, and Coon (1992) examined the situational and task variables that might control the spatial framework readers adopt. Their results suggest a "one place – one perspective" rule, in which a single consistent perspective is used for each location in the narrative world.

This analysis is consistent with the results of Black, Turner, and Bower (1979). They argued that readers generally select a default frame of reference whenever any information about spatial arrangement is encountered. If a different frame of reference is then encountered subsequently, readers may require additional time to adjust their representation. Black et al. compared sentences such as

6.1 Bill was sitting in the living room when John *came* into the living room.

to slightly different versions that suggest a different frame of reference, such as

6.2 Bill was sitting in the living room when John *went* into the living room [italics added].

In these examples, the deictic verb "came" is consistent with a frame of reference centered in the living room, while the verb "went" is not. If readers adopt such frame of reference by default while reading the first clause, sentence (6.2) should cause some difficulty. This is precisely the pattern of results observed: Reading time was substantially slower for sentences with an "inconsistent" deictic verb than with a "consistent" one. Presumably, the extra time for reading sentences such as (6.2) was used to alter the frame of reference. Black et al. assumed that readers construct a mental representation of the narratorial point of view and that processing time is needed to shift or alter that point of view. This analysis is related to that of Emmott (1997) who suggested that deictic verbs such as "come" and "go" determine the readers' "cognitive stance"; readers are assumed to enter the spatio-temporal world of the narrative and to move around in it according to the dictates of such cues.

Summary of the Evidence

The few results we have reviewed in this section suggest that speakers (and writers) have a range of methods of conveying information about spatial relations. However, only a single perspective may be adopted by the speaker or the hearer at a given time, and shifting perspective may take time or effort. In general, the relationship between the cues in the text for spatial perspective and the spatial representation constructed by the reader is likely to be loose: Any given utterance may be ambiguous by itself, and, in conversation, accurate identification of a common perspective system requires extended interaction and explicit signals. Further, without strong task demands to maintain detailed spatial representations, readers seem, at least in aggregate, to be sensitive to only coarse distinctions in spatial layout. Although this research in discourse processing on perspective and representations of space was not motivated by the distinctions and issues that have plagued narratology, we believe they have important implications in that context, and we develop these in the next section.

A Psychonarratological Approach to Focalization

We will not attempt to resolve here the debates concerning the classical problems of focalization in narratological theory, that is, the nature, mode, and agent of focalization. In our approach, we instead identify a related but somewhat different problem that we hope is more tractable: How do readers construct representations pertaining to the perceptual information in the text? Although the answer to this question is unlikely to resolve the problems of the nature, agent, and mode of focalization, we believe it will provide some valuable tools for furthering that debate. In our psychonarratological approach to this question, we first identify the features in the text that are relevant to such constructions and then generate some hypotheses concerning the nature and use of those constructions. The psychological literature on space and perspective provides some guidance in this effort. In particular, we assume that the text provides not a unique determination of spatial and perspective representations but rather a collection of overlapping constraints. In keeping with the seminal insights of Genette, as well as the evidence on perspective obtained by Tversky and others, we hypothesize that spatial location is a principle ingredient in readers' constructions concerning perceptual information. In the remainder of this chapter, we first provide a framework for understanding the relevant textual features; then we discuss some hypotheses for related reader constructions; and finally, we report some empirical evidence that supports these hypothesis. Each of these aspects is taken up in turn. (See also Bortolussi & Dixon, in press.)

Textual Features for Focalization

Our analysis of textual features for focalization is motivated by what seems important for actual readers, and paramount in this regard are implications regarding spatial positioning. Consider a simple example: The word "came" in the narrative fragment, "and then Mary came into the room," implies a spatial position that is internal to the room. From this perspective, it's as though the narrating agent were inside the room. If the sentence then continues, "Mary came into the room and looked at the rain falling outside her window," a natural reaction is to feel that although Mary is doing the seeing, the teller is "seeing" with her, for if the teller can be situated in the room with her, that same teller can also see the rain through the window. Although one can argue about who can really see or speak or how real the narrator and characters may be, one cannot dispute the fact that objects and events are described from given spatial perspectives, in this case, from inside the room. These kinds of implications are powerful for readers. Indeed, for all intents and purposes, and certainly from the perspective of the reader, *it is as if the narrating agent were there "seeing."* Saying that an omniscient narrator is "outside" the story world may not be a very intuitive way of describing narration at all, in spite of the fact that this view meets with the consent of some narratologists. To capture this intuitive importance of spatial positioning without getting lost in distinctions that are largely irrelevant to the reader, we focus on what we refer to as *perceptually salient descriptions*; a perceptually salient description is one *that could be interpreted* as sense perceptions arising from a spatial location. The term is intended to apply to all senses; vision is merely the most common. This definition allows us to discuss the textual features that are important in focalization even if an agent of focalization is not identified in the text.

An exhaustive description of all the features of the perceptually salient descriptions that might contribute to reader constructions related to focalization is an extensive task, and we will not attempt it here. However, from the relevant scholarship in narratology and linguistics, we have synthesized three categories of factors that seem to embrace a large proportion of the information pertaining to focalization in texts. We believe that these comprise a productive starting point for examining reader constructions. These categories are *descriptive reference frames, positional constraints,* and *perceptual attributions.* We outline each of these here.

Descriptive Reference Frames

There can be no description of anything that does not have implications for spatial vantage point. The literal seeing of an object by a character is certainly the clearest indicator of spatial positioning – if a character sees the front of a building, he or she is obviously not situated behind it. But this kind of intradiegetic "seeing" (as well as other kinds of perceptual information) are only one category of textual clues that indicate spatial positioning. A description of objects in an environment as being near or far is not obviously related to the direct "seeing" of a focalizing character, yet it nonetheless implies a spatial "view" or position with respect to the described objects. The spatial implications in both of these examples are captured by the notion of descriptive reference frames. In our usage, a reference frame is a set of axes that determine how spatial and relational information in a perceptual description is conveyed. As described earlier, there are a variety of subtleties concerning the nature and use of such reference frames. However, for the present purposes, it is principally useful to distinguish two categories of reference frames: *relative* and *external.*

Relative reference frames present or describe perceptual information relative to the location of a potential perceiver, as in the following two examples taken from *Madame Bovary,*

6.3 Sometimes a dog would howl in the distance
6.4 Then she would go back upstairs

As illustrated by both of these fragments, a relative descriptive reference frame implies a *descriptive position* that determines axes of the frame such as near / far, above / below, front / back, and left / right. So, for example, "in the distance" in (6.3) implies that there is a location (here) and the dog is far from that location. Similarly, in (6.4) the deictic verb "go" describes movement from the current location (here) to a location some distance removed ("upstairs" in this instance). We use the term "descriptive position" to refer to the implied location "here" in relative reference frames such as these.

In contrast, external descriptive reference frames are determined by axes found in the story world, independent of any potential perceiver. The axes of the external reference frame can be either intrinsic to the object or situation being described or based on known landmarks or directions. Consider these two examples:

6.5   The lamps shone from the summits of their tall poles. (Flaubert, *Madame Bovary*)
6.6   The photograph hung on the wall above the broken harmonium. (Joyce, "Eveline")

In (6.5), the adjective "tall" implies vertical extent and a vertical reference frame axis, and the "summit" indicates the top of that axis relative to the pole. In (6.6), "above" presupposes the vertical gravitational axis in the world. In both cases, the relative locations and their descriptions is unaffected by the position of a perceiver; that is, they could be described in the same way regardless of whether the scene is viewed from above, below, or the side. This is not the case with relative descriptive reference frames.

Our use of external reference frames collapses the common distinction between intrinsic and absolute reference frames. Our justification is that at a practical level, it is not always clear whether a given description involves intrinsic or absolute reference frames. For example, both sentences (6.5) and (6.6) could be classified as intrinsic because the directions implied by "summits" and "above" are intrinsic to the poles and harmonium, respectively. Alternatively, they both could be classified in terms of an absolute reference frame because they are using the canonical up–down dimension. Because our purpose is to find features in the text that constrain descriptive position, it is simpler to use the term "external" for both intrinsic and absolute reference frames since neither provides such constraint.

Positional Constraint

Typically, perceptually salient descriptions imply some constraint on the location of an agent who might have perceived the information. For example, relative descriptive reference frames entail that the perceiver must be at the center of the reference frame. However, the degree of such constraint on the actual location can vary considerably. For example, in (6.4), the descriptive position is constrained to be somewhere downstairs in a particular building; in (6.7), the descriptive position must merely be somewhere in Dublin:

6.7   The cars came skudding in towards Dublin (Joyce, "After the Race")

External reference frames may also imply some positional constraints, although the degree of constraint is typically less. For example, in (6.8), the descriptive position must simply be somewhere in the immediate vicinity if the information were to be perceived:

6.8   The sun shone coolly through the avenue of trees (Ellison, *Invisible Man*)

The general notion is that perceptually salient descriptions are interpreted as perceptions because readers construct a mental representation of the perceiver who of necessity must have been in the general region of the described scene, occupying a particular location in that scene. In other words, even if an external narrator is not physically present, readers may naturally attribute descriptive positions to him or her nonetheless. In particular, readers may construct a representation of the narrating agent who could have perceived the information if he or she had been present.

Perceptual Attribution

From a psychonarratological perspective, one of the most important aspects of perceptual information in the text is that it constitutes perceptual knowledge that may also be attributed to characters in the story world. We refer to the cues that support such inferences as perceptual attribution features. Some of the cues for attribution are obvious and clear to all; others are less overt but nonetheless suggestive of perceptual origin. *Perceptual verbs* constitute one such cue. For example, in (6.8), the presence of the verb "watched" clearly identifies

Emma as the perceiver; consequently, readers may infer that Emma has the perceptual knowledge corresponding to the description.

6.9   Sitting by the window, Emma watched the people of the village go by on the sidewalk (Flaubert, *Madame Bovary*)

In the absence of perceptual verbs, other cues can still suggest a perceiver. For example, Ann Banfield (1973) points out that in English, the transition to the past progressive is sometimes a sufficient cue. For example, if (6.9) is modified as in (6.10), one still has the impression that Emma is perceiving the people strolling:

6.10   Emma sat by the window; the people of the village were strolling by on the sidewalk

Intuitively, the tense shift suggests that the strolling is subordinate to and part of the Emma's observation from a sitting position; a possible inference then is that she must have been aware of this perceptual information. We also argue that another type of cue for perceptual attribution is simply *salient ability*. In other words, if it is clear that a character has the ability to perceive the information, then it may be plausible to attribute that perception to the character. This is illustrated in (6.11), also modified from (6.9):

6.11   Emma gazed out the window; the people of the village strolled by on the sidewalk

While the perceptual verb "gazed" does not explicitly associate the villagers strolling by with Emma's perception, the implicit connection may be sufficiently strong to lead readers to this inference.

In most contexts, these cues do not require that a character perceive a given object or scene; they only make it likely or plausible. Nevertheless, when these cues are sufficiently numerous and consistent, it can become clear that a given character is doing the perceiving. In such cases, we can speak of a narrator's *perceptual access* to that character. For the reader, if the narrator has perceptual access to a character, then for all intents and purposes the narrator perceives what the character perceives. This corresponds to a limited sense of Chatman's (1986) term "filter." However, for Chatman the notion of filter carries with it the idea that the character is the source of the perceptual information provided by the narration. In our usage, instead, perceptual access merely refers to a particular characteristic of the text, namely, the extended and consistent use of cues for perceptual attribution. The perceptual knowledge corresponding to the perceptual descriptions may then be consistently attributed to a character by a reader. However, identifying precisely what a character knows or recalls concerning the corresponding perceptual information involves inferential processing on the part of the reader (cf. Graesser, Bowers and Olde, 1999).

The features of descriptive reference frames, positional constraint, and perceptual attribution can be defined locally, over a collection of a few sentences, or globally. However, in extended texts, reference frames are likely to shift and be intermixed, so that attributions in any given case may be more or less clear, and positional constraints are likely to change, so that some will be mutually consistent, others not. As an aside, we note that this repeated shifting of descriptive reference frames and positional constraint may be a vital feature of omniscient narration. In this view, omniscience would not be caused by the narrator's ubiquitous presence or spatially unlimited position as some narratologists previously argued (e.g., Edmiston, 1989) but rather by the difficulty in localizing or constraining the narrator's position in a consistent manner.

Implications

A clear delineation of the various features strictly provided by the text, along the lines we have suggested, eliminates many of the conceptual difficulties that have plagued the treatment of focalization in classical narratology. First, it provides a resolution of the tension between minimalist and maximalist views of the nature of focalization. The minimalist perspective can be understood as a particular analysis of textual features; the approach taken here builds on many of these ideas. The maximalist perspective also includes a variety of notions concerning reader constructions, which must be interpreted as hypotheses that can only be verified with empirical evidence. Second, it eliminates the anthropomorphic connotations of terms such as "narrator" and "seeing." As we have argued, these concepts are better treated as reader constructions rather than as objective properties of the text. Although many of the cues that contribute to such constructions can be readily identified in the text, it is crucial to distinguish such features from what readers may or may not do with that information. Third, the distinction between internal and external focalization can be seen as an aspect of perceptual attribution. Internal focalization refers to the attribution of perceptual information to a character; external focalization refers to the absence of such attributions. Fourth, it illuminates the distinction between discourse (telling) and story (seeing). In our framework, the textual features for focalization are part and parcel of the discourse, that is, the telling. However, the property of seeing is construed as one aspect of what readers do with that information, in other words, a reader construction. One might say that based on what the text *tells* the reader, he or she constructs a representation of an entity that *sees*.

Reader Constructions for Focalization

Having discussed some categories of textual features related to perceptual information, the important question that should be considered is how such cues are processed by readers. What kinds of constructions do readers generate when they encounter perceptual descriptions in the text? There is unlikely to be a simple answer to such questions, and, as suggested previously, the evidence indicates that such constructions vary with the knowledge and goals of the reader. We present here several ideas concerning one aspect of the representations readers may construct in processing perceptually salient descriptions. Subsequently, we report some evidence in support of these ideas.

In our previous discussion of the nature, agent, and mode of focalization, it was clear that the relationship of the narrator to focalization was central to many of the conceptual difficulties that are apparent in this literature. Yet in many texts, there are no textual features that define the narrator or that relationship. Instead, as we argued in Chapter 3, the narrator should be thought of as a reader construction, that is, a mental representation the reader builds on the basis of information garnered from the text. Our hypotheses concerning reader constructions relevant to focalization are closely tied to that representation of the narrator. To reiterate our earlier argument, we assume that the mental representation of the narrator is analogous to the representation that people construct of other participants in a

conversation. Typically, this means that the narrator will be represented as (a) having sufficient knowledge of the story world;
(b) having a goal in presenting the narrative; (c) providing rational
and reliable information; and (d) cooperative in the sense of providing only necessary and sufficient information to understand the
narrative. Such assumptions are necessary for effectively engaging in
conversation, and one of the key hypotheses of this book is that they
are imported into readers' processing of the narrator.

Perceptual Knowledge

The processing of focalization features can be understood in terms of
this construction of a conversational narrator. In particular, perceptually salient descriptions would be interpreted in terms of the first
assumption that the narrator has knowledge of the fictional world;
they are cues to the perceptual knowledge that the narrator has. This
does not require that the narrator be thought of as belonging to the
story world, actually perceiving objects, scenes, and events. Instead,
it implies that readers imbue narrators with the perceptual knowledge that would result *if they were* a part of that world. For example,
when readers read a sentence such as (6.3), repeated here, they don't
necessarily assume that the narrator is a character in the story world
at that particular point in time and space, but they are likely to assume that he or she has the perceptual knowledge that would have
resulted from being there.

6.3   Sometimes a dog would howl in the distance

This kind of knowledge is required if the conversational assumption
of sufficient knowledge of the story world is to be sustained. Stanzel
expressed the same idea in different words, concluding that "what
is narrated by a teller–character claims, implicitly or explicitly, to be
a complete record of events, or a record as complete as the narrator
could or would, for the sake of the reader, make it"(Stanzel, 1981:8).

The features we identified previously provide the central ingredients for making inferences concerning perceptual knowledge. In
particular, positional constraint dictates that perceptual information
that is available at one location may be available to the narrator,
while other information would not be. For example, in (6.8), repeated

here, the reader may attribute other perceptual information about the locale, the trees, and the weather to the narrator, but may be less willing to attribute knowledge of other times and locations.

6.8   The sun shone coolly through the avenue of trees (R Ellison, *Invisible Man*)

Similarly, when relative reference frames imply a location in the story world, the narrator may be imbued with the perceptual knowledge that would be available at that location.

Narrator–Character Associations

As we mentioned in Chapter 3, specific perceptual access may lead readers to construct a narrator–character association. Specific perceptual access occurs when a large proportion of the perceptual descriptions are related as perceptual access only to a protagonist (e.g., Joyce's "Eveline"). We hypothesize that a consequence of such a narrative form is that readers come to form an association between the narrator and the character and to presume that in general, the perceptual knowledge of the narrator can also be attributed to the character, even when it is not explicitly marked as such in the text. A narrator–character association is related to the concept of a narrative "center" described by Chatman (1986), although in our framework this is clearly a reader construction rather than a feature of the text. One of the advantages of a narrator–character association is that it provides a heuristic for tracking perceptual knowledge. Rather than having to collate a variety of textual features for what perceptual information the narrator might have at any given point, the reader may adopt the shortcut of assuming that the perceptual knowledge of a character (who can typically be located at a specific point in the story world) is the same as that of the narrator. This is where we part ways with Stanzel, who claimed that because a reflector–character presents elements in an arbitrary fashion, owing to the fact that these elements are "determined by the reflector–character's experiential and existential contingencies," their perspective is less trustworthy than that of a teller-character (Stanzel, 1981:8).

As outlined in Chapter 3, a narrator–character association may also have other implications for reader constructions. Because in some sense the associated character stands for the narrator in the story world, readers may conflate the properties of the two. So, for example, the narrator may be presumed to share the character's age, gender, and social standing, and the conversational assumptions of cooperativeness, rationality, and reliability may come to be attributed to the character as well as the narrator. In this respect, we agree with William Nelles who, in his critique of Chatman's idea that narrators can't see, concluded that "the distinction between character and narrator ... would have to be a very subtle (or arbitrary) one and might serve little purpose. The narrator's seeing and conceiving appear to be identical with the character's" (Nelles, 1990:370–1).

In sum, we suggest that there may be three important aspects of reader constructions related to focalization. First, readers generally construct a representation of the narrator like that constructed of a conversational participant and endow that representation with the perceptual knowledge corresponding to perceptually salient descriptions. Second, in the presence of consistent perceptual access to a character, readers may construct an association between the narrator and that character, so that the character is presumed by default to share the perceptual knowledge of the narrator, and vice versa. And third, a perceptual association between the narrator and a character may lead the reader to assume that other attributes of the narrator and the character overlap as well: The character may share the narrator's rationality and cooperativeness, and the narrator may share the character's age, gender, and other physical attributes.

Empirical Evidence

In this section, we provide evidence related to one element of the framework we have described. In particular, we report an experiment devised to test whether readers form narrator–character associations on the basis of consistent perceptual access, and whether such associations have implications for the representations of the narrator and the character.[3] Ten stories were constructed involving an argument between a male and a female character. In all the stories, the point of contention was conveyed ambiguously, so that there were no clear

---

[3] These data were previously reported by Dixon and Bortolussi (1996b).

cues as to which of the two was in the right. The arguments ranged from trivial to dramatic. For example, in one a boy and a girl argue about whether someone was tripped intentionally in a relay race; in another, a husband and wife argue about whether the man is having an affair; and in another the argument revolves around a man's role in a murder. The language of the stories provided a wealth of perceptual descriptions with relative reference frames centered on one of the two characters. In addition, much of the perceptual information was unambiguously attributed to that character (e.g., "Julia glanced," "she watched," "she heard"). The consistent use of these features constitutes specific perceptual access to the character and suggests that the perceptual knowledge is shared by both character and narrator. The intent here was to make the cues for perceptual access as strong as possible; weaker or less consistent cues (such as positional constraints that don't correspond to the location of the character or the use of external rather than relative reference frames) might produce weaker effects. Two versions of each story were created, one that provided specific perceptual access to the male character and one that provided specific perceptual access to the female character. Examples of the two versions are shown in Table 6.1.

According to our hypothesis, consistent perceptual access should lead the reader to form an association between the narrator and the character. This in turn may cause the properties of the two to be conflated, so that the narrator takes on the properties of the character, such as gender, and the character takes on the conversationally appropriate attributes of narrators, such as cooperativeness, rationality, and reliability. To assess this prediction, we asked readers to answer four questions after reading each story. The first question pertained to the point of the argument and asked whether the reader thought the male or female character was right; the second question asked which character was more reasonable and rational, properties that would normally be associated with the narrator; the third question asked with which character the writer most sympathized; and the fourth question asked subjects to identify the gender of the writer. Readers responded to each question on a six-point scale, with 6 associated with the male character and 1 associated with the female character. Thus, we expected higher values when the perceptual attribution and relative reference frames were associated with the male character, and

TABLE 6.1. *Example of Perceptual Access Manipulation*

Female Perceptual Access
Julia was jogging back and forth on the track, the hot sun beating down against her face. She glanced briefly at the large crowd of people in the stands then looked to her left and noticed Brad Peterson, kneeling down on the track to tighten his shoelaces. She watched him as he stood up and began stretching his legs. The crowd suddenly went silent and, after a moment, she heard the blast of the gun then watched the first runner from her relay team burst out of the blocks.

Male Perceptual Access
Brad was kneeling down on the track to tighten his shoelaces, the hot sun beating down on his back. He glanced briefly at the large crowd of people in the stands then looked to his left and noticed Julia Williams jogging back and forth on the track. He began stretching his legs, feeling almost immediate relief from the tightness in his calf muscles. The crowd suddenly went silent and, after a moment, he heard the blast of the gun, then watched the first runner from his relay team burst out of the blocks.

we expected lower values when the focalization cues were associated with the female character. Twenty psychology undergraduates read the stories and provided responses. Each subject read one version of each passage in a random order. Version was counterbalanced over participants, so that each participant read five passages with the female perceptual access and five with male perceptual access, and across participants, each passage was read equally often in each version. (However, data for one passage was not used because of missing responses.)

The mean responses are shown in Figure 6.1. As can be seen, the results are consistent with our predictions: Providing specific perceptual access to the male character (for example) leads readers to side with the male character in the argument, to see the male character as more rational and reasonable, to infer that the writer is more sympathetic with the male character, and to assume that the writer is probably male. The evidence for these interpretations was assessed by calculating likelihood ratios as described in the Appendix. In this case, we compared the likelihood of the data based on the assumption that the observed difference represents a difference in the population means, with the likelihood of the data based on the assumption that

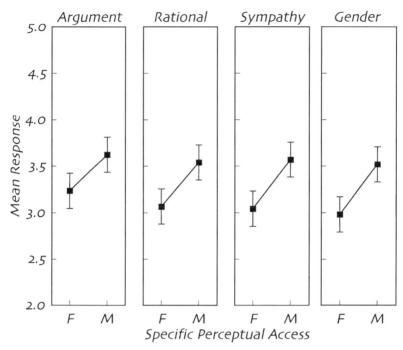

FIGURE 6.1. Mean response to the argument, rationality, sympathy, and gender questions as a function of specific perceptual access to the female (F) or male (M) character. Error bars indicate the size of 95% confidence intervals, adjusted for pairwise comparisons.

the obtained effects are due merely to chance variation. The value of the likelihood ratio was $\lambda = 4.58$ for the first question, $\lambda = 15.44$ for the second question, $\lambda = 46.01$ for the third question, and $\lambda = 65.67$ for the fourth. A likelihood ratio of 10 indicates relatively good evidence in favor of an interpretation of the data that includes an effect; thus, these calculations indicate that there is clear evidence for an effect of version on the response to the rationality, sympathy, and gender question. The evidence in favor of an effect of version on the argument question is weaker, although the pattern of results is similar to that for the other questions.

Although the size of the effects is small, it is perhaps as large as one might expect with a manipulation of this sort. For example, in deciding whom to side with in the argument, it seems likely that readers would be strongly affected by the actual content of the arguments made by the two characters, and only weakly affected by perceptual access. Similarly, readers may realize that there is no clear information provided by the text concerning the gender of the author and so may be reluctant to express a strong opinion based only on perceptual access. In general, we believe that the consistent effects of perceptual access, despite their small size, provide compelling evidence for our thesis that readers form perceptual associations between the narrator and the character on the basis of the manipulated features.

Summary

In this chapter, we reviewed some problems with the classical approaches in narratology to aspects of focalization: the nature of focalization, the agent of focalization, and the mode of focalization. In our view, a central shortcoming in this debate has been a failure to distinguish clearly the objective features of the text from the potentially variable reader constructions. This has produced a tension between what we refer to as the minimalist conception of focalization (based narrowly on what can be found in the text) and the maximalist conception (which includes a substantial amount of reader constructions). Moreover, at least some of the approaches would seem to require conceptual distinctions that many readers are likely to find unintuitive and to neglect what we believe to be the critical role of space and location in the story world.

Although research in discourse processing has generally not been concerned with these issues, some of the investigations provide valuable insights about the representation and processing of space and spatial perspective. The evidence indicates that speakers (and presumably authors) have a variety of techniques for providing spatial information, and although these techniques are generally used coherently, any given utterance may provide only ambiguous cues concerning the nature of the spatial framework being used. Similarly, readers may maintain a range of possible representations of space depending on their goals and the circumstances, ranging from precise representations of spatial relations and layout to much coarser representations. However, a variety of results suggest that readers represent the spatial location of the narrator or a perceiver: Information may be differentially accessible depending on its location relative to the narrator, and readers may assume a consistent spatial framework for the description of a given locale.

Based on these considerations, we suggested that many textual features for perceptually salient descriptions fall into three categories: descriptive reference frames, positional constraint, and perceptual attributions. We hypothesize two types of reader constructions based on these features: perceptual knowledge, that is, the perceptual information the narrator and characters have about the story world; and narrator–character associations, that is, a link between the perceptual knowledge of the narrator and that of a given character. The latter may lead to an expectation that the narrator and the associated character may share attributes as well as perceptual knowledge. In support of these hypothesized constructions, we reported a study in which specific perceptual access was manipulated in a number of passages. Consistent with our expectations, this manipulation affected both the rated rationality of the character and the rated gender of the narrator.

7

Represented Speech and Thought

Literary narratives in which only events are summarized are virtually nonexistent. In most narratives there are characters who speak and think; in fact, casual observation indicates that in many literary texts well over half of the words consist of dialogue or representations of character thoughts. The speech and thought of characters can be used for a wide range of purposes: It can advance the plot, provide direct information about the speaking characters and their reactions as well as indirect information about other characters, present the reader with a variety of perspectives or viewpoints, convey attitudes and judgments of the narrator, and communicate thematic content. Thus, the category of speech and thought intersects with those of narrator, plot, character, and focalization, and it is often impossible to speak of one without alluding to the others.

Because of the enormous variety of styles and techniques available to authors for the representation of speech and thought, the study of its forms and uses is a complex problem that, in our view, is still not fully understood. Within the fields of literary scholarship and linguistics, however, there have been a variety of important advances including typologies of speech and thought representation styles. Literary scholars in particular have been sensitive to the crucial issue of the effect of speech and thought representation styles on readers; however, they have been unable to frame hypotheses about reader constructions beyond the limits of purely speculative intuitions. For example, discussions about the techniques used to convey speech and thought often include assumptions about the effect of different styles of represented speech on readers (Prince, 1982; Corcoran, 1991; Danov, 1986; Emberson, 1986; Fort, 1985; Gross, 1993; McHale, 1978; Moore, 1993; Oltean, 1986; Prince, 1982; Sanders & Redeker, 1996; Tolliver, 1990). These assumptions are generally intuitions based on experience with literary texts. Although such insights are helpful, our view is that the generality and magnitude of such effects needs to be carefully considered. Indeed, we maintain that arguments about the effects of narrative techniques on readers should be the basis of hypotheses concerning reader constructions and as such need to be empirically validated. In this sense, scholarship on represented speech and thought contains a wealth of potential directions for empirical research. In discourse-processing research, on the other hand, the problem of represented speech and thought has not been thoroughly studied.

Our discussion of represented speech and thought begins with a brief description of some basic vocabulary and distinctions. Subsequently, we review some of the work on represented speech in narratology and linguistics, pointing out the difficulties inherent in these approaches. Based on this background, we propose several elements that we feel are important in a psychonarratological account of speech and thought and use these in an analysis of free-indirect discourse. Some empirical support for this analysis is presented.

Basic Distinctions

We use the term "represented speech and thought" to refer to the depiction of the content, wording, or manner of verbalization of characters' speech and thought. Such depictions can vary in terms of the techniques or style chosen by the author to convey that content and the amount and nature of information provided about the character's discourse. Here, we offer an overview of some of the possible distinctions and discuss some of the intuitions concerning their effects on readers.

Direct and Indirect Discourse

The most straightforward method of presenting speech or thought in narrative is by means of a transcription. This generally corresponds to quoted speech in the text in which the words of the character are presented verbatim; in some conventions, the speech of a character may also be set off by dashes rather than quotes. Either method is known as *direct* speech. In addition to the information concerning the words of the speech, a direct transcription may also include punctuation or other typographical conventions that depict something of the manner in which the words were conveyed. Direct speech generally includes tags that attribute the speech to a character or convey other information about the nature of the speech. In contrast *indirect* speech provides an indication that speech or thought has occurred in the story world and something of the content of that discourse but without precise information about word choice. An example is the following sentence from Emily Carr's *Klee Wyck*: "I told Aleck to ask if his mother would like to have me give her pictures of her poles" (1941:107). Conveyed indirectly in this sentence is the content of the speaker's message to Aleck, but not the precise words employed in the original utterance.

The distinction between direct and indirect discourse is sometimes associated with differential reader involvement with the characters. Prince (1982) observed that direct discourse reduces the "distance" between characters and reader to a minimum, thereby eliminating the presence of the narrator. In this respect, direct discourse creates a more dramatic effect, which may succeed in "heightening liveliness and the reader's involvement by *showing* what happened instead of *reporting* it" (Sanders & Redeker, 1996:297). Readers view the characters speaking directly, as in a play, and thus presumably experience a greater sense of immediacy or proximity to the characters.

In contrast, it is commonly thought that "we feel a greater distance and detachment from characters and their words when these are mediated via indirect speech" (Toolan, 1995:121) because "the indirect mode is less subjective in the sense that the utterance is less exclusively the embedded character's responsibility" (Sanders & Redeker, 1996:301). For example, consider the sentence from Willa Cather's short story, "Paul's Case": "The firm of Denny & Carson announced that the boy's father had refunded the full amount of his theft, and that they had no intention of prosecuting" (1951:171). Here, a summary of the content of the utterance is issued by some unspecified representative of the company, but no information is provided concerning

the precise vocabulary used, the length or style of the original pro-
nouncement, or the tone of voice with which it was spoken. The use
of indirect speech serves to render the speaker less accessible to the
reader which, intuitively, reduces the reader's involvement with that
speaker.

The Role of the Narrator

The narrator has an important role in the understanding and interpretation of represented discourse, regardless of whether it is conveyed
in a direct or indirect style. The narrator often conveys information
concerning, for example, the manner of the speech or thought or the
relation between the discourse and the surrounding events of the
narrative. Indirect speech would seem to provide greater opportunity for conveying such information because indirect speech may
be combined with other information provided by the narrator concerning beliefs, attitudes, or plot events. For example, consider this
passage from the same Cather story:

> After supper was over, and he had helped to dry the dishes, Paul nervously
> asked his father whether he could go to George's to get some help in his
> geometry, and still more nervously asked for car-fare. (1951:160)

In this case, the text provides information not only about Paul's general utterance, but also about the situation and his state of mind. Such
attributions might convey important cues about the character's communicative intent but can also create their own kind of ambiguity. For
example, while readers learn that Paul's state of mind is troubled, the
source of the trouble is not conveyed but left up to the reader to infer. Thus, allusions to his nervousness wouldn't necessarily help the
reader very much in understanding Paul's problem.

It is not clear whether direct or indirect speech would require more
processing effort on the part of readers to understand characters.
There are several possibilities. On one hand, direct speech might require more inferential processing because it is unaccompanied by
narratorial cues as to how to interpret the character's words. For this
reason, direct speech is sometimes thought to pose a greater interpretational challenge for the reader; he or she must "read between the
lines" without any assistance from the narrator. On the other hand,

as Rimmon-Kenan (1983) pointed out, the magnitude of that challenge depends not so much on the speech representation style as on the amount of additional information provided in the narrative. We agree with her conclusion that the "crucial distinction is not between telling and showing, but between different kinds of telling" (108). Further, the analysis and interpretation of naturally occurring speech is an activity in which readers commonly engage in real life with little effort, and one might suspect that the interpretation of transcribed speech would be accomplished with similar facility. Thus, while hearing characters speak directly may make us feel that we are physically closer to them, the ease of interpretation of that speech will depend on a variety of other properties of the narrative.

Another intuition concerning the effect of representation style pertains to the effort required on the part of readers to track changes in voice, that is, the speaker of the words of the text. In some cases, the utterance of a character may be signaled relatively obliquely, and, on the assumption that readers do indeed attempt to track shifts from narrator to character voice, an inference may be required to decide that a character has spoken. For example, the following passage from "Paul's Case" reflects this ambiguity: "Paul was startled for a moment, and had the feeling of wanting to put her out; what business had she here among all these fine people and gay colours?" (1951:153). On one hand, the entire sentence might be a rendition of Paul's thought, conveyed indirectly. On the other hand, the final clause ("what business had she here among all these fine people and gay colours?") might be a direct representation (i.e., verbatim transcription) of Paul's thoughts. Later in this chapter, we will discuss reader constructions pertaining to tracking such changes in voice.

Free Direct and Indirect Discourse

One variant of direct speech and thought may be termed *free-direct discourse*. In this case, the words of characters' speech or thought are conveyed directly, but without tags, quotation marks, or other markers (McHale, 1978:259; Prince, 1987:34). In Gioconda Belli's *The Inhabited Woman*, entire sections of the novel are written in free-direct speech to represent the voice of the spirit of an Indian woman who lived at the time of the Spanish conquest and who now inhabits the orange tree in the protagonist Lavinia's backyard. An example follows:

Poor Lavinia, looking at me, so absorbed in her love. She has not even noticed the orange blossoms, the aroma my white flowers give off.... Her sadness has penetrated me, spilling out through all my branches. (1995:301)

In its context, the passage is read as a transcription of the thoughts of the spirit, even though there are no quotation or other distinguishing markers.

An important theoretical problem in the analysis of represented speech and thought is *free-indirect speech*. In this narrative technique, the *narrator's* voice is used to convey the actual vocabulary and sentence structure of a character's speech without attribution tags, quotation marks, or other typographical cues. For example, in Toni Morrison's *Beloved*, the following passage, embedded in a conversation between Denver and Paul D., represents Denver's answer to Paul's question, "You on your way home?":

She said no. She had heard about an afternoon job at the shirt factory. She hoped that with her night work at the Bodwins' and another one, she could put away something and help her mother too.

The passage continues:

When he asked her if they treated her all right over there, she said more than all right. Miss Bodwin taught her stuff. (1998:266)

The last sentence is Denver's answer related in free-indirect speech. In these examples, the free-indirect speech style creates an impression of mimetic fidelity to Denver's actual utterance. However, details of the sentence structure (such as the tense and use of pronouns) are indicative of the narrator's voice and would be appropriate in indirect speech. Thus, "Miss Bodwin taught her stuff" would be a free-indirect rendering of the direct transcription, "Miss Bodwin teaches me stuff."

There is no perfect consensus on the precise features that signal instances of free-indirect discourse. McHale's (1978) review of the research demonstrated the inadequacies of purely grammatical accounts of free-indirect speech and led him to conclude that "no one kind of index is uniquely constitutive of FID [free-indirect speech] in all cases, but rather that some kinds are decisive for the reader's recognition of it in some cases, others in other cases" (McHale, 1978:264; see also, Rimmon-Kenan, 1983). Thus, it may be proper to conceive of the technique as consisting of a variety of subtypes or matters of degree. However, as a heuristic definition, we take free-indirect speech to consist of clear evidence that the words of the text provide information about the word choice and sentence structure that the character used (such as the use of vocabulary or dialect features that would be inappropriate for the narrator's voice), together with other indications that the text does not provide a transcription per se (e.g., tense shifts and the use of pronouns that would be appropriate for indirect speech).

Free-indirect speech can be used to convey a character's utterance with varying degrees of mimetic accuracy. In the following example from Gioconda Belli's *The Inhabited Woman*, the free-indirect style of the last two sentences is used to summarize the contents of Lavinia's direct thoughts. It appears in the context of the protagonist's awareness of her loneliness:

She had suddenly been left alone in the world. Alone and anxious. (342).... And where could Felipe be? Where were Flor and Sebastián? (1995:343)

We can surmise in the last two sentences, that only the verb tense marks the presence of the narrator, and that Lavinia's actual speech utterance would have probably been simply, "Where can Felipe be? Where are Flor and Sebastián?" Hence, in this example, the degree of mimetic accuracy is considerable.

Frequently, free-indirect speech appears in the context of the narrator's discourse, and only the use of particular vocabulary signals the change in voice. Under such circumstances, the mimetic accuracy may be less apparent. An example is the following passage from Angela Carter's short story "Black Venus" about the famed lover of the French poet Charles Bandelaire:

Therefore you could say, not so much that Jeanne did not understand the lapidary, troubled serenity of her lover's poetry but, that it was a perpetual affront to her. He recited it to her by the hour and she ached, raged, and chafed under it because his eloquence denied her language. It made her dumb, a dumbness all the more profound because it manifested itself in a harsh clatter of ungrammatical recriminations and demands which were not directed at her lover so much – she was quite fond of him – as at her own condition, great gawk of an ignorant black girl, good for nothing: correction, good for only one thing, even if the spirochetes were already burrowing away diligently at her spinal marrow while she bore up the superb weight of oblivion on her Amazonian head. (1996:9)

In this context, it seems inappropriate to attribute the words "great gawk of an ignorant black girl . . . one thing" to the narrator because her attitude toward the subject matter, Jeanne Duval herself, is highly respectful and sympathetic. Furthermore, the vocabulary and sentence structure in this portion of the passage is atypical of the narrator. For these reasons, one might infer that the words spoken are those of Jeanne Duval, recriminating herself. Unlike the previous example, there is no back shifting of tenses, and we are provided with only a few of the specific words of what might have been the protagonist's original speech or thought utterance.

An intuitive analysis of free-indirect discourse suggests that the voice of the character and the narrator are intertwined (McHale, 1978; Rimmon-Kenan, 1983). One might infer, then, that free-indirect discourse demands less interpretational effort on the part of the reader because the narrator provides some guidance, or, as Rimmon-Kenan put it, free-indirect discourse "can assist the reader in reconstructing the implied author's attitude towards the character(s) involved" (1983:114). Prince (1982) suggested that minimal distance between reader and character entails more demanding reader processing, which would presuppose that the greater the narrative distance, the lesser the interpretative effort required of the reader. Alternatively, free-indirect speech may tend to suggest that the narrator and character share a point of view. However, as Rimmon-Kenan pointed out, echoing McHale, free-indirect speech may act as a double-edged sword, because "the presence of a narrator as distinct from the character may create an ironic distancing," and readers cannot always choose between "the ironic and the empathetic attitude" (1983:114).

McHale's 1978 article on free-indirect speech made a significant contribution in acknowledging the role of readers' experiences of free-indirect speech. Arguing against purely grammatical approaches that focus exclusively on syntactical features, he demonstrated the important "bi-vocality" of free-indirect speech. Disparaging the meticulous linguistic analysis to track the minutest change in voice, McHale recognized that the reader "does not experience a text as a collection of syntactical patterns ... but as a sequence of signals, only some of which may lead him to discern the presence of 'other voices' in the text" (264). How precisely readers process free-indirect speech, especially when faced with ambiguities concerning whose voice or point of view is represented, is something that has still not been studied.

In some usages, the term "represented speech and thought" is reserved specifically for free-indirect discourse. As such, it is distinguished from *reported* speech and thought, corresponding to what we have referred to as direct discourse. The term "reported speech and thought" emphasizes the mediating activity of the narrator, that is, the fact that someone is directly attributing speech or thought to someone. Typically, this is achieved by means of a tag introduction (e.g., "he said," "Irma thought") followed by the speech or thoughts in quotation marks. In contrast, the term "represented speech and thought" is used to emphasize the speaking and/or thinking subject. It typically eliminates tags and summarizes the contents of the speech or thought indirectly while conserving some elements of the character's speech. Represented speech and thought conveys the gist of the speech or thought content, but because that content is still filtered through the narrator, it is often difficult to distinguish clearly between character and narrator voice. In our view, this more restricted understanding of the term "represented speech and thought" is confusing. Even in free-indirect speech, there is an element of narratorial reporting. By the same token, direct speech is representational in that the narrator selects the utterances and chooses tags, even though the content within quotation marks eliminates the narratorial voice. For this reason, we use the term "represented speech and thought" to refer simply to all styles of conveying speech and thought.

Nested Speech and Thought

Another complexity occurs when a character's speech refers to other speech and thought, for example as either direct or indirect discourse.

This is likely to be common in extended dialogue. For example, in John le Carre's *Smiley's People*, a character relates a previous telephone conversation:

> 'Get on with it, Mostyn,' Stickland growled.
> 'I said "Hullo" back, Mr. Smiley. That's all we do. We don't give the number. He said, "This is Gregory calling for Max. I have something very urgent for him. Please get me Max immediately." I asked him where he was calling from, which is routine, but he just said he had plenty of change.' (1992:67)

The relationship between the styles of nested speech can be complex. In this example, also from *Smiley's People*, Otto's speech is related in free-indirect style nested within the indirect description of Connie's speech:

> The Ginger Pig made his pitch so badly, said Connie, that Otto had at first to deride the proposal simply for the sake of verisimilitude: it was too crazy, too hole-in-the-corner, he said – secret lists, what nonsense! Why didn't Kirov approach the émigré organizations themselves and swear them to secrecy? Why employ a total outsider to do his dirty work? (1992:210)

In this instance, it is unclear precisely what the reader should infer about how Connie chose to relate Otto's speech: She may have quoted it directly, and it was then rendered in free-indirect style by the narrator; she may have used a free-indirect form comparable to that in the text; or it is conceivable that Connie only described the conversation indirectly and the information about wording and syntax were added by the (omniscient) narrator.

Of course, it is even possible for the nested speech itself to contain references to other speech and thought, as in this third example from *Smiley's People*:

> Grigoriev recalled being strangely touched by the priest's finality. 'Diagnosis and treatment are too often complicated by political considerations,' the priest went on. "In four years of treatment in our hospitals, the child Alexandra has been accused of many things by her doctors. 'Paranoid reformist and delusional ideas ... An over-estimation of her own personality ... Poor adaptation to the social environment ... Over-inflation of her capabilities ... A bourgeois decadence in her sexual behaviour.' Soviet doctors have repeatedly ordered her to renounce her incorrect ideas. This is not medicine," said the priest unhappily to Grigoriev. (1992:351)

Here, the priest quotes the Soviet doctors directly in his conversation to Grigoriev, but the surrounding context makes it clear that the entire direct speech of the priest is embedded in an indirect rendition of Grigoriev's description of this conversation to Smiley. Thus, there are three levels of speech being described, as follows:

Grigoriev → Smiley
   The priest → Grigoriev
      Soviet doctors → The priest

The ability of readers to sort out such complexities with little apparent difficulty provides important clues as to the nature of the language processing system and how it is used in processing narrative. Clark (1996; see also Bruce, 1981) argued that language is generally represented in "layers" that embed one speech act in another; in his analysis, even casual conversation can easily have two or three such layers. An important problem for the processing of narrative is the extent to which these layers are maintained distinctly in readers' representations. In particular, we suspect that the enduring representation of distinct layers may depend heavily on the supporting information provided by the narrator and the reader's representation of the narrator's point or message. However, we do not discuss in any detail these hypotheses, or the other complexities involved in nested speech and thought, in our present analysis.

Approaches to Speech and Thought in Narrative

Almost nine decades after Bally published his 1912 article on the free-indirect style in modern French, the study of reported speech and thought is far from exhausted, as indicated by the proliferation of scholarship on the topic. In the 1990s alone, dozens of studies have appeared, dispersed in books and journals in different disciplines: linguistics, narratology, stylistics, discourse analysis, and philosophy. An important development that has occurred over the years among the approaches has been the conceptual shift from an analysis of speech and thought based on the features of individual sentences (e.g., Banfield, 1981, 1993) to more context-based approaches. The latter fall into two broad classes: approaches based on larger units of text and approaches based on more pragmatic considerations in which the reader plays an important role. Each of these trends is discussed in turn.

Sentence-Level Models

We use the term "sentence-level models" to refer to approaches that seek to distinguish different styles of presenting speech and thought in terms of a fixed set of syntactic and typographical characteristics of individual sentences. A central element of such analyses is the distinction between "who sees" and "who speaks." The debate on the nature of the focalizer discussed in Chapter 6 bears on this distinction. However, since Genette (1973), "who sees" and "who speaks" have been considered separate issues. The distinction has been upheld by prominent narratologists such as Mieke Bal (1985), and formalist and grammatical models typically seek to specify the points in a text where a shift occurs in focalization and speech. Yet distinguishing between who sees and who speaks in a text is confusing even for narratologists, and instances of speech are often confounded with instances of "point of view" or perception. The connection between focalization and verbalization is easy to understand because changes in voice often co-occur with perceptual shifts and may signal shifts in emotional, evaluative, and ideological perspective as well. Rather than supporting the need to maintain a meticulous tracking of vision and voice, some narratologists have acknowledged that focalization is always tied to the notion of "voice" or speech (Fludernik, 1996:344, Sanders & Redeker, 1996). This recognition does not imply that the who sees / who speaks distinction is invalid, but it does suggest that for the reader the dissociation of who sees and who speaks may not be as obvious or meaningful as it is to some narratologists.

A prime example of a sentence-level approach is that of Banfield (1981). Her account depends on a distinction between "reflective" and "nonreflective" consciousness. Reflective consciousness refers to self-conscious awareness; nonreflective consciousness refers to (unspoken) tacit knowledge. Characters' utterances are examples of reflective consciousness when they are verbalized, either out loud or in thought, while nonverbalized thought, perception, or sentiment of that character would be nonreflective. Banfield maintained that syntactic features characterize each. Nonreflective consciousness (i.e., perceptions and nonverbalized thought) is marked by the past tense, whereas reflective consciousness is marked by the use of the imperfect or past progressive tenses. Nonreflective consciousness is also depicted through the use of "shifted" modals, such as "could," "would," "should," and "might" (as opposed to "can," "shall," "will," "may"). Reflective consciousness is suggested by lexical items associated with the character's speech, as well as by the use of exclamations, expressive words, direct questions, and parentheticals that make it clear that the character has such conscious thoughts or awareness (e.g., "he thought to himself," "she realized").

However, Banfield's account of the syntactical distinctions that mark the discursive representation of reflective and nonreflective consciousness is at times forced, and the distinctions are difficult to apply with certainty. As her own examples demonstrate, ambiguities regarding whether a clause or sentence falls into one or the other category cannot always be resolved purely on a textual basis. For example, Banfield claimed that the sentence, "she managed to re-fasten her veil," is not necessarily "pure narrative description," because it *"can be read* from the subject's point of view," as a representation "of the awareness" of this act of refastening the veil (1981:73; italics added). However, this claim would seem to imply an important role for reader interpretation, which in general is not determined solely by the text. Further, allowing textual distinctions to depend on unspecified predilections of the reader imbues the approach with a certain circularity.

Banfield's (1993) discussion of free-indirect discourse raises other problems. Rejecting the consensus that free-indirect speech is a blending of the narrator's and character's language and points of view, Banfield argued that sentences in fiction can represent *either* the "direct expression of a speaker's . . . point of view" *or* that of the narrator, although she acknowledged that fictional texts can alternate between the two kinds of sentence styles. Obviously uncomfortable with the term "free-indirect style," Banfield (1993) translated the French term "style indirect libre" as "represented speech and thought." One of her main arguments was that represented speech and thought (free-indirect discourse in our terms) is noncommunicational in the sense that it is not addressed to any interlocutor, but merely represents states of mind. For Banfield, the use of represented speech and thought can signal either reflective or nonreflective consciousness, both of which differentiate themselves from reported speech and thought by their lack of communicational scope.

Numerous scholars have argued that Banfield's distinction between communicational and noncommunicational sentences is simplistic and have disputed the claim that sentences cannot represent the voices of both narrator and character. For example, Sanders and Redeker (1996) claimed that "free indirect representation of consciousness (thought) is closely related to and often even indistinguishable from free indirect *speech*," and that "*direct* representation of thought, which combines a character's vision and narration, is functionally very close to free indirect thought" (292–3). They concluded that the duo-voiced nature of free-indirect discourse often renders the clear separation of narratorial and character voice impossible; this would suggest that it is pointless to attempt to determine whether an utterance related in this mode is an instance of the nonreflective consciousness of the character or an interpretation of the same by a narrator who undertakes to assume the character's point of view. From the reader's perspective, narrators have access to characters' thoughts and perceptions and therefore reflect those characters. Determining precisely whose voice is represented, or whether every utterance falls into the reflective or nonreflective category, may be an irrelevant consideration for readers. Indeed, the difficulty literary scholars have had in agreeing on Banfield's analyses and conclusions (e.g., Coulmas, 1986; Fludernik, 1996; McHale, 1978; Tolliver, 1990) suggests that distinguishing these categories would pose a challenge for readers in many cases.

McHale (1978) critiqued previous grammatical models of free-indirect discourse (e.g., Banfield, 1973) and demonstrated the inadequacy of the notion that indirect discourse is a transformed derivation of direct speech, and free-indirect discourse of indirect speech. Because free-indirect discourse in literature is not patterned on an original source utterance, and because writers use it freely in unlimited ways, this basic grammatical assumption proves to be of little value for the analysis of free-indirect discourse in fictional narrative. In particular, McHale's criticism draws attention to two limitations of the derivational model: its inadequacy for formulating grammaticality criteria suitable for a potentially infinite number of idiosyncratic derivations, and its unsuitability for differentiating between a variety of similar forms.

Related to purely grammatical models is the approach of Clark and Gerrig (1990). They argued that while indirect speech describes an utterance, direct speech provides a *demonstration* that depicts it. In their analysis of conversational discourse, demonstrations depict some aspects of a referent but not others, and speakers intend hearers to understand which is which. Further, demonstrations rely on the perceptual information that might be acquired from a particular vantage point. The argument that demonstrations depict selected aspects of the referent utterance provides a valuable insight into many uses of direct speech in textual narrative. For example, narrators may or may not convey information about intonation, pronunciation, or speech dysfluencies depending on whether such information is relevant to the narrator's communicative point.

Clark and Gerrig also used this framework to provide an analysis of free-indirect speech: The style is assumed to be a demonstration from the narrator's vantage point rather than that of the speaking character. Thus, free indirect discourse would provide the wording and syntax of the story-world utterance (as a demonstration), but would use tense and anaphors appropriate for the narrator's voice. The suggestion here is that those aspects of the utterance that are depicted (e.g., the wording and syntax of the utterance) are intended to be distinct from other aspects of the demonstration (e.g., the verb tense and pronoun use) and that readers should be able to recover that distinction. However, as discussed previously, the textual signs that distinguish the narrator's and the character's voice are not always clear. More generally, Clark and Gerrig do not detail how demonstrations are marked as such, and how, in literary narrative for example, the depictive aspects of a demonstration are distinguished from other aspects. Without such an independent delineation of how this is accomplished, the assertion that such distinctions are intended to be understood has an element of circularity. Thus, the analysis of represented speech and thought in terms of demonstrations by itself does not solve the general problem of distinguishing the voices of the narrator and characters.

Extended-Text Approaches

To avoid the pitfalls of purely syntactical models, and to better account for the range of representational styles found in literary texts, McHale (1978) argued that speech and thought representation styles can be charted on a continuum ranging from the most mimetic (imitative of characters' actual utterances) to the most diegetic (narratorial report of character's utterances) styles. Building on this assumption, he developed a typology of discursive possibilities which include: (a) *diegetic summary* ("the bare report that a speech event has occurred, without any specification of what was said or how it was said"; 258); (b) *summary* ("which to some degree represents, not merely gives notice of, a speech event in that it names the topics of conversation"; 259); (c) *indirect content-paraphrase* (which paraphrases the content of a speech act); (d) *indirect discourse* (which is "mimetic to some degree" in that it reproduces "aspects of the style of an utterance"; 259); (e) *free-indirect discourse* (which is situated between direct and indirect discourse, and can "be mimetic to almost any degree short of 'pure' mimesis"; 259); (f) *direct discourse* (which is the most mimetic in that it reproduces the actual words of the character); and (g) *free-direct discourse* ("which is nothing more than direct discourse shorn of its conventional orthographic cues"; 259). McHale went on to argue that the degree of mimesis that might be present in a given passage cannot be identified solely on the basis of tense or particular features of sentences but only by reference to larger segments of text.

More generally, the interpretation of individual utterances may be driven by a tendency for readers to identify a consistent voice in the text. So, for example, it may well be that the imperfect tense signals a character's perception and the aorist tense points to the narrator's perspective, as some have proposed, but on the basis of larger portions of text – a paragraph, page, or whole story – readers may conclude that it is predominantly the point of view of one or the other, or the two concurrently, that is represented. Thus, a more effective analysis of various speech styles, and of free-indirect discourse in particular, is more likely to be obtained by considering the impact of larger segments of text (cf. Shapiro, 1984).

Both the linguist Erlich (1990) and the literary critics McHale (1983) and Cohn (1978) have studied free-indirect discourse in relation to portions of individual texts. Others, such as Ramazani (1988) and Weinberg (1981) have examined free-indirect discourse in the context of the ironic import of certain texts. The dependence of free-indirect discourse on the larger, extratextual context in which it occurs is emphasized by its spontaneous occurrence in oral narrative. Labov (1972) and Polanyi (1982) collected samples of free-indirect discourse from oral narratives; this work strongly argues against the assumption that free-indirect discourse is an exclusively literary technique. Tolliver (1990) acknowledged that the conventions used to mark free-indirect discourse may be different in oral and written narratives but concluded that "these conventions are due to the differing modes of communication rather than to the literary or non-literary natures of the narratives in question" (266). Because literature is not limited in its potential selection of modes of communication, it is reasonable to posit substantial overlap between the two. Coulmas (1986) observed that the manner of reporting speech is language-specific and listed some of the grammatical features that are present or absent in reported speech in German, English, French, Japanese, and Russian. This raises the possibility that the markers used to signal free-indirect discourse in natural language may be flexible and vary with the language context.

Reader-Based Approaches

In our view, purely text-based models of represented speech and thought may not be directly relevant to how readers naturally process fictional narratives. Meticulous elaborations of complex syntactical models and rules that fail to reflect actual reading processes have become the object of critical scrutiny in the last quarter century. Numerous scholars (Lamarque, 1990; McHale, 1978; Prince, 1987; Tolliver, 1990) have drawn attention to the serious limitations of such exclusively grammatical models of represented speech and thought. Even when the social and historical context of a work is taken into account, text-based analyses may do little to illuminate the actual process of reading. For example, Corcoran (1991) argued that the direct discourse in Joyce's *Dubliners* suggests that women tended not to participate in conversation, in contrast to the social reality of the time. However, the impact of this particular textual feature on readers, and what inferences may be drawn from it, is uncertain and, we would argue, an open empirical question.

Within the field of literary studies, Monica Fludernik (1993) argued for the central role of the reader in the analysis of represented speech and thought. In response to Banfield's (1981, 1993) argument that free-indirect speech is not intended to communicate, Fludernik maintained that the act of attributing a teller function is a natural strategy that "regularly recurs in the practice of reading literary texts" (1993:440). Fludernik concluded that it is possible to "explain the entire communicative analysis of fiction as an (illicit) transferal of the frame of real-life conversational narrative onto literary personae and constructed entitites (such as the implied author)," and that "one can trace the recurrent personalizations of the narrative function... to the influence of the very same schema, namely that of the typical storytelling situation: if there is a story, somebody must needs tell it" (1993:448). Summarized very simply, the argument is that because in life we have a schema for story telling which includes a teller, as readers we expect all narratives to be told by someone.

Following on this analysis, Fludernik (1993) suggested that readers identify a narratorial voice over extended segments of text, and the reader's expectations regarding story-telling schemas are used in resolving the ambiguity inherent in free-indirect speech. For example, in a passage in which the narrator's voice predominates, any embedded representation of a character's thoughts or conscience will be interpreted as an instance of the narrator's voice. The attempt (e.g., by Banfield and others) to associate styles of speech representation with sentence-level features

ignores the evocation in some narrative clauses of the text of a narrator role which would then establish a default for the reader. Thus, a narrative that has a personalized teller figure in some passages establishes a situation of telling that is not cancelled out by the occurrence of 'neutral' description in other sections of the narrative. (Fludernik, 1998:438)

She argued that even in passages where a character's conscience is described, readers will infer the presence of a narrator's voice if "there is a clear narrative voice in the text" (450). Fludernik disputed Banfield's argument that sentences can only be centered on either a narrator or a character's point of view by pointing to the natural tendency of readers to infer a narratorial presence even in "reflectoral narratives," that is, texts where a percentage of sentences appear to be enunciated from a character's conscience. Following the work of Wiebe (1990) on context, Fludernik concluded that

> complex narrative situations tend to be resolved in terms of meaningfulness or relevance: if a specific free-indirect discourse sentence makes perfect sense as an utterance, it will be read in this way. If a certain formally ambiguous sentence makes sense as the narrator's exclamation but cannot reflect the character's verisimilar state of mind at that point in the story, the latent narrator will be said to have "uttered" that sentence. (1993:453)

Such inferences, of course, depend on the reading context. Fludernik argued that a reading context "is provided specifically by the narrated or prepresented plot-situation – a 'scene' that can be described in terms of the dynamics of human action and the expectations generated in the reader on the basis of such situational understanding" (1993:439).

In our view, this analysis, although insightful, stops short of the goal of understanding how readers process the represented discourse. For example, one needs to identify the features in the discourse or the larger textual context that contribute to one interpretation or the other. Further, it is important to understand the effects of different speech styles on readers. One might suppose, for example, that the readers will process speech differently when it is presented as direct discourse than when it presented as free-indirect discourse, even if the reader ultimately interprets the latter as a character utterance. Moreover, it still remains the case that conceptualizations of the reader in the studies of Fludernik and others are limited to hypothetical or ideal reader models, and evidence concerning the behavior of real readers is absent.

In the field of discourse processing, represented speech and thought has not been an important problem. However, the concept of "layering" has sometimes been discussed in connection with the concept of nested discourse. In this approach, the text of the story is viewed as a communication between the narrator and the narratee; conversations in the story world are layered on this communicative interchange. Clark (1996) argued that this layered interchange has the form of a *joint pretense* by the narrator and the narratee to assume the roles of the conversational participants in the story world (cf. Bruce, 1981). Within this framework, direct and indirect speech constitute different speech acts. For example, quoted, direct speech provides a demonstration of what was said (Clark & Gerrig, 1990), while indirect speech provides merely a description. The layers analysis involves the reader in that the story as a whole is assumed to be layered on a communicative interchange between the author and the reader. The approach provides a compelling analysis of irony and other subtle uses of language (Clark & Gerrig, 1984). Clark and Gerrig (1990) suggested that direct speech, because it provides a variety of perceptual information about the story-world utterance, may have distinct effects on the reader. For example, some information about the utterance, such as emotion or urgency, may be easier to appreciate in direct speech. Similarly, direct speech may engross the reader in the story world, while indirect speech may engross the reader in the narrator's thoughts and actions.

A common view is that readers represent the information concerning story-world conversations in a situation model of the narrative (e.g., Zwann, Langston & Graesser, 1995). Such representations would in principle be used to track who said what to whom and the knowledge each of the characters has of the interchange. In this approach, a much more active role of the reader is assumed because situation models are likely to be a product of the reader's knowledge-based inferences and subject to a variety of memory and processing constraints. As a consequence, such representations are more closely tied to the reader's processing of the text than to the details of the text itself. Several lines of research focused specifically on the representation of speech in narrative point to important effects of knowledge and memory. For example, Keysar (1994) argued that readers' knowledge of a character's intention in the story world affects the presumed interpretation of that character's utterances by others in the story world. If, for instance, a character intended a remark to be sarcastic, readers will commonly assume that other characters in the story world will appreciate that sarcasm, even if the narrative suggests they may have little basis for doing so (but see Gerrig, Brennan & Ohaeri, 2000). As another example, Graesser, Bowers, Olde, and Pomeroy (1999) examined source memory for story-world speech, that is, memory for who said what in a narrative. The results indicated that source memory is most accurate for first-person narrators, least accurate for third-person narrators, and intermediate for nonnarrator characters. We will have more to say about both of these studies in a later section. For the moment, though, we note merely that such work highlights the importance of knowledge and memory in understanding how represented speech will be interpreted and maintained.

Features in the Depiction of Speech and Thought

Our core hypothesis concerning represented speech and thought is that readers represent information concerning the story-world characters' intended messages. This hypothesis borrows from the notion of layering discussed by Clark (1996) in that the intended message of the character is layered on the message of the narrator. However, there are several important respects in which our analysis departs from that of Clark. First, in Clark's approach, the message of the narrator would also be layered on the message of the implied author, which in turn would be layered on the message of the historical author (see also Bruce, 1981). However, as discussed in Chapter 3, we do not assume that readers generally represent these additional levels of communication, and instead we hypothesize that readers often process the words of the narrator directly as if from a conversational partner. Further, we expect that the information concerning the intended messages of the characters can easily be incomplete and that the distinction between the message levels attributed to the narrator and the characters would not always be carefully maintained. Indeed, our analysis of free-indirect speech depends heavily on the failure of readers to distinguish the represented intentions of the narrator and the character.

A variety of different kinds of features are available in a narrative and are relevant to the goal of identifying intended story-world messages. For example, many of the forms and distinctions investigated in previous work in narratology on speech and thought comprise categories of text features that readers may use in processing the text and constructing such a representation. We divide such features into two broad categories: features that depict elements of the communicative situation and features that depict the manner of communication.

The Communicative Situation

In its simplest form, the communicative situation consists of who said what to whom. Often a great deal of such information is relayed explicitly in the text. Direct speech, of course, indicates precisely what was said, and indirect speech provides a summary of the gist at varying levels of detail. Tags or other conventions may indicate the speaker of an utterance and the recipient of the message may be clearly described. Other, more complex aspects of the situation may also be provided in the text. For example, an overhearer may be described in the narrative, as in this excerpt from *Cyteen: The Betrayal* by C. J. Cherryh:

> "Do you know," she said, over the dessert, a simple ice, tangy and pleasant. "We are going to have to make some far-reaching adjustments in staff."
>
> Amazing how many ears were pricked at table, and how quiet a room could get, when she was only speaking to Denys.
>
> "I really don't anticipate any difficulty with the Hope bill." They were all listening now, not pretending to do otherwise. (1988:53–4)

Another kind of complexity occurs when characters misunderstand utterances, either momentarily or for extended periods of time. For example, here the woman Tenar initially misinterprets who is being referred to by the pronoun "he":

> "Tell me," the woman murmured, and the child answered in her faint, hoarse whisper, "He came here."
>
> Tenar's first thought was of Ged, and her mind, still moving with the quickness of fear, caught that, saw who "he" was to her, and gave it a wry grin in passing, but passed on, hunting. "Who came here?" (Le Guin, *Tehanu: The Last Book of Earthsea*, 1990:109)

Although misunderstandings can have implications for understanding the mental states of characters, they are often corrected in the subsequent story-world conversation. At other times, though, misunderstandings persist and have an impact on the plot events. In this description from C. J. Cherryh's *Fortress of Owls*, many of the characters fail to understand the implications of a ghost's prophetic address:

> And *aetheling* she said, the lord of Amefel and the aetheling, as if they were not the same thing ... *the twain of you*, she said, *lord and aetheling* – which met his heart with a loud echo of all the wonderings he had had to himself. The

guards who heard might not have heard that salutation in the same way: the common folk attributed both titles to him. Perhaps even Crissand failed to gather the implied duality. (1999:62)

A range of detailed but important issues pertain to how various aspects of the communicative situation are marked in the text, and we do not offer a complete analysis of these issues here. Our overriding goal, though, would be to identify objective features of the text that signal such information and to carefully distinguish these from inferences and constructions readers may represent about the situation in the story world.

The Manner of Communication

A second class of features for represented speech and thought is information in a narrative concerning the manner in which that speech or thought is conveyed. Often, information about manner may be conveyed explicitly with adverbs describing the speech production (e.g., "He said angrily"; "She cried pitifully"). Such adverbs are typically found in tagged, direct speech (e.g., "'You're – you're writing to him, are you,' said Uncle Vernon in a would-be calm voice"; Rowling, *Harry Potter and the Goblet of Fire*, 2000:35), but they may be found in indirect speech as well, as in the following example from the same book:

In fact, the report continued, in a tone of unmistakable bewilderment, the Riddles all appeared to be in perfect health – apart from the fact that they were all dead. The doctors did note (as though determined to find something wrong with the bodies) that each of the Riddles had a look of terror upon his or her face (2000:9)

A second source of information concerning the manner in which a message is conveyed is the actual language used in transcribed speech. Direct, transcribed speech or thought can provide information not only about the choice of words and syntax but may also include indications of dialect or pronunciation, timing, or intonational contour. Pronunciation can be evoked by the use of phonetic spellings ("'Gawd, the poor girl!'"; Angela Carter, *Nights at the Circus*, 1994:143); information about timing can be conveyed with the use of commas, ellipses, dashes, or hyphens ("'I received a paper, yes,' Miss Emily said. 'Perhaps he considers himself the sheriff...I have no taxes in Jefferson'"; William Faulkner, "A Rose for Emily," 1961:51); and intonational contour may be indicated by punctuation, italics, or other typographical conventions. For example,

> "Forever?" said the stranger, solemnly.
> "Forever!" replied Wolfgang . . .
> "The fiend! the fiend has gained possession of me!" shrieked he.
> (Washington Irving, "The Adventure of the German Student," 1994, 42)

We assume that readers integrate such information into something resembling a phonological image of the speech; that is, readers would know something about how that speech would sound if spoken in the indicated manner. It is an open question as to how much fidelity and precision typically exists in such representations. However, work on reading tongue twisters (e.g., McCutchen & Perfetti, 1982) indicates that material that is difficult to articulate is read more slowly, suggesting that readers may commonly represent at least some information about how words are formed in speech.

Representing Intended Messages

In this section, we discuss some hypotheses concerning reader constructions with respect to represented speech and thought. As discussed in our review, a central theoretical problem in the scholarship on speech and thought has been identifying the voice associated with the text of the narrative. In our analysis, this amounts to distinguishing the conversational point and message of the narrator (as discussed in Chapter 3) from the messages that readers represent as intended by characters in the story world. In each case, the reader must identify elements of the communicative situation (i.e., who is speaking, who is hearing, what is being said) and information about the manner in which the communication takes place (i.e., the words, syntax, intonation, etc., of the utterance). Our discussion here is based on a simplistic analysis of the narrator's communicative circumstances: The narrator is represented as speaking to the reader, and information concerning intended messages in the story world is embedded in the narrator's message. The problem of voice, then, amounts to attributing the manner of the text (e.g., the words, syntax, and intonational contour) to either the narrator or the character.

Representing the Communicative Situation

The representation of intended messages can be complex. For example, messages may be directed to one individual but intended to be understood by a side participant; messages may be designed to convey misleading or partial information; or messages may be intended to be ironic or satirical. Although many of these complexities may be explicitly identified in the text, in general the textual information will be incomplete. Consequently, many aspects of the communicative situation will have to be inferred by readers, and such inferences will depend on their prior knowledge as well as their understanding of the circumstances of the story world.

One class of inferences concerning intended messages is based on narratorial implicatures. For example, consider the following exchange (from J. Le Carré's *Our Game*) in which the narrator attempts to identify when he had last seen Larry:

> "I've been trying to think. July, probably. We'd decided to give the wine vats an early scrub. The best way to get rid of Larry is put him to work. He scrubbed for an hour, ate some bread and cheese, drank four gin and tonics, and pushed off."
> "July, then," said Bryant.
> "I said. July."
> "Got a date at all? A day of the week, say? A weekend, was it?"
> "Yes, it must have been."
> "Why?"
> "No staff."
> "I thought you said we, sir."
> "Some children from the housing estate were helping me for a pound an hour," I replied, again delicately avoiding any mention of Emma. (1995:15)

Here, the narrator's final comment that he has avoided mentioning Emma is superficially unnecessary because he obviously has not mentioned anyone else by name. However, on the conversational assumption that the narrator is only providing necessary and sufficient information, one can infer that he *could* have mentioned Emma, and that his reply to Bryant was not completely honest. This implicature allows the reader to understand that the intent of the narrator's utterances was to mislead or conceal. In general, we suspect that a great deal of our understanding of intended messages comes from inferences based on the kinds of information the narrator provides or doesn't provide.

The role of narratorial implicatures sheds light on the phenomenon of "illusory transparency of intention" identified by Keysar (1994). Keysar argued that readers have a tendency to assume that characters will understand the intended meaning of utterances even when the situation in the story world might lead the utterances to be misunderstood. For example, readers often assume that utterances such as, "That was a great restaurant" will be interpreted by others in the story world as sarcasm when it follows a terrible restaurant experience, even when those characters have no other knowledge of the restaurant and apparently no basis for identifying the ironic intention. Keysar suggested that readers may not differentiate between their own knowledge of the speaker's intention and the common ground that exists for the characters in the story world. However, Gerrig, Ohaeri, and Brennan (2000) argued that such results can be explained by normal conversational processes because a speaker would not normally utter an ironic utterance unless the hearer had the knowledge to understand it as such. More to the point, from our point of view, the *narrator* is unlikely to relate a misunderstood utterance without commenting on the misunderstanding in some fashion. Thus, narratorial implicatures would normally allow the reader to infer that the conversational participants must have had sufficient common ground to understand the intended meaning, even if such common ground was not apparent from the text (cf. Gerrig, Brennan, & Ohaeri, 2000).

There is no guarantee that, on any given occasion, a reader will appreciate or infer characteristics of the communicative situation or recall them at a later time. Graesser, Bowers, Olde, and Pomeroy (1999) examined source memory for story-world speech, that is, memory for who said what in the story. Their results indicated that source memory was more accurate for the speech and thought of first-person narrators than it was for characters who were not the narrator. Readers were particularly poor at recalling the source of statements made by an absent, heterodiegetic narrator. Graesser et al. argued that the results supported an "agent amalgamation" hypothesis in which

the reader's representation of a narrator is richer and more elaborate when the narrator is also a story-world character. This richer
representation was hypothesized to support more accurate memory
retrieval. In contrast, we suggest that these effects can be parsimo-
niously explained by the assumption that readers track and maintain
information that is relevant to the narrator's message. Although the
mere fact of including information in the narrative is likely to signal
at least some importance to the narrator, we suspect that readers are
much more likely to maintain information about intended messages
that is expressly signaled as critical by the narrator. In particular, utterances spoken by the narrator in the story world on average are
likely to be more important for the narrator than other characters'
utterances, and thus it is not surprising that readers are better able to
remember such information. Our suspicion is that since statements
made by an absent narrator do not correspond to represented speech
and thought at all, readers would not explicitly represent their source
under most circumstances.

When readers encounter an indication of speech in the text, we
assume that they will ascribe an intended audience in the story world
for the utterance. For example, consider the following conversational
excerpt from Orson Scott Card's *Ender's Game*:

"Ender Wiggin, the little farthead who leads the standings, what a pleasure
to have you with us." The commander of Rat Army lay sprawled on a lower
bunk wearing only his desk. "With you around, how can any army lose?"
Several of the boys nearby laughed. (1977:108)

In this case, readers are likely to represent the target of the commander's statement to be to Ender, despite the fact that it is apparently
overheard by the boys nearby. Of course, in some cases, the audience may be ambiguous; for example, if there are several people in
a room it may be unclear from the text which of those people was
intended to be the recipient of the message. In this example, one
might guess that the commander actually intended the utterance to
be overheard by others in the room. The represented audience is
crucial for the reader's understanding of common ground, that is,
what the speaker and hearer commonly know and perceive in the
story world, which in turn bears on the reader's interpretation of

the utterance. For example, in the following example from the same book, Graff addresses one of a large group of recruits:

"What do you think is so funny, Wiggin?"
Graff's voice was sharp and angry. What did I do wrong, thought Ender. Did I laugh out loud?
"I asked you a question, soldier!" barked Graff. (1977:32)

By itself the exchange bears only on the relationship between Graff and Ender; however, the presence of a large group of recruits changes the nature of the comments to one of a demonstration or example to the group, with long-range implications for Ender's relationship with his peers.

We use the same analysis for the representation of character thoughts, except that in this case, the intended target is usually the character him- or herself. In the following example from Le Guin's *Tehanu* there is a clear indication of an (internal) speech event: "I'm sick of mourning, Tenar thought. Sick of mourning, sick of grief. I will not grieve for him! Didn't he come to me riding the dragon?" (1990:45). Here, an intended content and an intended manner is clearly marked in the text. However, the target of the communication cannot be any individual in the story world because the words are not spoken aloud; the communication must be intended for the character herself. Our working hypothesis is that with this exception, the representation of such internal verbalizations is similar to spoken utterances. (Of course, in some story worlds, some form of telepathy is possible, and verbalized thoughts may have an intended external audience).

In many instances, perceptions or reactions of a character may be described in a narrative without any explicit indication of a corresponding internal verbalization. For example, in the following passage also from *Tehanu: The Last Book of Earthsea* by Le Guin, the character doubts the wisdom of caring for a severely burned child:

Her anger with him, her stupid denial of the truth of what he told her, rose from disappointment. Though Lark had said ten times over that nothing could be done, yet she had hoped that Tenar could heal the burns; and for all her saying that even Ogion could not have done it, Tenar had hoped that Ged could heal Therru – could lay his hand on the scar and it would be whole and well, the blind eye bright, the clawed hand soft, the ruined life intact. (1990:74)

In this case, the reader is provided with a detailed and explicit indication of the character's insights and reactions. However, there is no indication of internal speech or (unvocalized) words and sentences. Although such information may be important in understanding the character and the plot events, we assume that this information is not represented as an (internal) speech event with an intended content and manner.

Representing Intended Manner

We assume that the representation of communicative intentions provides a basis for readers to distinguish the narrator's speech and thought from that of the characters. Consider, for example, the forms of direct, indirect, and free-indirect speech. In direct, quoted speech, the words are transcribed by the narrator, but the intention to express precisely those words lies solely with the character. In contrast, indirect speech provides an indication that a character intended to relay the message described in the text, but there generally is much less precise information about how the character intended to convey that message. In addition, the intentions of the character must be filtered through the communicative intent of the narrator, in whose voice the original communication is conveyed.

As suggested earlier, we hypothesize that readers attempt to construct a representation of intended messages in the story world and that part of such representation would be some indication of the manner in which the messages were conveyed. The information that readers have available to them is the wording of the text on the page, and they must identify to whom that wording should be attributed. In indirect speech, that wording should be attributed to the narrator, and further inferences may be needed to form a representation of the wording and manner of communication in the story world. Presumably, such inferences would be based on the information about the utterance provided by the narrator along with previous utterances by the character in the narrative. With direct speech, the process is potentially simpler because the words of the text should be attributed to the character rather than the narrator (although the narrator does decide how much of which speech utterances to include). However, further inferences concerning speed, volume, and intonation of the message may be necessary.

Free-Indirect Speech and Intended Manner

Our hypothesis is that free-indirect discourse provides ambiguous cues concerning to whom the wording should be attributed. On one hand, the vocabulary and syntax of free-indirect speech suggest that the manner of presenting the message is being depicted, and that the wording should be attributed to the character. On the other hand, the use of pronouns and tense in free-indirect discourse suggests that the text is not transcribed, and, as a consequence, the wording should be attributed to the narrator. The net result is that readers may end up attributing the wording to either or both in their representation of the intended message.

The ambiguity concerning the intention of wording may lead to other inferences concerning the narrator and the character. Intuitively, if a character shares intention with respect to the wording of speech and thought with the narrator, the character and the narrator may share other intentions and mental states as well. More generally, we assume that this ambiguity with respect to intention provides evidence for a narratorial association with the character. In Chapter 6, we suggested that narrator–character associations may be generated based on consistent perceptual access; speech style may provide another such cue. As discussed in Chapter 3, there are two implications of forming a narrator–character association. First, the narrator may be represented as having the traits and characteristics of the character. This might include properties such as age, gender, social status, and knowledge of the story world. Second, the character may be construed as having the characteristics commonly attributed to the narrator as a conversational participant. This would include the expectation that the narrator is cooperative and rational and providing necessary and sufficient information about the story world to understand the narrator's point or message.

In Dixon and Bortolussi (1996a), we argued that similar effects might be mediated by the represented position of the narrator in the story world. The argument was that different speech styles provide varying degrees of constraint on the position of the narrator. In particular, direct speech constrains the narrator to be in the immediate vicinity of the speaking character because the narrator must be able to perceive that speech; indirect speech would provide less constraint. Moreover, because the voice of the narrator and the character are intertwined in free-indirect discourse, the position of the narrator is constrained to be adjacent to the character. This close proximity of the narrator and the character was assumed to produce the overlap in characteristics of the narrator and the character mentioned earlier. Although we would still argue that such effects on positional constraint are important, our current view is that positional constraint by itself may not entail that the narrator and the character share characteristics other than position; a distinct step of forming a narrator–character association may be required.

Empirical Evidence

As evidence in support of our general approach to speech and thought, and our analysis of free-indirect speech in particular, we describe a study in which we manipulated the manner in which speech and thought were presented in the text.[4] The basis of this manipulation was the story "Rope" by Katherine Ann Porter. In the story, a man returns home from town and an argument with his wife ensues, nominally concerning the purchase of a coil of rope. The dialogue of the argument comprises almost all the story and is related entirely in free-indirect speech. In our experiment, additional versions of the story were created by changing the speech of the male character to direct, quoted speech; by changing the speech of the female character to direct speech; and by switching the story roles of the male and female characters, so that the woman returns from town rather than the man. Excerpts of two of the versions are shown in Table 7.1. Including the original, there were thus eight versions of the story consisting of the factorial combination of female speech style, male speech style, and male/female story role.

In the present context, the primary focus is on the hypothesized effect of free-indirect discourse on the formation of narrator–character associations and the attributes that might be attributed to the narrator and the characters. Thus, we asked readers about the apparent rationality of the male and female characters ("Is the man/woman in the story reasonable and rational or unreasonable and irrational?")

---

[4] These results are based on a reanalysis of those presented in Dixon and Bortolussi (1996a).

T A B L E 7 . 1 . *Example of Speech and Story-Role Manipulations*

Indirect Male Speech, Indirect Female Speech, Female at Home

Had he brought the coffee? She had been waiting all day long for coffee. They had forgot it when they ordered at the store the first day.

Gosh, no, he hadn't. Lord, now he'd have to go back. Yes, he would if it killed him. He thought, though, he had everything else. She reminded him it was only because he didn't drink coffee himself. If he did he would remember it quick enough. Suppose they ran out of cigarettes? Then she saw the rope. What was that for? Well, he thought it might do to hang clothes on, or something.

Direct Male Speech, Direct Female Speech, Male at Home

"Did you bring the tobacco?" he asked her. "I've been waiting all day long for a cigarette." They had forgot it when they ordered at the store the first day.

"Gosh, no, I didn't," she answered. "Lord, now I'll have to go back. Yes, I will if it kills me. I think, though, I got everything else."

"It's only because you don't smoke yourself," he reminded her. "If you did you would remember it quick enough. Suppose we ran out of coffee?" Then he saw the twine. "What's that for?" he asked.

"Well," she replied, "I thought it might come in handy, maybe for hanging plants or for tying up the bushes in the fall."

---

and the gender of the narrator ("Did you get the impression that the narrator was a man or a woman?"). Readers responded to these two questions on a nine-point scale after each of two readings of the story; we used the average of these two sets of responses in our analyses. Our expectation was that when an association is formed between the narrator and a character, that character will be seen as more rational (a characteristic normally associated with the narrator), and the narrator will be seen as sharing the gender and other attributes of that character. However, because the characters were having an argument, their rated rationality should interact: If one character is seen as rational, the holder of the opposing view is likely to be seen as less rational. Thus, we subtracted the rationality rating for the male character from that for the female character to produce a single index of relative rationality. (In this study, readers also responded to a variety of other questions concerning their evaluation of the story and the characters that are less relevant to our present concerns; see Dixon & Bortolussi, 1996a).

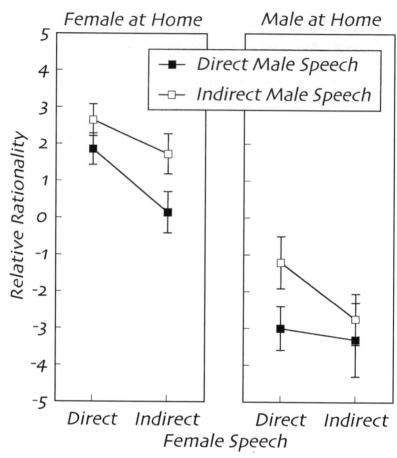

FIGURE 7.1. Relative rationality (Male−Female) as a function of speech style and story role. Error bars indicate the size of 95% confidence intervals, adjusted for pairwise comparisons.

The results for relative rationality are shown in Figure 7.1. As is clear from the figure, the relative rationality (in favor of the female character) increases with female free-indirect speech and decreases with male free-indirect speech. Our interpretation is that free-indirect speech causes the representation of the character to overlap with that of the narrator. Thus, when the female character's voice is expressed in free-indirect speech, she is seen as sharing some of the narrator's rationality; when the male character's voice is expressed in free-indirect speech, he is seen as relatively rational. It is also interesting to note that the effect of speech style is precisely the same for both male and female characters. There was also an overall effect of story role: The character who returns from town is seen as more rational, regardless of whether that character is male or female. Presumably, this effect reflects the content of the story. For example, the wife's actions and arguments in the original story seem to be portrayed as more emotional and less connected to the immediate situation than those of the husband. As a consequence, readers rate that role as less rational even when the genders associated with those roles have been switched.

These results were described with a linear model with two substantive parameters: the effect of speech style and the effect of story role. Likelihood ratios were used to assess the fit of several nested versions of this model. With only the effect of story role, the model fit better than a null model that predicts no differences ($\lambda > 1{,}000$). The effect of speech style was predicted with a single parameter. Relative rationality (in favor of the male character) should be higher when the male character's speech is in free-indirect and the female's is in direct, should be lower by the same amount if the speech styles are reversed, and should be unchanged if the speech styles are the same. Adding this parameter to the model improved the fit substantially ($\lambda > 1{,}000$). However, adding all other possible degrees of freedom to the model improved the fit only slightly ($\lambda = 4.82$). Thus, we conclude that there is good evidence for an effect of story role, good evidence for the hypothesized effect of speech style, and little evidence for other possible effects.

The results for narrator gender are shown in Figure 7.2; larger values are associated with a higher likelihood of being female. Although somewhat more complicated, the results are also broadly consistent with our analysis. In particular, there was an overall effect of speech style of the characters on the rated gender of the narrator: The narrator was seen as more likely to be male when the male speech was presented in free-indirect style, and the narrator was seen as more likely to be female when the female speech was presented in free-indirect style. On average, the magnitude of these two effects was comparable and similar to that for the effects found for rationality. However, there was a notable exception to this overall pattern: The narrator was rated as more likely to be female in the original version

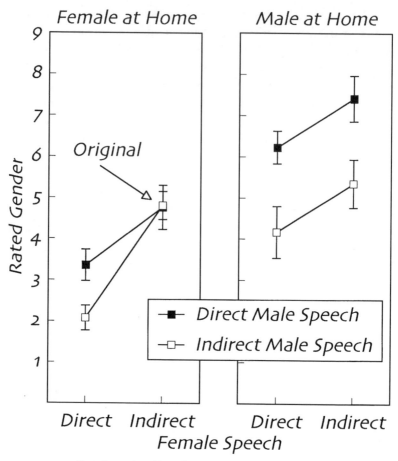

FIGURE 7.2. Rated gender (Female = 9, Male = 1) as a function of speech style and story role. Error bars indicate the size of 95% confidence intervals, adjusted for pairwise comparisons.

than would otherwise be expected on the basis of speech style. We have no simple explanation for this discrepancy. Perhaps the partic- ular constellation of features used in the original (i.e., both male and female voices presented in free-indirect style and a plot in which the male character returns from town) provided some indication of the characteristics of the narrator over and above that which could be gleaned from each factor independently. Despite this complication, the overall effects of the manipulations were quite clear and in line with our predictions.

To substantiate this interpretation of the results, we fitted nested linear models as before. A model with a single parameter of story role fit substantially better than the null model with no effects ($\lambda > 1{,}000$). Adding a parameter for the effect of speech style also improved the fit ($\lambda > 1{,}000$). The discrepancy discussed earlier was evaluated by adding another parameter to indicate that the narrator in the original seemed especially likely to be female relative to the other versions; this also had a substantial effect ($\lambda > 1{,}000$). Finally, this model was compared to a full model that included all possible degrees of freedom; the full model provided only a small improvement in fit ($\lambda = 5.85$). In sum, we conclude that the data provide strong evidence for the predicted effect of speech style on the perceived gender of the narrator, as well as an effect of story role. In addition, there is good evidence that the particular constellation of features used in the original also has an effect on the gender of the narrator over and above these general influences.

Summary

In this chapter, we discussed the nature and effects of different ways of depicting speech and thought in narrative. The basic distinctions consist of direct, indirect, free-direct, and free-indirect speech styles. A critical problem for the readers in processing these different forms is identifying the voice in the text. We reviewed three broad classes of approaches to this problem. In sentence-level models, one attempts to find characteristics of the syntax or wording that indicate whether the narrator or the character is speaking; in extended-text approaches, voice is apparent by considering the properties of larger segments of narrative; and in reader-based approaches, it is assumed that distinguishing the voice of the narrator and character can only be understood by considering the knowledge, expectations, and strategies of the reader.

The psychonarratology approach is to distinguish the features of represented speech and thought in the text from the attributions and inferences that readers might construct. We distinguished features that pertain to characteristics of the communicative situation – that is, who said what to whom – from features that provide information about the manner of that communication. Similarly, readers may need to construct inferences about elements of either the communicative situation or the manner of communication. These distinctions were used to provide an analysis of free-indirect speech: We hypothesized that free-indirect speech poses a problem for the reader because it is unclear whether features relating to the manner of communication should be attributed to the narrator or the character in the story world. We presented some evidence that this ambiguity leads readers to form an association between the narrator and the character so that, to some extent, the properties of the narrator are attributed to the character and vice versa.

8

Directions and Unsolved Problems

The title of this chapter is perhaps presumptuous because it suggests that some problems have been solved. In fact, even for issues we dealt with in some depth, such as narratorial implicatures and narrator–character associations, the present work merely scratches the surface. Thus, it is perhaps more appropriate to regard this work as an outline of an approach or framework, and the presented research provides only an illustration of the kind of work that can be done within that framework. Further, although we have attempted to cover a broad class of issues in the processing of narrative, there are many areas on which we have not touched. In this chapter, we discuss how psychonarratology could be developed to deal with some of these. First, we recapitulate what we see as the essential ingredients in our approach and summarize some of the specific ideas we have applied to the classic issues in narratology and literary studies. Following that, we discuss some important complications that we have glossed over in our treatment of these issues. Then, we describe some of the other obvious areas in which our treatment has yet to be applied but for which it seems ideally suited. Finally, we mention a few allied domains for which psychonarratology may have implications.

The Psychonarratology Approach

Core Assumptions

Psychonarratology is an interdisciplinary approach to the study of the processing of narrative form. As such it draws on the scholarship and insights of narratology, literary studies, and linguistics as well as the methods, epistemology, and findings of cognitive psychology and discourse processing. As we have said many times in this book, the basis of a scientific approach to the understanding of narrative involves carefully distinguishing textual features from reader constructions. The former are objectively defined properties of the text that can be identified and manipulated independent of any given reading or interpretation. The latter are inherently variable and depend on the reader and his or her knowledge and the reading context. Textual features are a matter of definition and cannot be true or false, only apt and less apt. On the other hand, reader constructions must be framed as hypotheses that need to be confirmed or disconfirmed on the basis of empirical evidence. With this distinction in hand, we have considered a wide range of scholarship on narrative. Some of this prior work identifies potentially important features of the text, while other work suggests plausible hypotheses about the nature of reader constructions. A central advantage of this approach is that it provides a method for assessing the value of this scholarship: Systems of textual features may be modified or discarded when they are not useful, and hypotheses concerning reader constructions may be supported or refuted by empirical evidence.

A distinction between the features of the text and the constructions readers make allows one to apply a powerful inferential technique: the textual experiment. The textual experiment involves manipulating features of the text and measuring concomitant changes in readers' constructions. As developed in Chapter 2, the textual experiment provides a basis for making strong inferences about causal relationships between features and constructions uncontaminated by confounds that would otherwise be difficult to rule out. The fact that naturally occurring texts are created by authors with some (at least partially) coherent plan and intent means that it is otherwise difficult to identify which of the plethora of textual features that might be found in the work might be responsible for the particular reactions that readers have. All of the studies reported in this work are textual experiments of one sort or another.

Within this framework, we developed an overarching hypothesis concerning the nature of many reader constructions: Readers treat the narrator as a conversational partner. As outlined in Chapter 3, this idea places a somewhat different interpretation of the relationship between the reader on one hand and the author and implied author on the other. Although readers can easily be aware of a distinction between the narrator and the implied author, and extratextual information about the historical author may sometimes be salient, we suggest that readers are typically and primarily concerned with identifying the message of the narrator, processed as if it were communicated to them. We suspect that most of the time, readers do not clearly distinguish the characteristics and intention of the narrator from that of the implied or historical author.

This hypothesis that the narrator is treated as a conversational participant suggests a wide range of ideas concerning reader constructions. Many of these fall under the general heading of narratorial implicatures, that is, inferences licensed by the assumption that the narrator is rational and is providing necessary and sufficient information for his or her point to be understood. We suggest that such inferences are used in understanding aspects of the plot and character, and in interpreting information concerning perception, speech, and thought. The experiment reported in Chapter 3 provides some direct evidence for this hypothesis: Eliminating some of the narratorial implicatures reduced the tendency to see the behavior of the narrator as justified, presumably because implicatures lead readers to attribute their own knowledge and experience to the narrator. Other evidence on the pivotal role of the narrator in interpreting the events of the story world was provided in Chapter 4. In this case, the narrator's point concerning the narrative seems to affect the inferences readers are inclined to make concerning character goals. We believe that there is a wide range of other fairly obvious empirical results that could be predicted based on this general perspective.

Specific Mechanisms

In addition to this broad perspective, we also discussed several more specialized ideas concerning reader constructions. One that was used in several contexts is the notion of a narrator–character association. The argument was that readers may explicitly associate the narrator with a particular character in the narrative. Such an association provides a heuristic for tracking the knowledge and perspective of the narrator, which in turn is necessary for an appropriate interpretation of the narrator's message. A narrator–character association may also lead the reader to attribute properties and characteristics of the narrator to the associated character and vice versa. The results reported in Chapters 6 and 7 provide some evidence for this analysis and suggest two features of the text that can lead to associations. In Chapter 6, specific perceptual access was shown to have these predicted attributions; in Chapter 7, free-indirect speech was shown to have similar effects.

Another idea pertains to the notion of reader "identification." As described in Chapter 3, we suggest that an important ingredient of what is intuitively thought of as identification is transparency, that is, the tendency to see the behavior and attitudes of a character as sensible and justified. We found evidence that narratorial implicatures contribute to transparency in autodiegetic narratives by licensing readers to attribute their own knowledge and experience to the narrator. Similar processes may contribute to the transparency of characters in other narrative styles when there is an association between the narrator and the character. These ideas do not provide a complete theory of identification, of course, but we suggest that it provides a start at a more detailed analysis of what might be meant by identification under some circumstances.

Unsolved Problems

Although we believe that the ideas and evidence presented here represent a certain amount of progress in the understanding of literary narrative, a very large number of different aspects remain to be developed. Here we provide a brief description of some of the more important ones.

Memory and Attention

What readers do with narratives must ultimately be a product of their own mental capacities. As we mentioned in Chapter 5, the experience and knowledge that readers use in interpreting characters must depend on what of their experience is retrieved and salient. Similarly, the nature of the story lines that readers construct in understanding the events of the story world depends on what they can remember of the events that were previously described in the text. Further, what readers represent concerning the perceptual knowledge presented in the text varies with how much and what readers attend to. There are a variety of well-developed accounts of working memory limitations, memory storage, and retrieval operations that are clearly relevant to understanding the processing of narrative (e.g., Ericsson & Kintsch, 1995; O'Brien, Lorch & Myers, 1998). Although we have not attempted to apply these ideas here, there are a number of obvious developments that one might pursue. For example, it is well established that a reader's representation of the content and structure of a passage depends on the strategies and heuristics one uses for maintaining information in working memory (e.g., Fletcher, 1986). Presumably, such heuristics have an impact on the reader's representation of the story line and other causal relationships (cf. van den Broek et al., 1996). However, we would hypothesize that the apparent point of message of the narrator would drive many of such processes. For example, readers may be much more likely to maintain information in working memory if the narrator marks it as important or relevant. In general, we anticipate that the processes we have touched on in this book would all interact in important ways with basic memory capacities and mechanisms.

A similar point can be made about attention: Readers are limited in terms of what they can attend to or selectively process in the course of reading. For example, the notion of a "discourse pointer" has often been used to describe what readers are currently focusing on during comprehension (Carpenter & Just, 1977a). Chafe (1972) suggested that only a subset of the entities described by a discourse are in focus at any one time (see also Halliday & Hasan, 1976). Sanford and Garrod (1998) suggested that a limited number of entities are in explicit focus at a given time while others are in implicit focus. Researchers have identified a variety of characteristics of the text that may determine what is currently in focus, such as the use of pronouns or cleft sentence structures (e.g., Sidner, 1983; Carpenter & Just, 1977b). However, such processes may interact with the attentional and memory capacities of the readers (e.g., Long & De Ley, 2000). Our contribution to this debate would be to suggest that at least some of the textual features that affect focus may simply mediate the conversational intent of the narrator, and that the manipulation of that apparent intent independent of those devices might produce similar effects.

Reading Context

One general class of problems we have not addressed is related to effects of context. Our theoretical framework allows for the possibility that reader constructions will vary depending on the context in which a narrative is encountered. In particular, the constraints of the reading situation and the goals the reader adopts are likely to be important determinants of how the narrative is processed. Novels, for example, are very rarely read in a single sitting, and the duration and timing of the readings is likely to have a large impact on the memory and interpretation of the work. If a long period of time intervenes between successive readings, it is very likely that some information from previous readings will be difficult to retrieve. On the other hand, the interpretation of a work may benefit from a period of reflection between readings. Glanzer, Fischer, and Dorfman (1984) have studied effects of short-term interruptions in reading; their results suggest that rereading the last sentence before the interruption ameliorates the effects of interruptions, but quite different processes might be involved with longer works and longer intervals. Reading aloud is another kind of situational constraint that might have important effects. Our impression is that this can have an effect on the appreciation of phonology and pacing of the text. By slowing the reader's pace, reading aloud might also cause the reader to attend to aspects of the wording and sentence structure that might otherwise go unnoticed, thereby potentially changing even the interpretation of a work.

Generally, we assume that readers do not read narratives for any one purpose. Rather, we imagine that a hierarchy of goals is relevant at any one time. These might include, for example, the aesthetic appreciation of the language of the narrative, an understanding of the events of the story world, an evaluation of the mental states of the narrator or characters, an appreciation of relations among characters or between characters and institutions, and an interpretation of the point or theme of the implied author. In academic contexts, reading goals may include the acquisition of very specific information, such as cataloging literary devices or the portrayal of culture or social roles. We assume that readers typically maintain several goals simultaneously and that the goals vary in relevance or importance from one reading to the next or from one moment to the next.

Readers' processing of the text is likely to vary in important ways depending on which goals are relevant or important. It is well known, for example, that varying reading goals can have important effects on memory for text (Anderson & Pichert, 1978; Postman & Senders, 1946). Thus, it seems reasonable to suppose that different kinds of information from a narrative will be salient or memorable depending on the particular reading goals that are active. In turn, the different information available could have significant effects on the interpretation or analysis of the story events or characters. Indeed, having students look for or attend to particular kinds of information is a common pedagogical technique in promoting literary appreciation. For example, Vipond and Hunt (1989) encouraged readers to engage in either "point-driven" reading in which they were to search for the point or message of a narrative or "story-driven" reading in which they were to assess the events and characters of the story world. They found that readers evaluated the story differently and rated the importance of story sentences differently depending on their goal. A more indirect manipulation is simply to ask readers to reread a story. Dixon et al. (1993) found that a difficult literary text was appreciated more on rereading, perhaps because the goals of the readers had shifted away from a concern with the surface story line.

Most of the analysis and research in this book is based on the assumption that readers have the goal of identifying the apparent point or message of the narrator. Our justification for the focus on this one goal is that it is likely to be salient for most readers most of the time. We suspect, for example, that the processing of the words of the narrative as originating with a conversational narrator is likely to be a relatively automatic process that cannot be wholly suppressed. Thus, although the goal may not be at the top of the goal hierarchy, it is likely to be generally present at some level of importance. Moreover, the processes implicated by other goals are likely to depend on the results of first understanding the narrator. Thus, appreciating the theme of the implied author is likely to be a product of who the narrator is and what the relationship is between the narrator and the implied author. For example, in the novel *The Family of Pascual Duarte*, by José Camilo Cela (1964), reading goals can have a profound influence on the interpretation of the narrator and the text. Most of the story consists of an imprisoned criminal writing his memoirs in first person. The protagonist relates episodes from his child and adult life, such as his troubled upbringing and the cold-blooded murder of his own mother. If readers rely exclusively on this first-person account, it is possible to interpret the protagonist as a victim of his times and circumstances. However, if one's goal is not merely to follow the events of the story world but to understand the techniques employed by the author, then one must necessarily relate the first-person narrative to the framing discourses that precede and follow it, such as the fictional editor–complier's note, the priest's letter, and so on. Extending one's scope of inquiry in this way enables readers to relate the perspectives created by the different voices and to perceive the ironic distance established between the implied author and the narrator. With this additional insight, the protagonist may be seen as an unreliable narrator.

Extratextual Information

In our analysis, we have generally assumed that readers process narrative texts in isolation, without reference to other knowledge about the work or the author. We argue that this is likely to be approximately true in many (most?) cases. Although how much extratextual knowledge readers typically have is an important empirical question, we suspect that often if a reader has any knowledge of the historical author at all, it may be limited to general knowledge of the type of writer he or she is, what kind of reputation his or her books have, and so on. However, there are certainly at least some cases in which readers clearly have knowledge or expectations about the work that affects its processing or interpretation. Indeed, Gibbs (1999) argued that this background of extratextual knowledge typically provides a firm basis for identifying intentions of the actual author. Our view, though, is that even when this is the case, it is usually more appropriate to analyze extratextual information as simply another feature that readers may have available for understanding the text. For example, prior knowledge of critical commentaries may bias the interpretation of characters and story-world events. We suspect, though, that only some of what readers know will be brought to bear on a given text, and that readers may disregard information that doesn't make sense in the context of the work.

Under some circumstances, a work may alter or inform the reader's knowledge of the author. For example, if a story is perceived as a departure from the author's previous work, readers may revise what they know about the author. In turn, this new knowledge of the author may lead them to new interpretations of other previously read works. Sometimes impressions garnered from a fictional work may suggest fallacious inferences based on a presumed correspondence between the story-world events and the life of the historical author. For example, in *One Day of Life* by Manlio Argueta, the main narrator is a woman, but the actual author is a man. We suspect that a workable analysis of the interplay of such influences can be based on the framework proposed in Chapter 3: Readers construct a representation of the author that may overlap to some extent with what may be suggested by the text. Clearly, the extent of the extratextual information readers have is crucial in determining the inferences about the author they are inclined to draw.

Interactions

It is clear that the division of psychonarratology into events and plot, characters and characterization, and so on, is simplistic. In general, the features and constructions we have discussed for all of these areas must interact in potentially complex ways. For example, specific perceptual access to a character can make that character seem more objective and rational; rationality, in turn, is a character trait that can influence how that character's actions are interpreted; that interpretation can then influence how the causal structure of the plot events is understood. As examples of some of the issues that arise in the discussion of such interactions, we describe two areas in which interactions seem important: narrator–character associations and narratorial presence.

Narrator–Character Associations

As we indicated earlier, narrator–character associations may be prompted by the use of specific perceptual access and free-indirect speech and thought. More generally, though, the kind of information provided about the story world could be an important influence. For example, associations might be formed with narratives that are focused on the events and circumstances of a single character. Sympathetic or defensive evaluations of a character by the narrator might also play a role. In general, we expect that clear narrator–character associations would be a product of the interaction of these features. Further, clear evidence for a narratorial association on one feature may bias the interpretation of other features. Thus, if a segment of narrative provides clear perceptual access to one character, the reader is more likely to construe other features as being consistent with a narrator–character association. Free-indirect speech, for example, may be more likely to be interpreted as the character's voice rather than the narrator's. This notion was discussed in a general way in Chapter 7 as the role of extended segments of text influencing the categorization of speech style. Here, however, we attribute such effects to a specific interaction between different classes of textual features. In general, we believe that the tendency for readers to form narrator–character associations would be a function of the constellation of features the text presents. Although the present work may have isolated a few of the variables that might be important, a complete account is likely to be much more complex.

Narratorial Presence

It is common to distinguish between narrator-present and narrator-absent narratives (e.g., Chatman, 1978, 1986). In the former, one has the impression of a distinct individual with a personality and judgments that are independent of other characters in the story world. In the latter, the act of telling the narrative seems to exist independently of events of the story world and does not appear linked to any identifiable persona. Such narratives are written in such a way as to give the impression of capturing events that happen by themselves, as if before a camera (hence the term "camera's eye" technique). Our analysis (described in Chapter 3) is that readers construct a representation of the narrator sufficient for the processes of conversational interaction. Thus, the reader's representation of the narrator is imbued with knowledge of the story world, a conversational point or message, and properties of rationality and cooperativeness. An absent narrator would have little else besides these bare necessities for conversational interaction. However, a present narrator could have a much deeper, more personal, representation that included personality traits, personal likes and dislikes, and explicit evaluations of the characters and events of the story world. The tendency to construct such deeper representations is likely to be a product of a wide range of features and influences. These might include the lack of consistent cues for a particular narrator–character association (creating an "omniscient" narratorial style), explicit and personal statements about the story world that would not be attributed to the characters, and explicit descriptions of the narrator.

The construction of a personal, present narrator might interact with other inferences involving the narrator. For example, in the study described in Chapter 5, self-evaluations by a personal narrator had little effect on the readers' trait ratings. Narratorial implicatures might also have a different force. To the extent that the narrator is represented as having different knowledge and memory from the reader, the inferences the narrator might draw about the story world could be different than those generated by the reader. Consider, for example, the short story "Haircut" by Ring Lardner. In this first-person, homodiegetic narrative, the narrator relates a sequence of reprehensible actions by another character in laudatory terms. Early in the narrative, the reader may be inclined to draw narratorial implicatures that justify the narrator's evaluations of the character. However, the burden of such inferences becomes too great as the story progresses, and different kinds of inferences are drawn about the narrator and his relationship to the character and the reader. The ability to make this switch may be supported by information in the narrative that allows the narrator to be represented more personally: The narrator exists in the story world, first-person pronouns are used consistently, and explicit references are made to the narrator's personal thoughts and interpretation of events.

Consistency

Although some narratives provide a consistent relationship between the narrator and the story world, many others do not. For example, the narrative may provide a variety of cues for a narrator–character association with one character in one segment of text, and then switch to another character in a subsequent segment. Or the identity or voice of the narrator may systematically change from one segment to another. Sometimes these switches may be marked by chapter boundaries, extra space between paragraphs, or changes in typeface. However, at other times the shifts may be abrupt and unheralded. These variations in narrator provide an analytical problem for the many of the issues we have dealt with in this book. For example, we assume that cues for narrator–character association are collated over extended segments of text; how long should one assume that segment is? Further, if the narrator changes or adopts a new association spontaneously, how is that identified by the reader? Undoubtedly, shifts in narrator can be signaled in a variety of ways, but one of these may be inconsistency in language, perspective, or circumstance.

Other Directions

In addition to the range of problems that we have raised so far, there are also a number of closely related issues for which psychonarratology may be a natural approach. We mention a few of these here.

Individual Differences

A broad class of variables that might be investigated concerns the nature of the reader. These include particular background or reader characteristics (such as gender), world knowledge, educational level, verbal ability, experience and expertise in literature or a particular genre, and dispositional tendencies to engage in various reading strategies. The incorporation of such variables in our general approach was explicitly anticipated in Chapter 2. However, we have pursued such factors only to a minor extent (cf. Dixon et al., 1993; Bortolussi & Dixon, 1996). Here we mention several important problems in this general area.

One obvious direction concerns background characteristics of the reader. At many points in the present work, we have suggested that narratorial implicatures invite readers to apply their own knowledge and experience to understanding the narrator's statements. Clearly, the kind of knowledge that readers are likely to bring to bear on such inferences depends on the idiosyncrasies of their own situation and experience. For example, to the extent that the lives of men and women differ, the kind of implicatures that men and women may draw in understanding a work may differ, perhaps leading ultimately to differing interpretations and evaluations of a work. Other variations may arise as a function of cultural differences. For example, Kinstch and Greene (1978), building on the classic work of Bartlett (1932), demonstrated that readers draw inappropriate inferences when reading literature from a different cultural tradition. Although this work did not specifically examine the role of narratorial implicatures, it seems intuitively clear that such cultural differences would have an impact on their processing.

Another important problem pertaining to individual differences is the understanding of the nature and effects of literary expertise. Undoubtedly, literary experts may engage in different kinds of processing or apply different knowledge than do unsophisticated readers. Some evidence supports this intuition. For example, Graves and Frederiksen (1991) compared the narrative descriptions of second-year undergraduates and English professors and found that the experts provided much more detailed and analytical descriptions of the language, text, communicative situation; Dorfman (1996) compared postgraduate students in literary studies to undergraduate computing science students and found substantial differences in the rated literariness and interest value of a range of stories. The results of these and similar studies confirm that literary experts provide more extensive, insightful analyses of literary works and suggest that they use a variety of more sophisticated analytical techniques. However, because these studies have been generally correlational in nature, it is difficult to be certain whether the differences between groups can be ascribed to experience at reading literary works, training in literature and literary criticism, aptitude and interest in literature, or simply general verbal ability.

One aspect of such expertise is likely to be knowledge of specialized genre form. Such knowledge would allow readers to better appreciate particular features of the text that they might not otherwise notice or understand. For example, Bortolussi and Dixon (1996) examined the effect of formal instruction in the genre of magical realism. Students in a class on magical realism read and evaluated a short story in the genre at both the beginning and end of the term. The responses indicated that after instruction, students were more likely to think that the narrator interpreted supernatural events at face value and less likely to interpret them as symbolism or metaphor. Such responses are broadly consistent with the content of the theoretical orientation developed in the class, but they were not explicitly taught. In contrast, students in a comparable course on science fiction showed no such changes over the term. Although this study rigorously demonstrated that genre-specific instruction can affect interpretation, a host of unanswered questions concerning the depth and generality of such effects remain.

We also suspect that a potent individual difference variable is simply sheer experience. Readers who read a lot are likely to have a greater range and depth of knowledge that is relevant to processing the narrative at hand. For example, in Dixon et al. (1993), we found that readers who reported reading more than three hours per week were sensitive to subtle variations in narrative technique in the Borges story, "Emma Zunz." Further, such readers appreciated the story more on second reading, but less-frequent readers did not. Although the reader samples in this study were not extensive, it did not appear that these effects could be attributed to differences in formal instruction or interest. It would be valuable to have a more precise understanding of the range of variations that such readers were sensitive to, what they were doing that was different than other readers, and how their more extensive reading experience supported such processes.

Our intuition is that an important individual difference is sensitivity to the role of the implied author. Certainly, in pedagogical contexts, it is common to sensitize students to the implied author by asking questions such as "What is the author trying to say?" or

"Why was the story constructed in this manner?" On the one hand, the fact that such reading strategies have to be deliberately taught reinforces our belief that a concern with the implied author is often not salient or important for many readers. On the other hand, the systematic tendency to generate representations of implied authors and their relationship to their stories may be an important distinction among groups of readers.

Literariness

Most work on narrative among literary scholars is focused on literary, as opposed to popular, narrative works. Thus, the scholarship often presupposes a concept of "literariness" even if it is not explicitly discussed. However, what precisely makes a work "literary" is difficult to identify. A useful (but fairly circular) operational definition of a literary work is one that literary critics find worthy of study. In turn, this suggests that literariness is not one thing but rather a collection of factors that make a work interesting or valuable for study. Moreover, it entails that criteria for literariness may not reside exclusively in the text but also in the reading context. For example, critics may find it valuable to study why a work produces the kind of reaction it does among readers, or works may be investigated because of their relationship to other works or societal events rather than because of specific properties of the texts on their own.

Beyond this fairly facile definition of literariness, though, it may be possible to identify characteristics of a text that are closely related to existing standards of literariness, and such a definition may be useful in understanding why readers appreciate some works more than others. In terms of the framework developed here, one would like to find textual features that are important for reader constructions related to literariness. Dixon et al. (1993) suggested that one such construction might be "depth of appreciation," defined as an increment in summary evaluations of a work on second reading. We assumed that depth of appreciation reflected some of the emergent, literary effects that a work might have. Further, we suggested that narrative ambiguity of various sorts might be one feature that is related to depth of appreciation: Works that are not obvious or clear-cut require more work on the part of the reader to understand. In a similar vein, we also suspect that narratorial implicatures and related techniques are important for literariness because they license the reader's use of his or her own knowledge and experience in interpreting the work. However, these ideas clearly relate to only one strand in the much larger question of literariness.

Genre

Another broad problem that we have not touched on is the nature and appreciation of literary genre. As it is commonly used, the term "genre" can refer either to a constellation of textual features or to a reader construction. On one hand, one can explicitly define different genres in terms of identifiable features. A substantial portion of the literary scholarship on genre would seem to have this goal. For example, inspired by biological taxonomies, some literary theories have focused on the identification of the necessary and sufficient features for a hierarchical classification of works (e.g., Symonds, 1970; Wellek, 1973). However, the rigidity of any given set of criteria fails to account for variations and evolution within any class and proves to be dysfunctional with respect to ambiguous or hybrid cases (e.g., Fowler, 1982; Fishelov, 1993). As an alternative, a number of scholars have discussed genre in terms of family resemblance rather than explicit criteria (e.g., Weitz, 1956, 1977). However, defining genres in terms of ill-specified family resemblance has the difficulty that we can no longer agree on what a given genre is and what works may or may not be in that genre.

On the other hand, genre can also refer to the particular constellation of properties and expectations a reader may have concerning works of a particular type, that is, a reader construction. We assume that readers' representations of genre are not different in kind to the representations of other categories that have been studied in cognitive psychology. In particular, it seems sensible to assume that readers have a collection of salient examples or prototypes available for each genre label with which they are familiar, and readers are usually able to assess the similarity between a given work and those prototypes (cf. Medin & Shaffer, 1978; Nosofsky, 1991; Rosch & Mervis, 1975). This perceived similarity provides the basis for classifying the work as being in or not in the genre.

Some important empirical work on aspects of genre as reader construction has been carried out in discourse processing. The general import of this research is that readers commonly have expectations concerning the conventions of different type of discourse, and that these expectations affect how the material is processed. For example, Olson, Mack, and Duffy (1981) found that readers of stories anticipated a causal structure in which upcoming events could be predicted on the basis of the events already encountered. In contrast, readers of essays assumed that a variety of evidence would be marshaled in support of an argument and, although succeeding elements could not be predicted, they should all relate to the central argument. Similarly, Einstein et al. (1990) argued that readers adopt relational or individual-item processing to varying degrees depending on the nature of the material; a fairy tale was presumed to invite relational processing, while expository prose was presumed to invite individual-item processing. Zwann (1994) demonstrated that these differences in processing can be attributed, at least in part, to the expectations readers have concerning the type of discourse rather than to the nature of the text itself: Different patterns of reading time and memory were found when the same text was introduced as either a news story or a narrative.

Based on work such as this, we would argue that there are three types of processes in which genre knowledge may be relevant. The first is cueing processes. Cueing processes are the mechanisms that allow a reader to identify a work as belonging to a particular genre. The second is schematic processes. Given that a work is identified as belonging to a particular genre, schematic processes would generate a collection of expectations and default assumptions pertaining to the themes, content, and style of the work. Finally, the third is contrastive processes. To the extent that a work does not conform to the expectations for the genre, contrastive processes allow the reader to identify the nature and degree of the similarity and differences between a work and prototypical or other salient works in a genre. However, beyond this general framework, many of the details of genre processing are unknown. In particular, the research in discourse processing has generally been concerned with distinctions between relatively broad categories of discourse (e.g., narrative versus newspaper stories; narrative versus essays). Consequently, these results do not have specific implications for the processing of finer grained distinctions within the overarching category of narrative (e.g., science fiction, romance novels, detective stories). In our view, those details would be amenable to the systematic application of the approach developed here. This would entail, for example, carefully identifying the textual features that are relevant to different aspects of genre processing and then investigating how reader genre constructions are related to those features.

Related Applications

Although the present work encompasses a broad selection of issues and problems, the horizon of new problems and issues is even broader, and there are many different allied areas for which our approach may have implications. These include the role of a narrator in nonnarrative discourse, the extension of psychonarratolgy to film narrative, and investigations into the process of writing of narrative.

Nonnarrative Discourse

Many of the processes we have implicated in the conversational processing of the narrator may also apply to the understanding of nonnarrative discourse. Traditionally, such discourse is analyzed in communicative terms as an interaction between the writer and the reader. Thus, conversational assumptions and inferences would be applied to understanding the point or message of the writer. The writer in turn would design the written communication with due consideration of the circumstances of the reader so that the intended message could be understood. A psychonarratological analysis becomes relevant, though, if the text is created from a different perspective or persona. The writer might create a "narrator," in effect, to present the arguments or information. The reader, in turn, would process such material as if it were presented by that narrator. Consequently, an analysis in terms of communication with the actual writer seems less apt, and it may be more insightful to adopt an approach in which one attempts to identify features of the text that contribute to readers' constructions.

Clear examples of this situation include ghost-written political speeches and advertising testimonials. It seems to us that in these kinds of works, writers attempt not to communicate with the reader, but rather to create an impression of a persona with a particular collection of beliefs and knowledge; those beliefs might differ substantially from their own. Readers for their part may have little appreciation of this distance between the actual author and the apparent author. Even essays and technical articles may have an element of this process because the author may in effect "put on" a voice or demeanor for the purpose to writing the text. For example, a researcher might write an article in which an argument or investigation is promoted simply for the purpose of the discourse, even though the researcher does not really subscribe to those beliefs. In such cases, there may be a significant difference between the knowledge and intentions of the writer and those which are represented by the reader. A variety of linguistic analyses might be applied to such texts; for example, the material might be construed as embodying a special register or as a form of pretense. However, it may also be useful to analyze the reading process in terms of features and reader constructions, without involving the actual author, using something like the framework developed here.

Film Narrative

The parallel between written and film narrative has been discussed by many authors (e.g., Bordwell, 1985; Magliano, Dijkstra & Zwann, 1996; Tan, 1994). As a consequence, it seems reasonable to ask whether the approach developed here for understanding written narrative might be profitably applied to film as well. Our guess is that the distinction between features and constructions is likely to be as important for understanding film as it is for written narrative. That is, it is critical to distinguish objectively defined properties of the film from the viewer's reactions and interpretations. However, we also suspect that our hypothesis concerning the conversational processing of the narrator would require some revision. The hypothesis that we developed here concerning the processing of the written narrative is that readers attempt to reconstruct, by virtue of normal conversational processes, the perceptual experience the narrator must have had in order to present the narrative as they do. However, in film, some analogue of the perceptual information is experienced directly, and there is much less reconstruction involved. This is sometimes referred to as the "diegetic effect" (Burch, 1979). Similarly, as Tan has noted, there is little in film that can be understood readily as speech acts. Nevertheless, one might suppose that film does have something akin to a narrator, or at least an implied director as it were, who selects the material and vantage to be presented. Indeed, Magliano et al. suggested that viewers interpret the information presented in terms of the conversational postulates of Grice. For example, when seemingly irrelevant information is presented, viewers may draw implicature-like inferences based on the assumption that it is actually relevant. Despite this commonality, though, our intuition is that the presence and characteristics of such a narrating agent are much more difficult to isolate in film than in text.

The notion of narrator–character association might also be relevant to film narration. We have suggested that some narrative techniques may lead the reader to form an association between the narrator and a character in the story world. These techniques include the selective use of perceptual access, free-indirect thought, and positional constraint. The result of such an association is often that the characteristics of the narrator and the character become less differentiated. There may be analogous techniques in film; for example, analogous to positional constraint, the camera may never show information that is not available to a character. However, because there is no obvious narrator in film, such processes may lead more directly to identification with the character (cf. Andringa et al., 1997).

Narrative Writing

The creation of written narrative is a broad and difficult problem. On one hand, it is an effortless, mundane experience: All of us routinely create narratives in conversation with apparent facility and little advance planning. On the other hand, the creation of valued, literary narrative is by all accounts a painstaking, extended process that only a very small portion of the population is capable of undertaking with any success. A first step in understanding this creative process might be to characterize the nature and range of the narratives that people produce, from informal, conversational narratives to extended (but unskilled) short stories to publishable fiction. Some good hypotheses about some of the properties of these products and the writing processes needed to create them can be garnered from the pedagogical literature: Generations of teachers have attempted to get students to write decent short stories, and one might suppose that such practical experience would lead to some understanding of what makes a good story and what it takes to write one.

Psychonarratology is well suited to undertake an empirical analysis of such hypotheses. For example, the pedagogical insights concerning good writing could be systematized as a collection of features, and then evaluations of readers could be measured as these features are manipulated. For example, one might conjecture that a narrative is more interesting when the circumstances of the story are presented indirectly in a piecemeal fashion rather than as an initial description of the setting. To test the hypothesis, a collection of amateur stories might be manipulated so that the setting is presented either explicitly or indirectly, and readers' reactions would be measured. Presumably, one of the things that accomplished writers have is a collection of techniques and strategies of this sort.

We anticipate that a critical element in the process of writing is likely to be the review process: A writer writes a segment of prose and then rereads it. Hayes and Flower (1986) divide up the writing process into planning, sentence generation, and revising; revision in turn involves detecting faults and diagnosing the problem. One might suppose that part of the goal of reading what you have written is to ensure that the intended message will be clear to the reader. This must entail some form of dissociation in which the processes used to understand the text must be compared to the original intention but not informed by it. In fact, Hayes et al. (1986; reported in Hayes & Flower, 1986) found that detecting writing flaws becomes more difficult with increased familiarity with the subject. We hypothesize further, though, that good creative writing may not be as planful as this characterization might suggest. The process of reviewing may actually suggest new ideas or directions that the writer did not have in mind at the outset. On reviewing the new revised text, further ideas are suggested, and so on. Thus, the narrative may seem to emerge without explicit intention from the processes of writing and reviewing. This process matches some of the introspections offered by accomplished novelists. For example, Cristina García indicated that writing her book, *Dreaming in Cuban*,

was like an archaeological dig, each time I went a little deeper and found something new that would somehow change everything that I had previously found, and then things couldn't be written quite the same way again. Even things I said had to be said in a different way. (López, 1994:611).

Le Guin (1985) also compared the writing of the novel *Always Coming Home* to an archeological dig and evoked images of discovery rather than creation.

To the extent that such processes occur, it becomes important to ask where the "new directions" come from. One possibility is that these were merely latent or undeveloped ideas that the writer already had. Another possibility is that the process of dissociation, necessary for effective reviewing, allows the writer to see things in a new way that would not have been possible before. Although we find such speculations intriguing, we are uncertain how they might be investigated.

Summary

In this chapter, we summarized what we see as the essential ingredients of the psychonarratology approach: One needs to distinguish objective features of the text from subjective constructions of readers, and the causal relation between features and constructions are best identified with textual experiments. We developed a general hypothesis about reader constructions: Under many circumstances, readers treat the narrator as a conversational participant and construct a representation of their point or intended message. This idea forms the backdrop for the consideration of a wide range of issues that have been of concern in narratology and literary scholarship. Although we have provided a certain amount of evidence in support of this general analysis, we have also ignored many issues. These include the detailed role of memory and attentional processes, effects of reading context and reading goals, how extratextual information is used, how the factors and areas we have discussed interact, and the identification of narrative consistency. We outlined briefly how we would be inclined to handle these issues. We also discussed possible directions in which research in psychonarratology might go. The former includes research on individual differences, the nature of literariness, and the treatment of literary genre. Some preliminary ideas were mentioned for each of these. Finally, we described a few more removed areas for which psychonarratology might have some relevance. These include the processing of some forms of nonnarrative discourse, the analysis of film narrative, and the investigation of narrative writing. We suspect that pursuing these connections will profit both the study of these other problems and the future development of psychonarratology.

Appendix

Evaluating Evidence

In this appendix, we outline some aspects of how the results of an experiment are evaluated. Although this clearly cannot be a comprehensive treatment of data analysis techniques, even as it applies to the results presented in this book, it at least may acquaint the reader with some of the relevant concepts. For readers with some background in statistical methods, the appendix also documents some procedures for calculating the likelihood ratios we use to compare models.

Experimental Design

In the vocabulary of experimental design, a manipulated independent variable is referred to as a *factor*, and each possible value of that variable is a factor *level*. For example, if one presents readers with two different versions of a story, one would say that the factor of story version has two levels. Often experiments have more than one factor. In a *factorial experiment*, each possible level of one factor is combined with each possible level of the other factors, and each combination of factor levels determines a particular experimental condition. For example, suppose the factor of story version was factorially combined with the factor of reading goal with two levels: reading to identify the narrator's point or reading to identify the plot events. In such a design, there would be four conditions: version 1 read for narratorial point; version 1 read for plot events; version 2 read for narratorial point; and version 2 read for plot events. Two types of results can be examined in a factorial experiment. On one hand, one can look for overall effects of the factors. For example, if recall of a particular story event were the dependent variable, one might find greater recall with the plot-events goal than with the narratorial point goal. Such overall effects are referred to *main effects*. On the other hand, one may also examine factor *interactions*. An interaction occurs when the effect of one factor depends on the level of another. For example, reading goal may only matter with story version 1 and may have no effect on the recall of events from story version 2. Factorial experiments are desirable precisely because they allow one to uncover important interactions of this sort.

An important distinction in experimental design is between factors that are manipulated between subjects and those that are manipulated within subjects. Between-subjects manipulations occur when different subjects participate in the different levels of a factor. For example, ten readers might read story version 1, and ten different readers might read story version 2. A within-subjects manipulation involves having the same subjects participate in each level of the factor. For example, each of the ten subjects might read both versions of the story. Within-subjects factors are sometimes referred to as *repeated measures*. A *mixed design* is one in which some factors are manipulated between subjects and others are manipulated within subjects. When practical, it is almost always better to manipulate factors within subjects because this allows for a more precise assessment of the effects of the variable. Essentially, a within-subjects manipulation allows the response of each individual to be compared to other responses of that same individual, thereby eliminating differences that might be caused by the particular characteristics of that individual. For example, any difference between a subject's recall of events from version 1 and that from version 2 cannot be attributed to the subject's general level of motivation and memory skill because those would be the same for both versions.

A difficulty in conducting within-subjects manipulations with many kinds of factors, and with manipulations of narrative materials in particular, is that exposure to one condition may affect the response to a subsequent condition. For example, readers' recall of a story is very likely to be affected by an earlier reading of another version of the same story. A common strategy for addressing this problem is *materials counterbalancing*. In this technique, there are different sets of materials, and subjects are exposed to only one set of materials in each condition, yet across subjects, all conditions and materials are used equally often. For example, one might manipulate whether the narrator offers a personal judgment of the events of the story world in two different stories. To counterbalance this manipulation, one set of subjects would read the personal-judgment version of story A and the impersonal version of story B, while another set of subjects would read the impersonal version of story A and the personal-judgment version of story B. In this way, each subject reads each story once, yet participates in both levels of the story version factor. The different groups of subjects in this scheme is referred to as a *counterbalancing factor*.

Analyzing Results

Analysis of Variance and Significance Testing

The most common tool for analyzing the results of factorial experiments, as well as other designs, is the analysis of variance (or ANOVA). The formal treatment of analysis of variance and related techniques is complex; only an intuitive outline of some basic elements is presented here. The essential notion in analysis of variance is that the scores one collects for one's dependent variable vary for a variety of reasons. They may vary because of the manipulated independent variable, they may vary because of characteristics of the individual, or they may vary because of other unknown or uncontrolled variables. The analysis of variance is a mathematical technique that allows one, given some assumptions about the nature and source of the data, to identify independent sources of variation. For example, in a simple experiment with a single between-subjects factor, variation may be divided into variation attributable to the manipulation and variation attributable to the individual subjects. (The latter is sometimes referred to as "error," although it is clear that very little of such variation is truly the result of what we might think of as random chance.) In a factorial design, variation can be partitioned into variation attributable to each factor (i.e., the main effects) and the interactions.

Analysis of variance results are often analyzed by the method of null hypothesis significance testing. In this approach, one begins by assuming that there is no difference among conditions (the so-called null hypothesis); then one calculates the probability of obtaining differences at least as extreme as those obtained; finally, if that probability is sufficiently small, one may reject the original assumption of no difference and conclude that the effect is "statistically significant." Statistical computer packages that perform analysis of variance typically produce a significance test for each interesting source of variation and summarize such tests in an "analysis of variance table"; examples are shown in Tables A.1, A.2, and A.4. In such tables, the total amount of variation attributable to each source is termed a *sum of squares* (abbreviated SS); each sum of squares is used to compute an estimate of the variance called a *mean square* (abbreviated MS); and then different mean squares are combined to calculate a test statistic, F. Associated with each F value is a probability or p value that allows one to test the significance of the effect.

Comparing Models

Despite its common use, null hypothesis significance testing has a number of well-known logical flaws and conceptual shortcomings (e.g., Cohen, 1994; Loftus, 1993). For example, in many contexts it is clear that there must be at least a miniscule difference among conditions, rendering the null hypothesis technically false a priori. Further, with sufficient power, the null hypothesis can be rejected even when the magnitude of the difference is trivial or uninteresting. Thus, by itself, rejecting the null hypothesis tells one nothing about the results of the experiment. We believe that a more appropriate and informative approach is first to identify competing interpretations or models of the data. The evidence for one model over another can then be summarized using a maximum likelihood ratio (Dixon, 1998; Dixon & O'Reilly, 1999); this approach is analogous to that advocated by Goodman and Royall (1988), Fisher (1955), and Edwards (1992) among others. The likelihood ratio indicates how likely the data would be, given one model, compared to how likely the data would be, given the other; when the ratio is high (e.g., greater than 10:1), one can be confident that the data provide reasonably strong evidence for the first model relative to the second.

Likelihood ratios provide precisely the same information that is used to compute test statistics such as F and in simple, prototypical designs lead one to draw comparable conclusions about the results. However, there is an important conceptual distinction between using hypothesis-testing methods and reporting likelihood ratios. Hypothesis testing is a method for making decisions and arguably was originally intended to be a formal, mechanical method for selecting an appropriate action purely on the basis of the data from an experiment. In contrast, likelihood ratios merely summarize the evidence. Despite the language of "significance" and "nonsignificance" that is typically adopted in research reports, we believe that, in reality, researchers generate decisions and interpretations by subjectively integrating the results of the experiment with a wide range of other considerations, including the results of previous research, theoretical plausibility, and interpretive parsimony. Although researchers commonly attempt to persuade others of their position by appealing to such factors, the quantitative assessment of the evidence from the experiment should remain separate. The likelihood ratio provides a clear, intuitive description of that evidence, divorced from what we believe is the misleading rhetoric of hypothesis testing. In the next section, we provide a brief introduction to this approach for readers familiar with the use of analysis of variance.

Calculating Likelihood Ratios

Comparing Two Conditions

To use likelihood ratios in analyzing the results of an experiment, it is essential to first identify different possible interpretations of the data. In the simplest possible experiment, there are two conditions and two possible interpretations or models. One interpretation is that there is no difference between conditions; we refer to this as the null model. A second interpretation is that there is some real, theoretically interesting difference between conditions; for the moment, we will refer to this as the condition model. To assess the evidence for one interpretation relative to the other, we would find the maximum

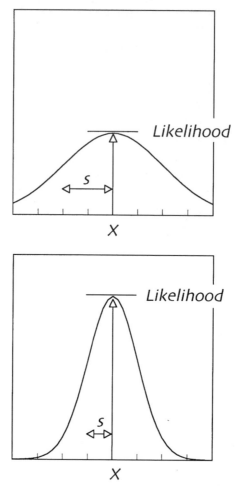

FIGURE A.1. Inverse relationship between likelihood and standard error.

likelihood given one model, the maximum likelihood given the other, and then calculate the ratio.

Likelihood ratios can be calculated in a straightforward fashion by recombining the numbers involved in standard statistical analyses. These calculations can be motivated by considering Figure A.1. Suppose in this case we were interested in determining the likelihood of an observation X. The likelihood of the observation is the height of the probability density function that represents the population distribution from which the observation was drawn. (In a

TABLE A.1. *ANOVA Table for Two-Condition Design*

Source	SS	df	MS	F	p
Condition	10	1	10.00	9.00	.008
Error	20	18	1.11		

discrete probability distribution, likelihood is simply the probability of the observation.) If we wished to maximize the likelihood of the observation and we had no other information about the mean of the population, we would center our estimate of the density function over the observation. In other words, we would select X as our maximum likelihood estimate of the mean. However, the likelihood of X, given that estimate, will depend on the standard deviation. This is shown in Figure A.1: Large standard deviations lead to low likelihoods, and small standard deviations lead to high likelihoods. More precisely, the maximum likelihood that we can find for X is proportional to $1/s$, where s is the standard deviation. In turn, s depends on how variable the data are, and variability can be thought of as unexplained variation. Putting this all together leads to the insight that the likelihood is inversely proportional to the square root of the unexplained variation.

Using this idea, we can calculate the likelihoods from the sum of squares in an analysis of variance table. An example for a simple two-condition design is shown in Table A.1. Each sum of squares in such a table can be understood as the amount of variation that can be attributable to a given source; in this case, SS_C refers to the variation attributable to the difference between conditions and SS_E is the variation attributable to error (i.e., variation across subjects within each condition). Under the condition model, in which it is assumed that there is a real difference between conditions, the only unexplained source of variation is error, so the maximum likelihood for each observation would be proportional to the square root of $1/SS_A$ or $(1/SS_E)^{1/2}$. Since there are n independent observations, the likelihood of all the observations would be found by multiplying together the likelihoods of each of the observations. Thus, the likelihood for the second model would be proportional to $(1/SS_C)^{n/2}$. The likelihood of the null model (in which it is assumed that there is no difference between conditions) would be calculated similarly. However, in this case, any difference between conditions is not explained by the model and must be attributed to chance. Thus, the unexplained variation would be $SS_A + SS_E$. In turn, this means that the likelihood for the null model would be proportional to $[1/(SS_C + SS_E)]^{n/2}$. Combining these two likelihoods in the form of a ratio leads to

$$\lambda = \left(\frac{SS_C + SS_E}{SS_C}\right)^{n/2} \qquad\qquad (A.1)$$

To illustrate this with the data shown in Table A.1, the calculation would be

$$\lambda = \left(\frac{10 + 20}{20}\right)^{20/2} = 57.7$$

In this case, the results lead to a large value of the likelihood ratio (i.e., substantially larger than 10). Thus, we can say that there is clear evidence that the condition model provides a better account of the results than the null model, and that the experiment provides clear evidence for an effect of condition. Notice that using traditional hypothesis testing procedures we would also have rejected the null hypothesis of no difference because the p value is smaller than the typical criterion of .05; hence, the results would be described as reflecting a "significant" effect. In this very simple case, then, the only difference between using likelihood ratios and testing hypotheses is conceptual: Rejecting the null hypothesis is a decision with presumed behavioral consequences, whereas the likelihood ratio merely summarizes the evidence with respect to the two models under consideration.

Factorial Designs

The same approach can be applied to more complicated designs. However, as the complexity in the dataset increases, so does the complexity in the theoretical analysis of possible interpretations. Our view is that there is no one fixed method of performing such an analysis, and that the models under consideration will depend on the theoretical context that motivated the experiment in the first place. However, one general strategy that we have used in this book is to consider nested linear models. In this approach, successively more

TABLE A.2. *ANOVA Table for Factorial Design*

Source	SS	df	MS	F	p
A	10	1	10.00	9.00	.005
B	8	1	8.00	7.20	.011
A × B	3	1	3.00	2.70	.109
Error	40	36	1.11		

complex theoretical interpretations are developed by adding linear components in a stepwise fashion. Likelihood ratios for such model comparisons are easily computed by recombining analysis of variance sums of squares.

Consider a (between-subjects) factorial design with two factors, A and B, each with two levels, and ten observations in each condition. If one conducted an analysis of variance of the data from such a study, one would get an analysis variance table such as that shown in Table A.2. Suppose further that, based on a theoretically motivated assessment of the possible interpretations of the results, we identified three interesting possible outcomes: a null model, in which none of the factors had an effect; an additive model in which both A and B had real effects and those effects simply added to determine the value of dependent variable; and a full model that also included an interaction between the factors. These three models are listed in Table A.3, along with the explained and unexplained sources of variation. In the null model, both factors and the interaction, as well as the error term, are unexplained and must be regarded as error; in the additive model, the unexplained sources include the error term and the interaction; and in the full model, only the error term is unexplained.

To evaluate the evidence for these three models, we would first compare the additive model to the null model. Using the formulation developed earlier, the likelihood ratio for this comparison would be

$$\lambda = \left(\frac{SS_A + SS_B + SS_{A \times B} + SS_E}{SS_{A \times B} + SS_E} \right)^{n/2} = \left(\frac{10 + 8 + 3 + 40}{3 + 40} \right)^{40/2} = 768.0$$

TABLE A.3. *Explained and Unexplained Sources of Variation in Factorial Design*

Model	Explained Sources	Unexplained Sources	Unexplained Variation
Null		A, B, A × B, Error	$10 + 8 + 3 + 40 = 61$
Additive	A, B	A × B, Error	$3 + 40 = 43$
Full	A, B, A × B	Error	40

Thus, there is strong evidence in favor of the additive model over the null model, and we would conclude that the factors together had some effect on the results. Second, we would compare the full model (that includes the interaction) to the additive model. In this case, the likelihood ratio would be

$$\lambda = \left(\frac{SS_{A \times B} + SS_E}{SS_E} \right)^{n/2} = \left(\frac{3 + 40}{40} \right)^{40/2} = 3.9$$

In this instance, the likelihood ratio is small (i.e., less than 10), and we would conclude that there is no clear evidence in favor of a model that includes an interaction between the factors. Notice that this corresponds to the nonsignificant effect for the interaction in the ANOVA table.

There is an important conceptual difference between this approach of comparing models and the traditional method of interpreting ANOVA tables. In the latter case, one typically identifies all the possible effects and interactions in the design and generates an independent test for each. Thus, Table A.2 includes F and p values for A, B, and the interaction. In the approach used here, we evaluate only models that provide plausible, interesting interpretations of the results. In the present example, we assumed that it was theoretically interesting to contrast the additive model (that included effects of both factors) with the null model; we did not bother, for example, to compare a model with only factor A to the null model, or to compare the additive model to one with only factor B, and so on. This is only an example of what one might want to do. We argue that the particular constellation of model comparisons that are appropriate can only be determined by considering the theoretical background that motivated the design and manipulations of that experiment, and that the appropriate comparisons cannot be specified in the abstract.

Repeated Measures and Mixed Designs

Repeated measures and mixed designs pose a small complication for this method of calculating likelihood ratios because the observations are not all independent; instead, one usually assumes that the observations for each subject are statistically dependent. An informal analysis of this situation that address the issue of dependence can be described as follows: Assume that there are n subjects divided among several between-subjects conditions and c repeated measures for each subject. One could then imagine recoding the data as a set of n subject means and $c - 1$ deviations from that mean for each subject. (Because the deviation scores must sum to zero, the cth deviation for each subject would be determined by the first $c - 1$ scores.) After this recoding, all the subject means and deviations would be independent of one another. Further, the likelihood of the original data is exactly the same as the likelihood of the recoded data since each exactly determines the other. The likelihood of the recoded data, though, is the likelihood of observing the pattern of subjects means *and* observing an independent set of deviations scores; thus, it can be written as $L_b \cdot L_w$, where L_b is the likelihood of the subject means and L_w is the likelihood of the deviations. The net result is that the likelihood ratio for comparing two models is the likelihood ratio for the subject means times the likelihood ratio for the deviation scores.

The values of the two likelihood ratios can be calculated from the sum of squares found in an analysis of variance table, as before. The only difference is that the sum of squares need to be first divided into those that are related to the between-subjects factors and those that are related to the within-subjects factors. Thus, in general, the likelihood ratio for a mixed-design comparison of model 1 and model 2 would be

$$\lambda = \lambda_b \cdot \lambda_w$$

$$= \left(\frac{SS_{b,1}}{SS_{b,2}}\right)^{n/2} \left(\frac{SS_{w,1}}{SS_{w,2}}\right)^{n(c-1)/2} \qquad (A.2)$$

TABLE A.4. *ANOVA Table for Mixed Design*

Source	SS	df	MS	F	p
A	10	1	10.00	6.00	.025
S	30	18	1.67		
B	5	1	5.00	4.50	.048
A × B	10	1	10.00	9.00	.008
B × S	20	18	1.11		

where $SS_{b,1}$ is the unexplained between-subjects sum of squares for model 1, $SS_{b,2}$ is the unexplained between-subjects sum of squares for model 2, $SS_{w,1}$ is the unexplained within-subjects sum of squares for model 1, and $SS_{w,2}$ is the unexplained within-subjects sum of squares for model 2. The exponents of the two terms depend on the number of independent observations: There are n independent subject means and $n(c - 1)$ independent deviations scores. The logic of computing each of these terms is the same as before: One identifies the factors or interactions that are left unexplained by either model and adds the corresponding sum of squares. (In a pure repeated-measures design, λ_b is identically 1, and one need only consider the sum of squares for the within-subject terms.)

As an example, consider a mixed design with one between-subjects factor, A, and one within-subjects factor, B. An ANOVA table for such a design is shown in Table A.4. In this example, there are ten subjects in each of two groups, and two repeated measures for each subject. Thus, S, the subjects factor, is nested within A. Suppose further that we were interested in comparing three models: a null model in which none of the factors were assumed to matter; a "groups" model in which only the between-subjects factor was assumed to have an effect; and a full model that also included the within-subjects factor and its interaction with groups. To identify the unexplained sources of variation, the sum of squares are first divided into those that pertain to the overall subject means (i.e., the between-subjects factors) and those that pertain to the pattern of observations for each subject (i.e., the within-subjects factors) as shown in Table A.5. The former consists of A and S; the latter consists of B, A × B, and B × S. For each model, the sums of squares in the two groups are divided into those that pertain to explained or unexplained sources of variation.

TABLE A.5. *Explained and Unexplained Sources of Variation in Mixed Design*

Model	Explained Sources	Unexplained Sources	Unexplained Variation
Between-Subjects Factors			
Null		A, S	$10 + 30 = 40$
Groups	A	S	30
Full	A	S	30
Within-Subjects Factors			
Null		B, A × B, B × S	$5 + 10 + 20 = 35$
Groups		B, A × B, B × S	$5 + 10 + 20 = 35$
Full	B, A × B	A × S	20

Using Equation A.2, the comparison between the groups and the null model is

$$\lambda = \lambda_b \cdot \lambda_w$$
$$= \left(\frac{SS_A + SS_S}{SS_S}\right)^{n/2} \left(\frac{SS_B + SS_{A \times B} + SS_{B \times S}}{SS_B + SS_{A \times B} + SS_{B \times S}}\right)^{n(c-1)/2}$$
$$= \left(\frac{10 + 30}{30}\right)^{20/2} \left(\frac{5 + 10 + 20}{5 + 10 + 20}\right)^{20(2-1)/2}$$
$$= 17.8$$

Similarly, the comparison between the full model and the groups model is

$$\lambda = \lambda_b \cdot \lambda_w$$
$$= \left(\frac{SS_S}{SS_S}\right)^{n/2} \left(\frac{SS_B + SS_{A \times B} + SS_{B \times S}}{SS_{B \times S}}\right)^{n(c-1)/2}$$
$$= \left(\frac{30}{30}\right)^{20/2} \left(\frac{5 + 10 + 20}{20}\right)^{20(2-1)/2}$$
$$= 269.4$$

Thus, one would conclude that there is clear evidence for an effect of the between-subjects manipulation A, as well as strong evidence for an effect of B that varies with group. As before, this summary of the evidence is comparable to the conclusions one might draw based on traditionally calculated p values.

References

Adams, D. The hitchhikers guide to the galaxy. London: Pan Books; 1979.

Ajzen, I., and Fishbein, M. A. Bayesian analysis of attribution processes. Psychological Bulletin. 1975; 82:21–77.

Anderson, N. H. Foundations of information integration theory. New York: Academic Press; 1981.

Anderson, R. C. and Pichert, J. Recall of previously unrecallable information following a shift in perspective. Journal of Verbal Learning and Verbal Behavior. 1978; 17:1–12.

Andringa, E.; Tan, E.; van Horssen, P.; and Jacobs, A. Effects of focalization in film narration. in: Totosy de Zepetnek, T. and Sywenky, I., editors. The systemic and empirical approach to literature and culture as theory and application. Edmonton: University of Alberta; 1997; pp. 203–15.

Argueta, R. One day of life, Vintage International Edition, 1991, translated from original, Un Día en la Vida, San Salvador: UCA Editores; 1980.

Aumonier, S. "Miss Bracegirdle does her duty." in: Priestley, J. B., editor. Great British short stories. London: Reader's Digest Association; 1974; pp. 26–39.

Baddeley, A. Working memory. Oxford: Clarendon; 1986.

Bal, Mieke. The narrating and the focalizing: A theory of the agents in narrative. Style. 1983; 17(2):234–69.

Narratology: Introduction to the theory of narrative. Boheemen, C. van, translator. Toronto: University of Toronto Press; 1985.

Bally, C. Le style indirect libre en français moderne. Germanisch-Romanisch Monatsschrift. 1912; 4(549–56):597–606.

Banfield, A. Narrative style and the grammar of direct and indirect speech. Foundations of Language. 1973; 10:1–39.

Reflective and non-reflective consciousness in the language of fiction. Poetics Today. 1981; 2(2):61–76.

Where epistemology, style, and grammar meet literary history. in: Lucy, J. A., editor. Reflexive language: Reported speech and metapragmatics. Cambridge, UK: Cambridge University Press; 1993; (3):339–64.

Barthes, R. Introduction à l'analyse structurale des récets. Communications. 1966: 8:1–27.

Introduction à l'analyse structurale des récits. Barthes, R.; Kayser, W.; Booth, W. C., and Hamon, P., editors. Poétique du récit. Paris: Edition du Seuil; 1977; pp. 7–57.

Bartlett, F. C. Remembering: A study in experimental and social psychology. Cambridge, UK: Cambridge University Press; 1932.

Bates, E. The emergence of symbols: Cognition and communication in infancy. New York: Academic Press; 1979.

Bauer, W., et al. Text und Rezeption: Wirkungsanalyse Zeitgenössischer Lyrik am Beispiel des Gedichtes "Fadensonne" von Paul Celan. Frankfurt: Athenäum; 1972.

Beach, R. A teacher's introduction to reader-response theories. Urbana, IL: National Council of Teachers of English; 1993.

Belli, G. The inhabited woman. March, K., translator. Willimantic, CT: Warner Books Edition; 1995.

Black, J. B. and Wilensky, R. An evaluation of story grammars. Cognitive Science. 1979; 3:213–30.

Black, J. B.; Turner, T. J.; and Bower, G. H. Point of view in narrative comprehension, memory, and production. Journal of Verbal Learning and Verbal Behavior. 1979; 18:187–98.

Bleich, D. Subjective criticism. Baltimore: John Hopkins University Press; 1978.

Booth, W. The rhetoric of fiction. Chicago: University of Chicago Press; 1961.

Bordwell, D. Narration in the fiction film. Madison, WI: University of Wisconsin Press; 1985.

Borges, J. L. "Emma Zunz." in: Borges, J. L. Labyrinths. New York: Modern Library; 1983; pp. 132–7.

Bortolussi, M. and Dixon, P. The effects of formal training on literary reception. Poetics Today. 1996; 23:471–89.

Science and the study of literature. Rusch, G., editor. Spiel: Siegener Periodicum Zur Internationalen Empirischen Literaturwissenschaft. 1998; 16(1/2):67–70.

A psychonarratological revision of the theory of focalization. Language and Style. in press.

Bower, G. H. Experiments on story understanding and recall. Quarterly Journal of Experimental Psychology. 1976; 28:511–34.

Bower, G. H.; Black, J. B.; and Turner, T. J. Scripts in memory for text. Cognitive Psychology. 1979; 11:177–220.

Bremond, Claude. La logique des possibles narratifs. Communications. 1966; 8:60–75.

Logique du récit. Paris: Seuil, 1973.

The logic of narrative possibilities. New Literary History. 1980; 11:398–411.

A critique of the motif. Todorov, T., editor. French literary theory today. Carter, R., translator. New York: Cambridge University Press; 1982; pp. 124–46.

Brodzki, B. She was unable not to think: Borges' "Emma Zunz" and the female subject. MLA. 1985; 100(2):330–47.

Bronzwaer, W. Mieke Bal's concept of focalization: A critical note. Poetics Today. 1981; 2(2):193–201.

Brown, N. R. Estimation strategies and the judgment of event frequency. Journal of Experimental Psychology: Learning, Memory, and Cognition. 1995; 21:1539–53.

Bruce, B. A social interaction model of reading. Discourse Processes. 1981; 4:273–311.

Bryant, D. J.; Tversky, B.; and Franklin, N. Internal and external spatial frameworks for representing described scenes. Journal of Memory and Language. 1992; 31:74–98.

Burch, N. To the distant observer. Berkeley, CA: University of California Press; 1979.

Card, O. S. Ender's game. New York: Tom Doherty Associates; 1977.

Carpenter, P. A. and Just, M. A., Integrative processes in comprehension. in: LaBerge, D. and Samuels, J., editors. Basic processes in reading: Perception and comprehension. Hillsdale, NJ: Erlbaum; 1977a.

Reading comprehension as eyes see it. in: Just, M. A. and Carpenter, P. A., editors. Cognitive processes in comprehension. Hillsdale, NJ: Erlbaum; 1977b.

Carr, E. Klee Wyck. Toronto: Irwin Publishing; 1941.

Carter, A. Nights at the circus. London: Vintage; 1994.

Black Venus. London: Vintage; 1996.

Cather, W. "Paul's Case." in: Cather, Willa. Five stories. New York: Vintage Books; 1959; pp. 149–74.

Cela, J. C. The Family of Pascual Duarte. Kerrigan, A., translator. Boston: Little, Brown and Co.; 1964.

Chafe, W. L. Discourse structure and human knowledge. in: Freedle, W. O. and Carroll, J. B., editors. Language comprehension and the acquisition of knowledge. Washington, DC: Winston & Sons; 1972.

Chafe, W. L. Some things that narratives tell us about the mind. in: Britton, B. K. and Pellegrini, A. D., editors. Narrative thought and narrative language. Hillsdale, NJ: Erlbaum; 1990; pp. 79–98.

Chang, F. Active memory processes in visual sentence comprehension: Clause effects and pronominal reference. Memory and Cognition. 1980; 8:58–64.

Chatman, S. On the formalist–structuralist theory of character. Journal of Literary Semantics. 1972; 1:57–79.

Story and discourse: Narrative structure in fiction and film. Ithaca, NY: Cornell University Press; 1978.

Characters and narrators: Filter, center, slant, and interest-focus. Poetics Today. 1986; 7(2):189–204.

Coming to terms. Ithaca: Cornell University Press; 1990.

How loose can narrators get? (And how vulnerable can narratees be?). Narrative. 1995; 3(3):3.

Cherryh, C. J. Cyteen: The betrayal. New York: Popular Library; 1988.

Fortress of owls. New York: Harpe Prism; 1999.

Chomsky, N. Syntactic structures. The Hague: Mouton; 1957.

Review of Skinner's Verbal Behavior. Language. 1959; 35:26–58.

Aspects of the theory of syntax. Cambridge, MA: MIT Press; 1965.

Clark, H. H. The language-as-fixed-effect fallacy: A critique of language statistics in psychological research. Journal of Verbal Learning and Verbal Behavior. 1973; 12:335–59.

Using language. Cambridge, UK: Cambridge University Press; 1996.

Clark, H. H. and Carlson, T. B. Hearers and speech acts. Language. 1982; 58:332–73.

Clark, H. H. and Chase, W. G. On the process of comparing sentences against pictures. Cognitive Psychology. 1972; 3:472–517.

Clark, H. H. and Gerrig R. J. On the pretense theory of irony. Journal of Experimental Psychology: General. 1984; 113:121–6.

Quotations as demonstrations. Language. 1990; 66:764–805.

Clark, H. H. and Schaefer, E. F. Contributing to discourse. Cognitive Science. 1989; 13:259–94.

Clark, H. H.; Cohen, J.; Smith, J. E. K.; and Keppel, G. Discussion of Wike and Church's comments. Journal of Verbal Learning and Verbal Behavior. 1976; 15:257–66.

Cohen, J. The Earth is round (p < .05). American Psychologist. 1994; 49:997–1003.

Cohn, D. Transparent minds: Narrative modes for presenting consciousness in fiction. 1978: Princeton: Princeton University Press.

Corcoran, M. G. Language, character, and gender in the direct discourse of *Dubliners*. Style. 1991; 25(3):439–53.

Coste, D. Narrative as communication. Minneapolis: University of Minnesota; 1989.

Coulmas, F. Direct and Indirect Speech. Berlin: Mouton de Gruyère; 1986.

Craig, C. "In the hills." in: Mordecai, P. and Wilson, B., editors. Her true-true name: An anthology of women's writing from the Caribbean. Oxford: Heinemann; 1990; pp. 56–9.

Craik, F. I. M. and Lockhart, R. S. Levels of processing: A framework for memory research. Journal of Verbal Learning & Verbal Behavior. 1972; 11:671–84.

Craik, F. I. M. and Watkins, M. J. The role of rehearsal in short-term memory. Journal of Verbal Learning and Verbal Behavior. 1973; 12:599–607.

Culler, J. Defining narrative units. in: Fowler, R., editor. Style and structure in literature: Essays in the new stylistics. Ithaca, NY: Cornell University Press; 1975a.

Structuralist poetics: Structuralism, linguistics, and the study of literature. London: Routledge and Kegan Paul; 1975b.

Cupchik, G. C. Identification as a basic problem for aesthetic reception. in: Tötösy de Zepetnek, S. and Sywenky, I., editors. The systemic and empirical approach to literature and culture as theory and application. Edmonton: University of Alberta Press; 1997; pp. 11–22.

Cupchik, G. C.; Oatley, K.; and Vorderer, L. Emotional effects of reading excerpts from short stories by James Joyce. Poetics. 1998; 25:363–78.

Danov, D. Dialogic structures in *Crime and Punishment*. Russian, Croatian and Serbian, Czech and Slovak, Polish Literature. 1986; 19(3):291–314.

Deighton, L. Berlin game. London: Grafton Books; 1984.

de Man, P. Blindness and insight: Essays in the rhetoric of comparative criticism. Minneapolis: University of Minneapolis Press; 1983.

Dillon, G. Language processing and the reading of literature. Bloomington: Indiana University Press; 1978.

Dingwall, W. The species-specificity of speech. in: Dato, D. P., editor. Developmental psycholinguistics: Theory and applications. Washington, DC: Georgetown University Press; 1975.

Dixon, P. Why scientists value p values. Psychonomic Bulletin & Review. 1998; 5:390–6.

Dixon, P. and Bortolussi, M. Literary communication: Effects of reader-narrator co-operation. Poetics. 1996a; 23(6):405–31.

The narrator in the text and the narrator in the reader. Paper presented at the meeting of the International Society for the Empirical Study of Literature. 1996b; Nakoda Lodge, Alberta, Canada.

I metodi della psiconarratologia. in: Nemesio, A., editor. L'esperienza del testo. Rome: Meltemi Editori; 1999c; pp. 126–43.

Narratorial relevance and character goals. Paper presented at the meeting of the International Society for the Empirical Study of Literature. 2000; Toronto.

Text is not communication: A challenge to a common assumption. Discourse Processes. 2001a; 31(1):1–25.

Prolegomena for a science of psychonarratology. in: W. van Peer and S. Chatman, editors. New perspectives on narrative perspective. Albany, NY: State University of New York; 2001b; pp. 275–88.

Dixon, P. and O'Reilly, T. Scientific versus statistical inference. Canadian Journal of Experimental Psychology. 1999; 53:133–49.

Dixon, P.; Bortolussi, M.; Twilley, L. C.; and Leung, A. Literary processing and interpretation: Towards empirical foundations. Poetics. 1993; 22:5–33.

Doležel, L. Possible worlds and literary fictions. in: Allén, S., editor. Possible worlds in humanities, arts and sciences. Berlin: Walter de Gruyter; 1989; pp. 221–42.

Dorfman, M. H. Evaluating the interpretive community: Evidence from expert and novice readers. Poetics. 1996; 23:453–70.

Dressler, W. U. The cognitive perspective of 'naturalist' linguistic models. Cognitive Linguistics. 1990; 1:75–98.

Duchan, J. F.; Bruder, G. A.; and Hewitt, L. E. Deixis in Narrative. Hillsdale, NJ: Erlbaum; 1995.

Ebert, T. L. The romance of patriarchy: Ideology, subjectivity, and postmodern feminist cultural theory. Cultural Critique. 1988; 10.

Eco, U. The role of the reader: Explorations in the semiotics of texts. Bloomington: Indiana University Press; 1979.

Edmiston, W. F. Focalization and the first-person narrator: A revision of the theory. Poetics Today. 1989; 10(4):729–43.

Edwards, A. W. F. Likelihood. Baltimore: John Hopkins Univeristy; 1992.

Einstein, G. O.; McDaniel, M. A.; Owen, P. D.; and Coté, N. C. Encoding and recall of texts: The importance of material appropriate processing. Journal of Memory and Language. 1990; 29:566–582.

Ellison, R. Invisible man. New York: Random House; 1952.

Emberson, J. Reported speech in medieval German narrative. Paregon: Bulletin of the Australian and New Zealand Association for Medieval and Renaissance Studies. 1986; 4:103–16.

Emmott, C. Narrative comprehension: A discourse perspective. Oxford: Oxford University Press; 1997.

Ericsson, K. A. and Kintsch, W. Long term working memory. Psychological Review. 1995; 102:211–45.

Erlich, S. Point of view: A linguistic analysis of literary style. London & New York: Routledge; 1990.

Faulkner, W. Honor. Collected stories of William Faulkner. New York: Random House; 1950; pp. 551–64.

   A rose for Emily. Selected short stories of William Faulkner. New York: The Modern Library; 1961; pp. 49–61.

Fetterley, J. The resisting reader: A feminist aproach to American fiction. Bloomington: Indiana University Press; 1977.

Findley, T. Not Wanted on the Voyage. Toronto: Penguin Books; 1984.

Fisch, H. Character as linguistic sign. New Literary History. 1990; 21:593–606.

Fish, S. Literature in the reader: Affective stylistics. New Literary History. 1970; 2:123–62.

   Is there a text in this class: The authority of interpretive communities. Cambridge, UK: Cambridge University Press; 1980.

   Being interdisciplinary is so very hard to do. Profession. 1989; 89:15–22.

Fishelov, D. Types of characters, characteristics of types. Style. 1990; 3:422–39.

   Metaphors of genre: The role of analogies in genre theory. State College, PA: Pennsylvania State University; 1993.

Fisher, R. A. Statistical methods for research workers. Edinburgh: Oliver & Boyd; 1925.

   Statistical methods and scientific induction. Journal of the Royal Statistical Society, Series B. 1955; 17:69–78.

Flaubert, G. Madame Bovary: A story of provincial life. Russell, A., translator. Harmondsworth: Penguin Books; 1950.

Fletcher, C. R. Strategies for the allocation of short-term memory during comprehension. Journal of Memory and Language. 1986; 25:43–58.

Fletcher, C. R. and Bloom, C. P. Causal reasoning in the comprehension of simple narrative texts. Journal of Memory and Language. 1988; 27:235–44.

Fludernik, M. The fictions of language and the languages of fiction: The linguistic representation of speech and consciousness. London: Routledge; 1993.

Towards a "natural" narratology. London: Routledge; 1996.

Forster, E. M. Aspects of the novel. London: Edward Arnold; 1974.

Fort, B. Manon's suppressed voice: The uses of reported speech. Romanic Review. 1985; 76(2):172–91.

Fowler, A. Kinds of literature: An introduction to the theory of genres and modes. Boston, MA: Harvard University Press; 1982.

Franklin, N. and Tversky, B. Searching imagined environments. Journal of Experimental Psychology: General. 1990; 119:63–76.

Franklin, N.; Tversky, B.; and Coon, V. Switching points of view in spatial mental models. Memory & Cognition. 1992; 20:507–18.

Frazier, L. and Rayner, K. Making and correcting errors during sentence comprehension: Eye movements in the analysis of structurally ambiguous sentences. Cognitive Psychology. 1982; 14:178–210.

Frow, J. Spectacle binding: On character. Poetics Today. 1986; 7(2):227–50.

García, C. Dreaming in Cuban, New York: Ballantine Books; 1992.

Genette, G. Figures III. Paris: Editions du Seuil; 1973.

Narrative discourse. Oxford: Basil Blackwell; 1980.

Narrative discourse: An essay in method. McDowell, R. S. and Velie, A., translators. Lincoln: University of Nebraska Press; 1983.

Gergen, K. J. Textual considerations in the scientific construction of human character. Style. 1990; 24(3):17–31.

Gerrig, R. J. Experiencing narrative worlds. New Haven, CT: Yale University Press; 1993.

Gerrig, R. J. and Allbritton, D. W. The construction of literary character: A view from cognitive psychology. Style. 1990; 24:380–91.

Gerrig, R. J.; Brennan, S. E.; and Ohaeri, J. O. What can we conclude from speakers behaving badly? Discourse Processes. 2000; 29:173–8.

Gerrig, R. J.; Ohaeri, J. O; and Brennan, S. E. Illusory transparency revisited. Discourse processes. 2000; 29:137–159.

Gibbs, R. Comprehending figurative referential descriptions. Journal of Experimental Psychology: Learning, Memory and Cognition. 1990; 16:56–66.

Intentions in the experience of meaning. New York: Cambridge University Press; 1999.

Gibson, W. All tomorrow's parties. New York: Ace Books; 1999.

Glanzer, M.; Fischer, B.; and Dorfman, D. Short-term storage in reading. Journal of Verbal Learning and Verbal Behavior. 1984; 23:467–86.

Glenn, C. G. The rules of episodic structure and of story length in children's recall of simple stories. Journal of Verbal Learning and Verbal Behavior. 1978; 17:229–47.

Glenberg, A. M. What memory is for. Behavioural and Brain Sciences. 1997; 20:1–55.

Glenberg, A. M. and Robertson, D. A. Indexical understanding of instructions. Discourse Processes. 1999; 28:1–26.

Glenberg, A. M.; Robertson, D. A.; and Members of the Honors Seminar in Cognitive Psychology. Symbol grounding and meaning: A comparison of high-dimensional and embodied theories of meaning. Journal of Memory and Language. 2000; 43:379–401.

Glenberg, A. M.; Meyer, M.; and Lindem, K. Mental models contribute to foregrounding during text comprehension. Journal of Memory and Language. 1987; 26:69–83.

Goodman, S. N. and Royall, R. Evidence and scientific research. American Journal of Public Health. 1988; 78:1568–74.

Graesser, A. C.; Bowers, C.; Olde, B.; and Pomeroy, V. Who said what? Source memory for narrator and character agents in literary short stories. Journal of Educational Psychology. 1999; 91:284–300.

Graesser, A. C.; Bowers, C. A.; Olde, B.; White, K.; and Person, N. K. Who knows what? Propagation of knowledge among agents in a literary storyworld. Poetics. 1999; 26:143–75.

Graesser, A. C.; Singer, M.; and Trabasso, T. Constructing inferences during narrative text comprehension. Psychological Review. 1994; 101:371–95.

Graves, B. and Frederiksen, C. H. Literary expertise in the description of a fictional narrative. Poetics. 1991; 20:1–26.

Greimas, A. J. Narrative grammars: Units and levels. MLN. 1971; 86:793–806.

Grice, H. P. Logic and conversation. in: Cole, P. and Morgan, J. L., editors. Syntax and semantics: Speech acts. New York: Academic Press; 1975; pp. 41–58.

Gross, J. B. A telling side of narration: Direct discourse and French women writers. The French Review. 1993; 66(3):401–11.

Gross, S. Cognitive readings; or, the disappearance of Literature in the Mind. Poetics Today. 1997; 18(2):271–97.

Hakala, C. Accessibility of spatial information in a situation model. Discourse Processes. 1999; 27:261–80.

Halliday, M. A. K. and Hasan, R. Cohesion in English. New York: Longman; 1976.

Hamon, P. Pour un statut sémiologique du personnage. Littérature, 1972; 6:86–110.

Pour un statut sémiologique du personnage. in: Barthes, R.; Kayser, W.; Booth, W. C.; and Hamon, P., editors. Poétique du récit. Paris: Editions du Seuil; 1977; pp. 115–80.

Hartley, J. Invisible fictions: Television audiences, paedocracy, pleasure. Textual Practice. 1987; 1(2):121–138.

Harvey, W. J. Character and the novel. Ithaca, NY: Cornell University Press; 1965.

Hauptmeier, H.; Meutsch, D.; and Viehoff, P. Empirical research on understanding literature. Poetics Today. 1989; 10(3):563–604.

Haviland, S. E. and Clark, H. H. What's new? Acquiring new information in comprehension. Journal of Verbal Learning and Verbal Behavior. 1974; 13:512–21.

Hayes, J. R. and Flower, L. S. Writing research and the writer. American Psychologist. 1986; 41:1106–13.

Hayes, J. R.; Schriver, K. A.; Spilka, R; and Blaustein, A. If it's clear to me it must be clear to them. Paper presented at the Conference on College Composition and Communication; New Orleans, LA; 1986.

Hemingway, E. The snows of Kilimanjaro. New York: Charles Scribner's Sons; 1927.

Hirsch, E. D. The aims of interpretation. Chicago: University of Chicago Press; 1976.

Hochman, B. Character in literature. Ithaca, NY: Cornell University Press; 1985.

Holland, N. 5 readers reading. New Haven, CT: Yale University Press; 1975.

Recovering "The Purloined Letter": Reading as a personal transaction. in: Saleiman, S. R. and Crossman, I., editors. The reader in the text: Essays on audience and interpretation. Princeton, NJ: Princeton University Press; 1980; pp. 350–70.

Fantasy and defense in Faulkner's "A rose for Emily." in: Staton, S., editor. Literary theories in praxis. Philadelphia: University of Pennsylvania Press; 1987; pp. 294–307.

Holub, R. C. Reception theory: A critical introduction. London: Routledge; 1989.

Irving, W. "The adventure of the German student." in: Litz, A. W., editor. Major American short stories, 3rd ed. New York: Oxford University Press; 1994; pp. 38–43.

Iser, W. The implied reader: Patterns of communication in prose fiction from Bunyan to Beckett. Baltimore: Johns Hopkins University Press; 1974.

The act of reading: A theory of aesthetic response. Baltimore: Johns Hopkins University Press; 1978.

Interaction between text and reader. in: Suleiman, S. R. and Crossman, I., editors. The reader in the text: Essays on audience and interpretation. Princeton, NJ: Princeton University Press; 1980; pp. 10–19.

Jahn, M. Frames, preferences, and the reading of third-person narratives: Towards a cognitive narratology. Poetics Today. 1997; 18(4):441–68.

Jauss, H. R. Literary history as a challenge to literary theory. New Literary History. 1970; 2(1):7–37.

Levels of identification of hero and audience. New Literary History. 1974; 5(2):283–312.

Johnson-Laird, P. N. Mental models. Cambridge, MA: Harvard University Press; 1983.

Johnson, N. S. and Mandler, J. M. A tale of two structures: Underlying and surface forms in stories. Poetics. 1980; 9:51–86.

Jones, E. E. and Davis, K. From acts to dispositions: The attribution process in person perception. in: Berkowitz, L., editor. Advances in experimental social psychology. New York: Academic Press; 1965; pp. 219–66.

Jost, F. Narration(s): En decà et au-delà. Communications. 1983; 38:192–212.

Joyce, J. Dubliners. New York: Penguin Books; 1991.

Just, M. A. and Carpenter, P. A. The psychology of reading and language comprehension. Boston: Allyn and Bacon; 1987.

Kamau, K. A. Flickering shadows. New York: Henry Holt and Company; 1996.

Kaschak, M. P. and Glenberg, A. M. Constructing meaning: The role of affordances and grammatical constructions in sentence comprehension. Journal of Memory and Language. 2000; 43:508–29.

Kelley, H. H. Attribution in social psychology: Nebraska Symposium on Motivation. 1967; 15:192–238.

Kenny, D. A. A general model of consensus and accuracy in interpersonal perception. Psychological Review. 1991; 98:155–63.

Keysar, B. The illusory transparency of intention: Linguistic perspective taking text. Cognitive Psychology. 1994; 26:165–208.

Kincaid, J. Marbles. in: Mordecai, P. and Wilson, B., editors. Her true-true name: An anthology of women's writing from the Caribbean. Oxford: Heinemann; 1990; pp. 112–16.

Kintsch, W. The representation of meaning in memory. Hillsdale: Erlbaum; 1974.

Kintsch, W. and Greene, E. The role of culture-specific schemata in the comprehension and recall of stories. Discourse Processes. 1978; 1:1–13.

Kintsch, W.; Kozminsky, E.; Streby, W. J.; McKoon, F.; and Keenan, J. M. Comprehension and recall of text as a function of content variables. Journal of Verbal Learning and Verbal Behavior. 1975; 14:196–214.

Knapp, J. V. Family systems as psychotherapy, literary character, and literature: An introduction. Style. 1997; 31(2):223–54.

Introduction: Self-preservation and self-transformation: Interdisciplinary approaches to literary character. Style. 1990; 24(3):349–64.

Krieger, M. Arts on the level: The fall of the elite object. Knoxville: University of Tennessee Press; 1981.

Kushigian, J. La economía de las palabras: Disipador del miedo inefable en Borges y Silvina Bullrich. Inti: Revista de Literatura Hispánica. 1989 Spring–1989 Fall; 29–30:207–214.

Labov, W. Language in the Inner City: Studies in the Black English Vernacular. Philadelphia: University of Pennsylvania; 1972; pp. 354–96.

Lakoff, G. and Johnson, M. Philosophy in the flesh: The embodied mind and its challenge to Western thought. New York: Basic Books; 1999.

Lamarque, P. Narrative and Invention: The Limits of Fictionality. in: Nash, C., editor. Narrative in culture: The uses of storytelling in the sciences, philosophy, and literature. London: University of Warwick Centre for Research in Philosophy and Literature; 1990; pp. 131–53.

Lanser, S. The narrative act: Point of view in fiction. Princeton, NJ: Princeton University Press; 1981.

Sexing the narrative: Propriety, desire, and the engendering of narratology. Narrative. 1995; 3(1):85–94.

Lardner, R. The love nest and other stories. New York: C. Scribner's Sons; 1926.

Larsen, S. F. and Seilman, U. Personal remindings while reading literature. Text. 1988; 8:411–29.

Larsen, S. F. and Viehoff, R. Introduction: "Empirical" – What does it mean in IGEL studies? in: Rusch, G., editor. Emprical approaches to literature: Procedings of the fourth conference of the International Society for the Empirical Study of Literature – IGEL; Budapest. Siegen: Lumis Publications; 1995:21–27.

Larsen, S. F.; László, J.; and Seilman, U. Across time and place: Cultural-historical knowledge and personal experience in appreciation of literature. in: Ibsch, E.; Schram, D.; and Steen, G., editors. Empirical studies of literature: Proceedings of the second IGEL Conference, Amsterdam, 1989. Amsterdam: Rodopi; 1991.

le Carré, J. The naive and sentimental lover. London: Pan Books; 1972.

Smiley's people. London: Penguin Books; 1992.

Our game. Toronto: Penguin Books; 1995.

The tailor of Panama. Toronto: Penguin; 1997.

Le Guin, U. K. "The wife's story." in: The Compass Rose. New York: Bantam Books; 1983.

Always coming home. Toronto: Bantam Books; 1985.

Tehanu: The last book of Earthsea. New York: Atheneum; 1990.

Lehnert, W. G. Plot units: A narrative summarization strategy. in: Lehnert, W. G. and Ringle, M. H., editors. Strategies for natural language processing. Hillsdale, NJ: Erlbaum; 1982; pp. 375–412.

Lenneberg, E. The biological foundations of language. New York: Wiley; 1967.

Levelt, W. J. M. Speaking: From intention to articulation. Cambridge, MA: MIT Press; 1989.

Perspective taking and ellipsis in spatial descriptions. in: Bloom, M. A.; Peterson, N. L.; and Garret, M. F. Language and space. Cambridge, MA: MIT Press; 1996; pp. 77–108.

Levine, W. H. and Klin, C. M. Tracking of spatial components of situation models. Memory & Cognition. 2001; 29:327–35.

Limon, J. The place of fiction in the time of science: A disciplinary history of American writing. New York: Cambridge University Press; 1990.

Linde, C. and Labov, W. Spatial netwoks as a site for the study of language and thought. Language. 1975; 51:924–39.

Loftus, G. R. A picture is worth a thousand p values: On the irrelevance of hypothesis testing in the microcomputer age. Behavior Research Methods, Instruments, & Computers. 1993; 25:250–6.

Long, D. L. and De Ley, L. Implicit causality and discourse focus: The interaction of text and reader characteristics in pronoun resolution. Journal of Memory and Language. 2000; 42:545–70.

López, I. H. . . . And there is only my imagination where our history should be: An interview with Cristina García. Michigan Quarterly Review. 1994; 33:3.

Mackie, J. L. The cement of the universe: A study of causation. Oxford: Clarendon; 1980.

Magliano, J. P.; Dijkstra, K.; and Zwann, R. A. Generating predictive inferences while viewing a movie. Discourse Processes. 1996; 22:199–224.

Makaryk, I. R., editor and compiler. Encyclopedia of contemporary literary theory: Approaches, scholars, terms. Toronto: University of Toronto Press; 1993.

Mandler, J. M. A code in the node: The use of a story schema in retrieval. Discourse Processes. 1978; 1:14–35.

Stories, scripts, and scenes: Aspects of schema theory. Hillsdale, NJ: Erlbaum; 1984.

Mandler, J. M. and Goodman, M. S. On the psychological reality of story structure. Journal of Verbal Learning and Verbal Behavior. 1982; 21:507–23.

Margolin, U. Characterization in narrative: Some theoretical prolegomena. Neophilologus. 1983; 67:1–14.

The doer and the deed: Action as basis for characterization in narrative. Poetics Today. 1986; 7(2):205–25.

Structuralist approaches to character in narrative: The state of the art. Semiotica. 1989; 75(1/2):1–24.

Individuals in narrative worlds: An ontological perspective. Poetics Today. 1990a; 11(4):843–71.

The what, the when, and the how of being a character in literary narrative. Style. 1990b; 24(3):453–68.

Fictional individuals and their counterparts. Andrew, J., editor. Studies in Slavic Literature and Poetics. 1992; 1743–56.

Changing individuals in narrative: Science, philosophy, literature. Semiotica. 1995; 107(12):5–31.

Characters in literary narrative: Representation and signification. Semiotica. 1998; 106(3/4):373–92.

McCutchen, D. and Perfetti, C. A. The visual tongue-twister effect: Phonological activation in silent reading. Journal of Verbal Learning and Verbal Behavior. 1982; 2:672–87.

McDaniel, M. A.; Hines, R. J.; Waddil, P. J.; and Einstein, G. O. What makes folk tales unique: Content familiarity, causal structure, scripts, or superstructures? Journal of Experimental Psychology: Learning, Memory, and Cognition. 1994; 20:169–84.

McHale, B. Free indirect discourse: A survey of recent accounts. PTL: A Journal for Descriptive Poetics and Theory of Literature. 1978; 3:249–87.

Unspeakable sentences, unnatural acts: Linguistics and poetics revisited. Poetics Today. 1983; 4(1):17–45.

McKoon, G. and Ratcliff, R. Inference during reading. Psychological Review. 1992; 99:440–66.

McRobbie, A. Feminism and youth culture. Cambridge, MA: Hyman; 1990.

Medin, D. L. and Schaffer, M. M. Context theory of classification learning. Psychological Review. 1978; 85:207–38.

Meyer, B. J. F. The organization of prose and its effect on memory. Amsterdam: North Holland; 1975.

Miall, D. S. and Kuiken, D. Aspects of literary response: A new questionnaire. Research in the Teaching of English. 1995; 29:37–58.

Moore, R. E. Performance form and the voices of characters in five versions of the Wasco Coyote cycle. in: Lucy, J. A., editor. Reflexive language: Reported speech and metapragmatics. New York: Cambridge University Press; 1993.

Morrison, T. Beloved. New York: Plume, Penguin Putnam; 1998.

Morrow, D. G.; Bower, G. H.; and Greenspan, S. L. Updating situation models during narrative comprehension. Journal of Memory and Language. 1989; 28:292–312.

Morrow, D. G.; Greenspan, S. L.; and Bower, G. H., Accessibility and situation models in narrative comprehension. Journal of Memory and Language. 1987(26):165–87.

Mukarovsky, J. Aesthetic function, norm and value as social facts. Ann Arbor: University of Michigan Press; 1970.

Munro, A. The office. in: Munro, A., editor. Collected short stories. New York: Random House; 1996; pp. 59–74.

Murillo, L. A. The Cyclical Night: Irony in James Joyce and Jorge Luis Borges. Cambridge, MA: Harvard University Press; 1968.

Myers, J. L. and O'Brien, E. J. Accessing the discourse representation during reading. Discourse Processes. 1998; 26:131–58.

Nash, C. Narrative in culture. London: Routledge; 1994.

Nelles, W. Getting focalization into focus. Poetics Today. 1990; 11(2):365–82.

Newell, A. and Simon, H. A. Human problem solving. Englewood Cliffs, NJ: Prentice Hall; 1972.

Neyman, J. and Pearson, E. S. On the use and interpretation of certain test criteria for purposes of statistical inference. Biometrika. 1928; 20A:263–94.

Nosofsky, R. M. Tests of an exemplar model for relating perceptual classification and recognition memory. Journal of Experimental Psychology: Human Perception and Performance. 1991; 17:3–27.

Oatley, K. A taxonomy of the emotions of literary response and a theory of identification in fictional narrative. Poetics. 1994; 23:53–74.

O'Brien, E. J. and Albrecht, J. E. Comprehension strategies in the development of a mental model. Journal of Experimental Psychology: Learning, Memory, and Cognition. 1992; 18:777–84.

O'Brien, E. J.; Lorch, R. F., Jr.; and Myers, J. L. Memory-based text processing. Discourse Processes. 1998; 26:2–3.

Olson, G. M.; Mack, R. L., and Duffy, S. A. Cognitive aspects of genre. Poetics. 1981; 10:283–315.

Oltean, S. Functions of free indirect discourse: The case of a novel. Revue Roumaine de Linguistique. 1986; 31:153–64.

A survey of the pragmatic and referential functions of free indirect discourse. Poetics Today. 1993; 14(4):691–714.

Omanson, R. C. An analysis of narratives: Identifying central, supportive, and distracting content. Discourse Processing. 1982; 5:195–224.

O'Neill, P. Points of origin: On focalization in narrative. Canadian Review of Comparative Literature. 1992; Sept:331–50.

Fictions of discourse: Reading narrative theory. Toronto: University of Toronto Press; 1994.

Ortega, R. P. Intento de interpretación psicoanalítica de un cuento de Jorge Luis Borges. Eco. 1971; 23(138–139):587–99.

Pavel, T. G. Fictional worlds. Cambridge, MA: Harvard University Press; 1986.

Phelan, J. Reading people, reading plots: Character, progression, and the interpretation of narrative. Chicago: University of Chicago Press; 1989.

Pinker, S. The language instinct. New York: Morrow; 1994.

Piwowarczyk, M. A. The narratee and the situation of enunciation: A reconsideration of Prince's theory. Genre. 1976; 9:161–77.

Polanyi, L. Literary complexity in everyday storytelling. in: Tannen, D., editor. Spoken and written language: Exploring orality and literacy. Norwood, NJ: Ablex; 1982.

Pollard-Gott, L. Attribution theory and the novel. Poetics. 1993; 21:499–524.

Porter, K. A. Rope. in: Cahill, S., editor. Women and fiction: Short stories by and about women. New York: New American Library; 1975; pp. 78–84.

Postman, L. and Senders, V. L. Incidental learning and generality of set. Journal of Experimental Psychology. 1946; 36:153–65.

Potter, J. and Wetherell, M. Discourse and social psychology. London: Sage; 1987.

Prince, G. A grammar of stories. The Hague: Mouton; 1973.

Dictionary of narratology. Lincoln: University of Nebraska Press; 1987.

Narratology: The form and functioning of narrative. Amsterdam: Mouton; 1982.

On narratology: Past, present, future. French Literary Studies. 1990; XVII.

Propp, V. Morphologie du conte. Derrida, M.; Todorov, T.; and Kahn, C., translators. Paris: Editions du Seuil; 1965.

Morphology of the folktale. Austin: University of Texas; 1968.

Raap, D. N.; Gerrig, R. J.; and Prentice, D. A. Readers' trait-based models of characters in narrative comprehension. Journal of Memory and Language. 2001;45:737–50.

Rabinowitz, P. J. Other reader-oriented theories. in: Selden, R., editor. The Cambridge history of literary criticism: From formalism to poststructuralism. Cambridge, UK: Cambridge University Press, 1995; 375–403.

Ramazani, V. The free indirect mode: Flaubert and the poetics of irony. Charlottesville: Univeristy Press of Virginia; 1988.

Reeder, G. D. and Brewer, M. B. A schematic model of dispositional attribution in interpersonal perception. Psychological Review. 1979; 86:61–79.

Richard, J.-P. Littérature et sensation. Paris: Aux Editions du Seuil; 1954.

Richards, E. and Singer, M. Representation of complex goal structures in narrative comprehension. Discourse Processes. 2001; 31:111–37.

Richardson, B. Beyond poststructuralism: Theory of character, the personae of modern drama, and the antinomies of critical theory. Modern Drama. 1997; 40:86–99.

Ricoeur, P. Temps et récit. Paris: Seuil; 1983.

Riffaterre, M. Describing poetic structures: Two approaches to Baudelaire's "Les Chats." Yale French Studies. 1966; 36/37:200–42.

Rimmon-Kenan, S. Narrative fiction: Contemporary poetics. New York: Methuen; 1983.

Rosch, E. and Mervis, C. B. Family resemblances: Studies in the internal structure of categories. Cognitive Psychology. 1975; 7:573–605.

Ross, L. The intuitive psychologist and his shortcomings: Distortions in the attribution process. in: Berkowitz, L., editor. Advances in experimental social psychology. New York: Academic Press; 1977; pp. 173–220.

Ross, L. D.; Amabile, T. M.; and Steinmetz, J. L. Social roles, social cognition, and biases in social-perception processes. Journal of Personality & Social Psychology. 1977; 35:485–94.

Rowling, J. K. Harry Potter and the goblet of fire. London: Raincoast Books; 2000.

Rumelhart, D. E. Notes on a schema for stories. in: Bobrow, D. G. and Collins, A., editors. Representation and understanding: Studies in cognitive science. New York: Academic Press; 1975; pp. 211–36.

Rusch, G. The notion of "empirical": Knowing how. in: Rusch, G., editor. Empirical approaches to literature: Proceedings of the fourth biannual conference of the International Society for the Empirical Study of Literature – IGEL; Budapest. Siegen: Lumis Publications; 1995; pp. 103–8.

Sanders, J. and Redeker, G. Perspective and the representation of speech and thought. in: Fauconnier, G., editor. Worlds and grammar. Chicago: University of Chicago Press; 1996; pp. 290–317.

Sanford, A. J. and Garrod, S. Understanding written language: Explorations in comprehension beyond the sentence. Chichester: Wiley; 1981.

Sanford, A. J. and Garrod, S. C. The role of scenario mapping in text comprehension. Discourse Processes. 1998; 26:159–90.

Schank, R. C. and Abelson, R. P. Scripts, plans, goals and understanding. Hillsdale, NJ: Erlbaum; 1977.

Schegloff, E. A.; Jefferson, G.; and Sacks, H. The preference for self-correction in the organization of repair in conversation. Language. 1977; 53:361–82.

Schmidt, S. J. Receptional problems with contemporary narrative texts and some of their reasons. Poetics. 1980; 9:119–46.

Empirical studies in literature: Introductory remarks. Poetics. 1981; 10:317–36.

The empirical science of literature ESL: A new paradigm. Poetics. 1983; 12:19–34.

What can "empirical" mean in a constructivist context? 10 considerations. in: Rusch, G., editor. Empirical approaches to literature: Proceedings of the fourth biannual conference of the International Society for the Empirical Study of Literature – IGEL; Budapest. Siegen: Lumis Publications; 1995: 109–112.

Schober, M. F. Spatial perspective-taking in conversation. Cognition. 1993; 47:1–24.

Seidenberg, M. S. and McClelland, J. L. A distributed, developmental model of word recognition and naming. Psychological Review. 1989; 96:523–68.

Selden, R. The Cambridge history of literary criticism: From formalism to poststructuralism. Cambridge, UK: Cambridge University Press; 1995.

Shapiro, M. How narrators report speech. Language and Style. 1984; 17(1):67–78.

Shaw, H. E. Thin description: A reply to Seymour Chatman. Narrative. 1995; 3(3):307–14.

Shepard, L. Life during wartime. New York: Bantam Books; 1987.

Shklovsky, V. Art as technique. in: Lemon, L. T. and Reis, M. J., editors. Russian formalist criticism: Four essays. Lincoln: University of Nebraska Press; 1965; pp. 3–24.

Sidner, C. Focusing and discourse. Discourse Processes. 1983; 6:107–30.

Sinclair-de Zwart, H. Language acquisition and cognitive development. in: Moore, T., editor. Cognitive development and the acquisition of language. New York: Academic Press; 1973.

Singer, M. and Ferreira, F. Inferring consequences in story comprehension. Journal of Verbal Learning and Verbal Behavior. 1983; 22:437–48.

Slatoff, W. With respect to readers: Dimensions of literary response. Ithaca, NY: Cornell University Press; 1970.

Sophocles. Oedipus the king and Antigone. Arnott, P. D., translator. New York: Appleton-Century-Crofts; 1969.

Spilich, G. J.; Vesonder, G. T.; Chiesi, H. L.; and Voss, J. F. Text processing of domain-related information for individuals with high and low domain knowledge. Journal of Verbal Learning and Verbal Behavior. 1979; 18:275–90.

Spolsky, E. Gaps in nature: Literary interpretation and the modular mind. Albany: State University of New York Press; 1993.

Stampfl, B. Filtering Rimmon-Kenan, Chatman, Black, Freud, and James: Focalization and the divided self in "The beast in the jungle." Style. 1992; 26(3):388–99.

Stanzel, F. K. Teller-characters and reflector-characters in narrative theory. Poetics Today. 1981; 2(2):4–15.

Stein, N. L. and Glenn, C. G. An analysis of story comprehension in elementary school children. in: Le Freed, R., editor. New directions in discourse processing (Vol. 2). Norwood, NJ: Ablex; 1979; pp. 53–120.

Suleiman, S. and Crosman, I. The reader in the text: Essays on audience and interpretation. Princeton, NJ: Princeton University Press; 1980.

Symonds, J. A., On the application of evolutionary principles to art and literature. in: Essays speculative and suggestive. New York: AMS Press; 1970; pp. 197–224.

Tan, E. S. H. Film-induced affect as a witness emotion. Poetics. 1994; 23:7–32.

Tannen, D. Oral and literate strategies in spoken and written narratives. Language. 1982; 58(1):1–21.

Conversational style. Analyzing talk among friends. Norwood: Ablex; 1984.

Taylor, H. A. and Tversky, B. Perspective in spatial descriptions. Journal of Memory and Language. 1996; 35:371–91.

Thorndyke, P. W. Cognitive structure in comprehension and memory of narrative discourse. Cognitive Psychology. 1977; 9:51–86.

Thury, E. M. and Friedlander, A. The impact of expertise: The role of experience in reading literary texts. in: Rusch, G., editor. Empirical approaches to literature: Proceedings of the fourth biannual conference of the International Society for the Empirical Study of Literature – IGEL; Budapest. Siegen: Lumis Publications; 1995; p. 22.

Tolliver, J. Discourse analysis and the interpretation of literary narrative. Style. 1990; 24(2):266–83.

Tomachevsky, B. Thématique. in: Todorov, T., editor and translator. Théorie de la littérature. Paris: Aux Editions du Seuil; 1965.

Toolan, M. J. Narrative: A critical linguistic introduction. New York: Routledge; 1995.

Trabasso, R. and Sperry, L. L. Causal relatedness and importance of story events. Journal of Memory and Language. 1985; 24:595–611.

Trabasso, T. and van den Broek, P. Causal thinking and the representation of narrative events. Journal of Memory and Language. 1985; 24:612–30.

Trope, Y. and Burnstein, E. Processing the information contained in another's behavior. Journal of Experimental Social Psychology. 1975; 11:439–58.

Turner, M. Reading minds: The study of English in the age of cognitive science. Princeton, NJ: Princeton University Press; 1991.

Tversky, B. Spatial perspective in descriptions. in: Bloom, P.; Barret, M.; Hadel, L.; and Peterson, M., editors. Language and Space. Boston: MIT Press; 1996; pp. 463–91.

Uleman, J. S.; Hon, A.; Roman, R. J.; and Moskowitz, G. B. On-line evidence for spontaneous trait inferences at encoding. Personality and Social Psychology Bulletin. 1996; 22:377–94.

van den Broek, P.; Risden, K.; Fletcher, C. R.; and Thurlow, R. A. "Landscape" view of reading: Fluctuating patterns of activation and the construction of a stable memory representation. in: Britton, B. K. and Graesser, A. C., editors. Models of understanding text. Hillsdale, NJ: Erlbaum; 1996; pp. 165–87.

van Dijk, T. A. Philosophy of action and theory of narrative. Poetics. 1976; 5.

van Dijk, T. A. and Kintsch, W. Strategies of discourse comprehension. New York: Academic Press; 1983.

Vipond, D. and Hunt, R. A. Literary processing and response as transactions: Evidence for the contribution of readers, texts, and situation. in: Meutsch, D. and Viehoff, R., editors. Comprehension of literary discourse: Interdisciplinary approaches. Berlin: de Gruyter; 1989; pp. 155–74.

Vitoux, P. Le jeu de la focalisation. Poétique. 1982; 51:359–68.

Notes sur la focalisation dans le roman autobiographique. Etudes Littéraires. 1984; 17(2):261–72.

Walsh, R. Who is the narrator? Poetics Today. 1997a; 18(4):495–513.

Why we wept for Little Nell: Character and emotional involvment. Narrative. 1997b; 5(3):306–21.

Warren, W. H.; Nicholas, D. W.; and Trabasso, T. Event chains and inferences in understanding narratives. in: Freedle, R. O., editor. Advances in discourse processes: New directions in discourse processing, Vol. 2. Norwood, NJ: Ablex; 1979.

Weinberg, H. H. Irony and "style indirect libre" in *Madame Bovary*. Canadian Review of Comparative Literature. 1981; 8(1):1–9.

Weitz, M. The role of theory in aesthetics. Journal of Aesthetics and Art Criticism. 1956; 15(1):27–35.

The opening mind. Chicago: University of Chicago Press; 1977.

Wellek, R. The concept of evolution in literary history. in: Wellek, R., editor. Concepts of criticism. New Haven, CT: Yale University Press; 1973.

Werth, P. N. How to build a world (in a lot less than six days, and using only what's in your head). in: Green, K., editor. New essays in deixis: Discourse, narrative, literature. Amsterdam: Rodopi; 1995; pp. 49–80.

White, H. The value of narrativity in the representation of reality. in: Mitchell, W. J. T., editor. On narrative. Chicago: University of Chicago Press; 1981; pp. 1–24.

Whitehurst, G. Language development. in: Wolman, B., editor. Handbook of developmental psychology. Englewood Cliffs, NJ: Prentice-Hall; 1982.

Wiebe, J. M. Recognizing subjective sentences: A computational analysis of narrative text. Buffalo, NY: SUNY, Department of Computer Science; 1990.

Wieder, L. Telling the code. in: Turner, R., editor. Ethnomethodology. Harmondsworth, UK: Penguin; 1974.

Wike, E. L. and Church, J. D. Comments on Clark's "The language-as-fixed-effect fallacy." Journal of Verbal Learning and Verbal Behavior. 1976; 15:249–55.

Wilder, D. Perceiving persons as a group: Effects on attributions of causality and beliefs. Social Psychology. 1978; 1:13–23.

Wilson, S. G.; Rinck, M.; McNamara, T. P.; Bower, G. H.; and Morrow, D. G. Mental models and narrative comprehension: Some qualifications. Journal of Memory and Language. 1993; 32:141–54.

Winograd, T. A framework for understanding discourse. in: Just, M. A. and Carp, P. A. Cognitive processes in comprehension. Hillsdale, NJ: Erlbaum; 1977; pp. 63–88.

Wolff, E. Der intendierte Leser: Uberlegungen und Beispiele zur Einfuhrung eines literaturwissenschaftlichen Begriffes. Poetica. 1971; 4(2):141–66.

Zwann, R. Effect of genre expectations on text comprehension. Journal of Experimental Psychology: Learning, Memory, and Cognition. 1994; 20:920–33.

Zwann, R. A.; Langston, M. C.; and Graesser, A. C. The construction of situation models in narrative comprehension: An event-indexing model. Psychological Science. 1995; 6:292–7.

Index